According to Baba

A Collaborative Oral History
of Sudbury's Ukrainian Community

Stacey Zembrzycki

UBCPress · Vancouver · Toronto

22 21 20 19 18 17 16 15 14   5 4 3 2 1

Printed in Canada on FSC-certified ancient-forest-free paper
(100% post-consumer recycled) that is processed chlorine- and acid-free.

Library and Archives Canada Cataloguing in Publication

Zembrzycki, Stacey, 1978-, author
   According to Baba : a collaborative oral history of Sudbury's Ukrainian community /
Stacey Zembrzycki.

(Shared : oral and public history series, 2292-3020)
Includes bibliographical references and index.
Issued in print and electronic formats.

ISBN 978-0-7748-2695-2 (bound). – ISBN 978-0-7748-2696-9 (pbk.)
ISBN 978-0-7748-2697-6 (pdf). – ISBN 978-0-7748-2698-3 (epub)

   1. Ukrainian Canadians – Ontario – Sudbury – Social conditions. 2. Ukrainian
Canadians – Ontario – Sudbury – Biography. 3. Ukrainian Canadians – Ontario –
Sudbury – Interviews. 4. Zembrzycki, Olga – Interviews. I. Title.

FC3099.S83Z7 2014   971.3'13300491791   C2013-908445-2
                                                          C2013-908446-0

Canadä

UBC Press gratefully acknowledges the financial support for our publishing program of the Government of Canada (through the Canada Book Fund), the Canada Council for the Arts, and the British Columbia Arts Council.

This book has been published with the help of a grant from the Canadian Federation for the Humanities and Social Sciences, through the Awards to Scholarly Publications Program, using funds provided by the Social Sciences and Humanities Research Council of Canada.

UBC Press
The University of British Columbia
2029 West Mall
Vancouver, BC V6T 1Z2
www.ubcpress.ca

For Baba

*An extensive community photo album is available
at www.sudburyukrainians.ca*

Contents

Illustrations

Acknowledgments

EVERY BOOK HAS A STORY, and I would be remiss if I did not share the one that led me to write *According to Baba*, or the "Baba book," as it is known among my friends, colleagues, and family members.

In December 2002, I read Franca Iacovetta's *Such Hardworking People*. I devoured it in an afternoon. I loved it – the narrative, the voices, and the community that came alive in its pages. Great books inspire, excite, and leave you dreaming about new projects, and this was no exception. *Such Hardworking People* led me to think about where I was from and the community with which I associated. Mining had drawn thousands of immigrants to northern towns, yet most historians either failed to mention them or referred to them only in the footnotes of their studies. Why wasn't there a history of Sudbury's Ukrainian community? Could I write one? These thoughts remained in the back of my mind for a couple of months as I tried to convince myself to stick to my original plan. I had gone to Carleton University to write about foreign policy, and that was what I would do. After all, I had nearly completed my coursework, and this made switching specialties difficult, though not impossible, as Norman Hillmer reassured me in a memorable afternoon meeting. As Norman spoke to me about the importance of being passionate about my project and reminded me of how much time it would require, I knew that I had no choice but to change directions. I would never have made this bold move, to study Sudbury's Ukrainian community, without Norman's wise words and the enthusiasm of Kerry Abel, Marilyn Barber, and John C. Walsh. Kerry helped me build the historiographical foundation I needed to move forward, and Marilyn and John shepherded me through the rest of the process. I was both lost and behind when I began this project, but they never wavered in their support for it and its unconventional methodology. Thank you for giving me the space I needed to come into my own as a scholar. Additionally, I would like to thank Franca Iacovetta for all the time and effort she devoted to mentoring me and making this book better. You are one of the most generous scholars I know, and I am a better historian because of you. Steven High has also been a formidable figure in my journey. We met in the North, when Steve was teaching at Nipissing University, and I have since been lucky enough to work with him at Concordia University, particularly at the Centre for Oral History and Digital Storytelling (COHDS). The time we spent together, both talking about and doing oral history, has pushed me to hone my craft as an oral historian. Steve, thank you for challenging me with your tough questions, reminding me of the nuances of listening, and pushing me to think about why the stories we hear matter so much.

If it takes a village to raise a child, I think the same can be said of writing a book, especially one that is community-based and collaborative in nature. Myron Momryk, who was a senior archivist at Library and Archives Canada while I researched this book, was instrumental in getting it off the ground. He engaged me in insightful conversations, directed me to sources that I would not otherwise have found, translated sources that I could not read, and most importantly, shared a love of the North with me. Larissa Stavroff also played an integral role, painstakingly translating nearly every Ukrainian source I used. Ukrainian Canadianists Jars Balan, Suzanne Holyck Hunchuck, Andrij Makuch, and Orest Martynowych ensured that my version of the Ukrainian experience was just right. Furthermore, I owe a debt of gratitude to Father Peter Bodnar, Jim Fortin, Olia Katulka, Heather Lewis, Monsignor Theodore Pryjma, and Mary Stefura, all fellow Sudburians who directed me to invaluable local sources. I also thank Léo L. Larivière, at Laurentian University, for preparing the maps used throughout this book. Shanna Fraser, a childhood friend who is now the archivist at the City of Greater Sudbury Archives, welcomed my oral history collection with open arms and, in the process, made it possible for community members to enjoy the fascinating stories that kept Baba and me on the edge of our seats. It was always my intention to give these stories back to the community, and I thank you for accommodating my wish.

After I moved to Montreal, COHDS became a second home to me. As an oral historian, I can think of no better place to be. Since 2007, I have spent nearly every day either doing or thinking or talking about oral history. If I am a better oral historian, it is because of the community of scholars I befriended at COHDS. My relationship with Anna Sheftel is a case in point. She helped me understand who I am as an oral historian and why this discipline is so important to me. Thank you, Anna, for giving me the encouragement I need not only to dream big dreams but also to accomplish them. I also appreciate the countless conversations we had about the book's title. In the end, I think your suggestion, to use the phrase *According to Baba,* truly captures Baba's indelible spirit.

In March 2011, shortly after sending this manuscript out for review, I had a great idea: to host a "trash the book" party. I was surrounded by a wonderful circle of engaged oral historians, so I invited a group of them to my home to critique the book while we enjoyed a buffet of Eastern European food, including Baba's perogies and cabbage rolls. The night was an incredible success, and I thank Hourig Attarian, Steven High, Jessica Mills, Anna Sheftel, Luis van Isschot, and Alan Wong for their engaged critiques and perceptive comments. This book has improved because of your suggestions. Though not an oral historian, Kristina Guiguet, a friend and colleague from my days at Carleton, made a special trip to Montreal to be a part of this conversation. Thank you for your smart observations and considerate feedback, Kristina. You are a true friend!

Financial support from Carleton University, the Canadian Institute of Ukrainian Studies' Helen Darcovich Memorial Doctoral Fellowship, and the Ontario Graduate Scholarship Program was critical to making this project possible. I am also indebted to Melissa Pitts at UBC Press for gently steering this project to completion. Melissa, thank you for taking a special interest in Baba's stories and in oral history in general. You certainly did not have to, but since you did, it has made sharing these tales a real pleasure. I also thank the editorial team at UBC Press, namely, Lesley Erickson and Deborah Kerr, as well as my three anonymous reviewers for providing insightful suggestions that helped me strengthen the text.

Oral historians often find it difficult not to get swept up by the lives of interviewees. Their fascinating tales tend to consume and carry us off to other places and past times. I thank my friends and family for helping to ground me and remind me of the importance of having my own experiences so that I could make my own memories, my own stories. There is life beyond our computer screens! My best friend, Laura Grover, always seems to know when I need a quick e-mail or a long telephone conversation. Brian and Tina Douglas, my second set of parents, welcomed me into their family, supported me, and worked hard to give me a near perfect summer setting, overlooking Lake Kipawa, in which to write. I had no sisters growing up, but I am lucky to have three now. Two of them, Ellen and Lori – along with Ashlyn, Gavin, Jessica, Jim (Burlingham) and Jim (Roy), Leah, and Sawyer – make my life a whole lot richer. My brother Andrew, my other sister Kayla, and their girls, Amileah and Anella, do the same. All these little munchkins bring me great joy and seem to know just how to put a smile on my face. Where would I be without FaceTime dance parties? My parents, Dan and Gail Zembrzycki, have always been there whenever and at whatever time I needed them, providing emotional, financial, and intellectual support. I cannot thank you enough for your love, enthusiasm, encouragement, and understanding. And yes, Dad, the book is finally done! Most of all, I must thank my partner, Robert Douglas. Although he has lived with this project for far too long, he remains my biggest fan, getting me over each bump (and there have been many) on this long road and remaining positive every step of the way. Thank you for your patience, for your engagement, and for just being you.

According to Baba was possible because eighty-two gracious women and men welcomed Baba and me into their homes and shared their stories. I appreciate your honesty and willingness to participate in this project. Although some of you may not agree with what I have written, I hope that you can appreciate my interpretation of your stories. For those who are no longer with us – and sadly there are far too many – know that your stories live on in the pages of this book.

Last, but certainly not least, I must thank Olga Zembrzycki, my baba. Although it has taken me many years to recognize her impact on my life, I now realize that her stories played a central role in shaping the person I have become. Baba, by sharing your stories with me, you not only sparked my imagination but also instilled in me a love of the past. For this, and for all the time and energy you gave to this project, I am forever grateful. This book, with much love and appreciation, is for you.

A PORTION OF THE Introduction was published as "Sharing Authority with Baba," *Journal of Canadian Studies* 43, 1 (Winter 2009): 219-38; part of Chapter 4 was published as "'There Were Always Men in Our House': Gender and the Childhood Memories of Working-Class Ukrainians in Depression-Era Canada," *Labour/Le travail* 60 (Fall 2007): 77-105; and lastly, excerpts from Chapter 5 were published in "Bringing Stories to Life: Using New Media to Disseminate and Critically Engage with Oral History Interviews," *Oral History* 41, 1 (Spring 2013): 98-107.

Abbreviations

AER	Algoma Eastern Railway
AUUC	Association of United Ukrainian Canadians
CCC	Canadian Copper Company
CPR	Canadian Pacific Railway
CSO	Canadian Sitch Organization
FUSD	Federation of Ukrainian Social Democrats
INCO	International Nickel Company
MNC	Mond Nickel Company
OUN	Organization of Ukrainian Nationalists
RCMP	Royal Canadian Mounted Police
UHO	United Hetman Organization
ULFTA	Ukrainian Labour Farmer Temple Association
ULTA	Ukrainian Labour Temple Association
UNF	Ukrainian National Federation
URA	Ukrainian Rifleman's Association
USDP	Ukrainian Social Democratic Party
USRL	Ukrainian Self-Reliance League
UWVA	Ukrainian War Veterans Association

According to Baba

Introduction

WHEN I THINK ABOUT the afternoons I spent in 2004-05 with my Ukrainian Catholic grandmother, my baba, conducting interviews with her friends and acquaintances in Sudbury, I can now smile and even laugh out loud. Looking back, I can see that our experiences together were hilarious. In those moments, however, they were often frustrating, emotionally charged, and exhausting. Every interview seemed to present new challenges, especially because I was constantly struggling to juggle my roles and responsibilities as both an oral historian and a granddaughter. Sometimes the two were compatible, but in other instances, they were not. The line between the personal and the professional was always blurred. Although this project required a great deal of hard work, our tenaciousness, a trait that Baba and I share, forced us to go on. Her goal was to interview as many Ukrainian men and women as possible.[1] Mine was to complete my studies. "We'll get there!" Baba would say. And eventually, we did.[2]

My research was about the social history of Sudbury's Ukrainian community between 1901 and 1939. Baba was supposed to be just another interviewee, but when no one responded to my advertisements for interviews, she became an integral part of the project. To put it simply, the project would not have existed without her. Our work together was deeply collaborative, filled with trials and rewards. This book uses Baba's narratives to form the historical backbone to the story of Sudbury's Ukrainians, but it also provides a frank account of my efforts to share authority with her. It is not a conventional oral history but a reflective one that seeks to place practice and process at the centre of the discussion. It is about giving up control and discovering where that leads, an often frightening and disconcerting process. Sharing authority with Baba required constant negotiation; what I initially deemed to be mistakes were often later revealed as important lessons about the theoretical and methodological foundations of oral history.

Our afternoon encounters began and ended with a car ride. After scraping the ice and snow off my windshield, I would drive across the city to pick up Baba; Sudbury, a working-class mining community in northern Ontario, tends to have incredibly bright but bitterly cold, dry winters, and that of 2004-05 was no exception. Sometimes she was ready to go, standing in the window and waiting for me to pull into her drive- way, and other times, I waited for her to make herself presentable. "Is it cold outside?" she would ask. Depending on my answer, she either grabbed the jacket she had worn the day before or searched for gloves and a scarf to be worn on her head, in typical *babushka* fashion. As I waited impatiently, checking my watch and warning that we would be late for our interviews, I scanned the Post-it Notes on her kitchen table, trying to ascertain what appointments she had booked for the rest of the week. Baba spent most evenings on the telephone, convincing her peers that they ought to be interviewed and arranging meeting times. She often referred to herself as "my secretary" and unabashedly joked that, at the end of the project, she would earn a PhD. When we finally made it out of her postwar brick bungalow, Baba would lock the back door, check and recheck it, and ensure that her keys were safely in her purse before heading toward the car. After unlocking the driver's door, I would press the button that automatically unlocked the passenger door. "It's open," I would call out. Without fail, Baba lifted her door handle at that precise moment, preventing the automatic locks from working. "It's locked!" she would answer. I would roll my eyes, and we would repeat this process a number of times before Baba actually got into the car. Then there was the seatbelt. As she tried to buckle it up, it would partly lock into place, and then slowly, as we drove away, wind back across her body and into its holder. "Baba, just make sure it clicks!" I would remark after pulling over to the side of the road and reaching across to buckle her in. Often Baba would try to be sneaky, pretending that the belt had clicked into place. At some point, usually when she was tired of holding it, the belt would snake back across her waist. She hoped that I wouldn't notice, dodging the exasperated "Baba!" that would invariably fly out of my mouth. We did seventy-two interviews together, and she never managed to buckle herself in! Thankfully, she did figure out the door locks – well, most of the time.

After going through these motions, Baba and I would start talking about our interviewees. As she briefed me on some of the stories that I could expect to hear, she craftily managed to weave herself into the narrative, telling me about her relation to the interviewees and the role they played in her past. In many respects, listening to Baba was like conducting pre-interviews, allowing me to prepare my questions in advance and making me aware of any issues that required sensitivity. Whereas oral historians meet with interviewees prior to pressing the start buttons on their recorders, my pre-interviews took place in my car with Baba. They were a mixed blessing – the talking never seemed to stop. I either listened intently, bearing in mind that I was lucky to have such an engaged grandmother, or I fixated on my feelings of anger and frustration, focusing on my inner monologue rather than the one uttered by Baba. For her part, Baba was often oblivious to my feelings. As she spoke, she stared out the passenger window, watching the world go by. She rarely attached as much meaning to these episodes as I did. They were just a part of everyday happenstance, a regular exchange between the two of us. And, ultimately, she was not the one trying to write a book about these moments.[3]

Her stories continued as we moved from the car and into interviewees' homes. When she interrupted them, I would cringe, shuffle in my seat, and glare at her before trying politely and subtly to get the conversation back on track. My actions either silenced Baba or encouraged her to go on. Listening to others was difficult for her and sometimes seemed futile to me, especially when she insisted on sharing stories that contradicted those told by interviewees. In other instances, however, her perspectives on the past were welcome additions to our conversations, encouraging people to expand on their remarks. There were definitely benefits and drawbacks to collaborating with Baba. By offering readers a play-by-play of the conversations that occurred during some of our interviews, this book shows how the dynamics of our relationship and the ways that we interacted affected how others remembered the past. When Baba decided that she had had enough of these "visits," we packed up our things and returned to the car. My desire to leave or our interviewees' fatigue rarely had an effect on her decisions.

When I was irritated, I dreaded the car rides home. This was when my bad behaviour reared its ugly head. There was never any time to stop and reflect on what we had heard. Baba always had an opinion, and she insisted on voicing it, whether I wanted to hear it or not. Depending on how an interview had gone, I either bit my tongue or let loose. When I was at my wit's end, I raised my voice and asked Baba why she insisted on interrupting people. "They have a story to tell too!" I would say. "This project isn't just about you!" Baba either denied her intrusion or merely stated that she would try to be quieter next time. Then, the conversation would be over. I was her granddaughter, after all, and Baba was well aware of my character flaws and the best ways to appease and tolerate me.

On these kinds of days, I could not get to Baba's house fast enough, only too happy to pull into her driveway, mumble a quick goodbye, and hammer on the automatic lock button. Baba always managed to free herself from the seatbelt and quickly exit the car. As I threw the car into reverse, wrapped my white fists around the steering wheel, and took in some much needed silence, I often wondered why I was doing this project. What was it about? Who was it for? Sometimes, instead of pulling into Baba's driveway every afternoon, I wanted to tear past it and leave her at home. I acted on this impulse a couple of times, telling her that I didn't need her in the interviews. This approach was always temporary. Before long, I would find myself back in the car with Baba, picking up where we had left off.

I went back for two reasons. She was my grandmother and our relationship always came first. We had "put up" with each other for twenty-plus years, and this project was not going to tear us apart. We are, I now realize, very much alike, and we knew just which buttons to press, so to speak. To be fair and balanced, I must point out that the car rides were filled with lots of pleasant moments too. We had many wonderful conversations that helped me make sense of the stories our interviewees told us. There were also lots of memorable side trips on the way home – we would go for late lunches, shop, and sometimes wander through the region's many cemeteries. Gravestones served as memory aids for

FIGURE I.1   Olga and Stacey Zembrzycki, c. 2008. Baba and I pose for a photograph after our final formal interview together; this exchange is discussed in depth in Chapter 6. *Photo by Stacey Zembrzycki*

Baba, prompting her to tell new stories and giving her ideas for expanding our interviewee list. Baba brought Sudbury's Ukrainian community to life in these places, reminding me of the important role she played as a gatekeeper of its memory. This is, therefore, a book about working with my Baba and listening deeply to stories about her home, her identity, and ultimately her community. Our entertaining and troubling process is just as important as the outcome, demonstrating the contested ways that we negotiated and eventually arrived at this narrative. It was necessary for us to wear each other down in the car and to wrestle in the interview space if I were to understand who Baba was and why she saw the past as she did. This is where the hard work of sharing authority took place, her experiential authority coming to blows with my scholarly expertise.

Coined by Michael Frisch in 1990, "shared authority" is a neat term that captures the essence and highest ideal of the oral history enterprise. Emphasizing the collaborative nature of the discipline, it forces us to think about making oral history a more democratic cultural practice.[4] Developed at a time when social history was revolutionizing history departments, the term referred to the interview itself: "the dialogic nature of the interview, in the history-making offered by both interviewer and narrator, [and] in the answer to the always appropriate question 'who is the author of an oral history?'"[5] In the years since, practitioners have adopted a more expansive understanding of Frisch's term. Shared has become "sharing": whereas "sharing authority is an approach to doing oral history ... a shared authority is something we need to recognize in it."[6] When it comes to sharing, interviewers make "a deliberate decision to give up some control over the product of historical inquiry," involving interviewees in decisions about the research, interpretation, and presentation phases of their projects.[7]

In many respects, sharing authority has become both a "mantra" and a black box among oral historians.[8] Although it is often invoked, practitioners rarely offer the transparency and reflection that this imperfect process demands.[9] Collaboration is personally and intellectually demanding work that, depending upon the project, can produce mixed results.[10] This book shows how issues pertaining to authority, both shared and sharing, come up in practice inside and outside the interview space. Given the flexibility and creativity that every oral history project demands, I cannot offer a model on the best ways to share authority. Instead, I provide an honest reflection on how my particular process, my attempts to balance my scholarly authority and Baba's experiential authority, evolved over time, warts and all. This book is about the perils, pitfalls, and potential of collaborative practice. It is about the give and take – the power struggle – that is central to this methodology. Some of the interviews that Baba and I conducted were better than others. But since there is no right or wrong way to either listen or share authority, I view our blunders as lessons, not mistakes. As Baba says, "We didn't know what we were doing! We were fumbling along the whole time!" Indeed. Being honest and self-critical about these sorts of challenges does not compromise our scholarship. Rather, it makes it more realistic and rigorous.[11]

Although I recognized that collaboration was central to the interview process – namely, the co-creation of the interview itself – I did not plan to share authority with interviewees in any other way. A lack of funding, and hence limited time, forced me to establish a clear set of priorities. I wanted to conduct one hundred single life story interviews with fifty Ukrainian men and fifty Ukrainian women during a one-year period; these oral histories would supplement the limited written records in the public archive.[12] It was not until I placed my first advertisement in the bulletin at Baba's church, St. Mary's Ukrainian Catholic Church, and failed to receive a single response that my priorities changed. Whether I wanted to or not, I would, in the end, learn to share authority with Baba. My methodology evolved from necessity, as a result of the circumstances I faced in the field.[13]

I grew up in Sudbury in a home with two working parents. Fortunately, my maternal and paternal grandparents lived in the city, so there was never any need to send me to a babysitter. I developed close relationships with all my grandparents but spent most of my time with Baba, my paternal grandmother. As a result, my first words were in Ukrainian. Although Baba was born and raised in Sudbury, her immigrant father insisted that his children speak Ukrainian in the home, stressing that they ought to know where they had come from. Like her father, Baba believed that I too must learn the language, so she spoke only Ukrainian when she babysat me. Because I had a difficult time transitioning from Ukrainian to English when my parents arrived home from work, these early language lessons ended soon after I began to speak.

My memories of the time we spent together come into focus around my sixth birthday. Baba and my grandfather, my Gigi, lived on Marymount Hill, a neighbourhood overlooking Sudbury's Downtown. We were close to everything, so Baba and I walked everywhere together. Unless the weather was inclement, we strolled downtown every afternoon, whether Baba needed something or not. This was a social outing, an opportunity to get out of the house and pass the time. Baba is an outgoing and active lady, a lifelong member of St. Mary's and various volunteer organizations within it, and thus she has always known many Sudburians. Wherever we were, she always seemed to meet someone with whom she could chat, sharing the latest news and reminiscing about the past. After she introduced me to them, and finished doting over me,

I would stand to the side and listen as they talked. Clearly, our afternoon interview sessions, and the power dynamics that ordered them, were firmly rooted in this well-established routine.

Baba's stories were the best part of these daily excursions. As we walked down the hill, through the shopping centre, and then back up the hill and home, she told me exciting stories about when she was young, transporting me back to a time and a place that no longer existed. Although I never forgot these stories, as I grew older and spent more time away from Baba, I also distanced myself from them. Returning to them, viewing them "intellectually rather than emotionally," would take time.[14]

Unlike Baba, I was not an active member of Sudbury's Ukrainian community. I attended Ukrainian language school in the basement of St. Mary's for a number of years, but like so many other Ukrainian Canadian children from third and fourth generations, I became involved in other activities, effectively dissociating myself from my ethnic roots. My connection to the community and my knowledge about it were therefore premised upon Baba's memories. I participated imaginatively in her world and shared her vision of the past.[15] Historically, Ukrainian grandmothers have acted as important storytellers in their families. Custodians of traditions, arts, and culture, they have played central roles in defining the Ukrainian identities of their descendants.[16] Had it not been for Baba, I would not identify as a Ukrainian today. Her role in my life, her experiences in the Ukrainian Catholic community, and her stories about the past formed the basis of my identity and my imagined Ukrainian community. When I began this project, I believed that I was both a community insider and an outsider, maintaining not only a subjective connection to it through Baba, but also a real distance from it because I had not participated in it. I was a Sudburian too, so I knew what it was like to grow up in this small and somewhat insular mining community in northern Ontario. I hoped that my familiarity with Sudbury and my family's ethnic roots would help me solicit interviewees. In hindsight, I was naive to believe that people would throw open their doors and welcome me into their homes. I quickly realized that interviewing Baba – my first subject – would be nothing like those to come.[17] Whereas we spent a couple of hours easily conversing about the past, others were not as forthcoming. Before I could address the dynamics in the interviews, however, I had to deal with the fact that no one answered my call to participate in this project.

My first response was to panic. My ethnicity and my relationship with Baba would not necessarily help me forge an easy connection to this community. After all, my link was an imagined one, grounded in Baba's stories rather than my own participation. I was a stranger to those with whom I wanted to speak. This was certainly not the sole reason why no one came forward. Shyness, apathy, and a tendency to devalue personal stories were among the other reasons. If I were going to continue with this research, I needed help from someone whom community members trusted. I turned to Baba. She was eager to help, highlighting names in the church directory and constructing a list of her friends and acquaintances. I called a handful of these individuals but few wanted to participate. Fearing that the project would end before it began, I asked Baba how to proceed.

She had done pastoral visits at local hospitals and nursing homes on behalf of the church for thirty-five years, and she offered to help me approach their residents. She was happy to facilitate these meetings, hoping that we could replicate our own positive interviewing experience of a few weeks earlier. These people were friendly and thrilled to have visitors. Baba would greet them, introduce me, and then describe my project. They often insisted that we sit down and do the interview right there and then, rather than waiting until another day. Although I had intended to return later, without Baba, I did not want to miss the opportunity to speak with them. Many were quite sick, so if they were feeling well on the day of our visit, we just stayed and interviewed them. Many of these individuals passed away shortly afterward, a fact that reinforced the time-sensitive nature of the project.

Sharing authority with Baba began immediately, although I must admit that, at the outset, it often felt more like giving up authority. She spent the first part of these early interviews getting caught up with her friends and acquaintances, asking how they were feeling, if they had had many visitors, and whether they enjoyed living in a long-term-care facility. They complained about their age and then started to reminisce about the good old days. Having Baba there put them at ease and often made the inter-action feel like a meeting between old friends rather than a formal inter-view. There was no need to build trust; it was already there. The problem, however, was that Baba and the interviewees would get swept up in their conversations. They told anecdotal stories while I sat on the sidelines and watched. I was actually quite powerless during these times, feeling more like that young child holding Baba's hand in the middle of the shopping centre than a trained historian. To be honest, I worried that Baba was ruining my project. In my mind, there was a right and a wrong way to do oral history, and this was definitely not the right way. Would our interviews have any historical worth? The project always seemed to teeter on the brink of disaster. Although I jumped into the conversations from time to time and asked questions, people would answer them and then proceed to speak with Baba, not me. At other times, I asked questions, interviewees answered them, and then Baba would answer the questions as well, telling and retelling the stories I had heard throughout my life and in our interview together. Instead of remembering their own experi-ences, people became wrapped up in Baba's story. By interrupting them, she dominated the discussion.

Coming home and listening to the interview tapes was difficult and frustrating. Instead of hearing new stories, I heard those recounted by Baba. Feeling as if I were outside the interview space listening in, I tried to regain authority by excising her stories and frequent interruptions from my transcripts.[18] When I did this, the interviews felt more legitimate. This was my way of salvaging the worthwhile pieces of the project. After a couple of these interviews, I began to think about the roles that Baba and I had played in them. I had to establish, with her and interviewees, that I was not just a granddaughter. I had to figure out how authority could be shared. Collaboration "does not require agreement in all things, but a mutual commitment to talk things through, to reach a common understanding, and to respect considered differences."[19] Baba and I had to learn how to collaborate before we could listen to interviewees. We had to share some of the same purposes if we were going to move forward.

Henry Greenspan states that "a good interview is a process in which two people work hard to understand the views and experiences of one person: the interviewee."[20] In this case, Baba and I had to come together to appreciate the significance of the stories that interviewees recalled. In the car ride home, after we had conducted nearly a dozen interviews, I worked up the courage to face Baba and tell her how she was both helping and hindering the process. One interview, in particular, brought me to this point. "Helen" was a difficult person to read.[21] From the moment she opened her door to the time we left, she was quiet, reserved, and for the most part, unwilling to discuss the past in any depth. I wondered why she had agreed to talk to us. Was she doing Baba a favour? Did she know what an interview entailed? She constantly brushed my questions aside, quickly answering them and then refocusing our conversation on the present. She wanted to catch up with Baba, making it clear that in recent years she had become quite lonely and detached from the community. For her part, Baba did not disappoint. She and Helen had a lovely talk about the church, their grandchildren, and their health. I tried to interject many times, but nothing I said made Helen want to share her memories with us.[22] In the car afterward, I was careful but deliberate in my remarks to Baba, speaking about the trust she brought to the interaction, the implicit power struggle between her and me and the interviewees, and her frequent interruptions during our interviews. Baba did not see things in quite this light. She was only trying to help, she shot back, and there was no problem with how the interviews were going. For her, they were conversations among friends, not formal oral history interviews with all their inherent academic baggage. However, she did respect my feelings and my desire to adhere to the "rules" I had learned during my training, vowing to listen more and speak less in the future. Despite this "understanding," Baba continued to behave in the same manner. Ukrainian grandmothers have been characterized as stubborn, highly individualistic, opinionated, and at times slightly irreverent beings, and certainly Baba was guilty of possessing all these attributes.[23] I now see that she was sometimes much better at "rolling with the punches" than I was. Whereas I was guilty of over-thinking every conversation, she quickly adapted to challenges in interviews. She is a good conversationalist and a skilled storyteller, so she seamlessly transformed uncomfortable silences and digressions into new threads that enabled us to move past awkward moments. If an interviewee, such as Helen, did not want to talk about the past, she would not push her to do so. This approach had its benefits and drawbacks. Although silences make people uncomfortable, and we normally try to avoid them, they tend to be incredibly interesting for oral historians. They remind us of the complexities of remembering and give us an alternative point of reference from which to interpret the stories we hear.[24] Baba and I discussed this aspect of oral history on a number of occasions, but she had a hard time with it in practice. For her, it was simple. A good interview was about having good conversations about good times.

Given our conflicted understanding of oral history, I began to conduct interviews on my own. However, they were neither as rich nor as detailed as when Baba was present. Speakers were shy, and although they warmed up to me, they did not seem to trust me completely.[25] After a handful of these solo ventures, I decided to include Baba once again. I made this decision for a number of reasons. First, she was essential to the project. Without her, these interviews would never have taken place. I also felt a responsibility to enable her as a community historian. Like me, she became obsessed with documenting the history of Sudbury's Ukrainians. During this intense period, we rarely thought about anything else. While I pored over the discoveries I made in local archives and in the basements and attics of our interviewees, Baba kept notes about the memories she had forgotten to tell me in our exchanges and made extensive lists of potential interviewees. She spent nearly every evening on the telephone, calling these people and trying to convince them to be a part of our project. She welcomed the chance to leave her home and visit with friends whom she had not seen in years. Additionally, the project enabled her to establish her place as a caretaker of the community's memory. Baba often declared that few people remembered the past as well as she did. Just as Barbara Myerhoff discovered while exploring the process of aging among a group of elderly Jewish people, I began to see that this was a means through which Baba could demonstrate her existence and worth in no uncertain terms.[26] I had no wish to disconnect Baba from this process, so I walked a fine line when addressing her role in the interviews. Emotional attachments were central to the project, and as I stated above, our grandmother-granddaughter relationship had to be maintained throughout, whatever the cost.[27]

After discussing, yet again, the subtle ways that Baba consciously and unconsciously changed the course of each interview, we decided to give our partnership a second chance. This time we dealt with how the interviews themselves would work and how power could be shared in them. We agreed that Baba would remain silent during the formal part of the conversation, and then, at the end, she could ask questions and add any relevant memories of her own. We decided to keep the digital recorder on throughout this process, so that everything could be preserved. Collaboration had to be structured. Without clear rules, Baba would have continued to act as before. We both came away from this conversation with renewed excitement, knowing that we had a framework to follow as we moved ahead.

Baba and I conducted many interviews before we began to share authority in a fruitful way. Speaking about our rules was one thing, but implementing them was another. Collaboration requires time, patience, and practice to develop, regardless of whether it is with someone you know and love. We never perfected our three-way exchange, but we managed to transform it into a working relationship that eased my frustrations and suited my needs as well as those expressed by Baba and our interviewees. Whereas Baba and I had to learn to work together, I also realized that I had to trust my methodology. Projects often take on a life of their own, whether we care to admit it or not. They evolve organically and out of necessity, and this is acceptable. Unlike anthropologists, historians, who are concerned with maintaining a degree of objectivity, have spent little time reflecting on their experiences in the field.[28] Our project taught me that oral history is a subjective craft that is made more interesting when unconventional approaches form its basis. I used to be embarrassed about discussing Baba's role in the interview, worrying about the implications of this personal, untraditional, and seemingly haphazard style, but I have come to see it as a rigorous, authentic, and valid attempt to gain a sense of the past through a process of "knowing with" Baba rather than simply "knowing from" or "knowing about" her.[29] The time we spent together changed both of us and deepened our relationship. We came to know each other and ourselves in new ways through our shared experiences.

"Single-session oral histories," Donald Ritchie writes, "are like 'audio snapshots.' It often takes more than one interview just to break the ice. Repeated visits help establish an intimacy that encourages candidness. Both interviewer and interviewee need some time together to develop the rapport necessary to ask difficult questions and to give honest answers."[30] Although I agree with Ritchie and recognize that multiple interviews would have been beneficial, this approach was not feasible and would have completely changed our project and its outcome. That said, Baba brought an unusual degree of trust to interviews. She may not have been a trained historian, but her questions and memories made a difference, enabling interviewees to recall stories, mostly about their childhoods, that my questions did not help them remember.[31] Also, my conversations with Baba prepared me for the interviews, allowing me to personalize my questions and maximize the time we spent with each person. Certainly, discrepancies between Baba's tales and those told by interviewees reminded me of the subjective and layered nature of memories, and particularly of the importance of asking how variables, such as gender and class, mould both the construction of historical memories and the telling of stories.[32] To this end, they allowed me to identify some of the silences implicit in interviewee narratives. Through her insider knowledge of the time, the place, and the culture, Baba was often able to speak to them, relying on subtle hints dropped during the course of an interview; she became more comfortable and aware of the importance of these moments as the project progressed. With her help, I was able to understand some of these conscious and unconscious gaps in memory.

Although bringing Baba to the interviews had its benefits, it also complicated matters. When she was in the room, some people were quite selective in sharing their memories. For instance, according to Baba, a few individuals had been victims of domestic abuse. Despite the horrendous stories that she told me, they never mentioned this aspect of their lives, choosing instead to focus on the positive nature of their relationships. Even when they hinted at the abuse they had suffered, I chose not to broach this subject. I trusted that Baba would remain silent when it came to interview content, but I did not want to risk ruining interviewees' reputations. I did not want these sorts of private memories to become public, something that could potentially slip out in conversations Baba had later with her friends. I was bound by the ethical obligations of my university. Baba was not. Nor did I want to make people uncomfortable by putting them on the spot and mentioning stories that, frankly, could have been wrong, misleading, and even offensive. Had I conducted multiple interviews, the first with Baba and subsequent ones alone, I would have felt more comfortable delving into such issues if the conversations went in those directions. Revealing difficult experiences is often easier when interviewers commit to deep listening. Interviews require us to build relationships, demonstrate understanding, and show compassion; they cannot be interrogations.[33] Baba may have brought trust to the conversation, but this did not always create the conditions that individuals needed if they were to share personal or intimate memories.

Baba was well known to the Ukrainian Catholic community, and her infrequent interactions with members of the Ukrainian National Federation (UNF) and St. Volodymyr's Ukrainian Greek Orthodox Church had allowed her to build relationships among these organizations as well. Thus, she accompanied me to most of the interviews with people from these associations. However, she was an outsider when it came to the Ukrainian Left – a group opposed by members of St. Mary's, the UNF, and St. Volodymyr's – so I tried to speak with these progressives on my own, often taking the time to conduct multiple interviews to develop sound connections with them. I did not want my relationship with Baba, and her Catholic roots, to limit or impede our conversations.

When Baba was a child, her strict Ukrainian Catholic father forbade her from associating with the "communists," as she called those on the Ukrainian Left, and their Spruce Street Hall; although they formed distinct communities, Catholic, Orthodox, and nationalist Ukrainians sometimes united against the "evil" progressive Ukrainians and their organization, the Ukrainian Labour Farmer Temple Association (ULFTA), later renamed the Association of United Ukrainian Canadians (AUUC). Hearing negative stories about ULFTA members, I assumed that Baba had not formed relationships with them. However, sustained conversations with her revealed that the boundaries of her Ukrainian community were more fluid than I had imagined. Her father's rules had not stopped her from becoming friends with a number of progressives. She interacted with them in a variety of neutral locations outside the Catholic church, such as schools, workplaces, and shopping centres. Her status as both an insider and an outsider was complex, layered by her experiences and the multiple identities that she assumed over time. A "neighbourhood's bricks and mortar," as Talja Blokland points out, can provide "the building blocks for the production of collective memories."[34] These places also offer spaces in which relationships, like those maintained by Baba and a number of progressive Ukrainians, may flourish. In reflecting upon the project, I admit that it was foolish to believe that Baba's community was simply structured upon equalities and similarities. Her narrative about the past may have excluded progressives, but its silences, and specifically her relationships with members of this community, speak to a more complicated notion of the past and a broad view of the community to which she belonged.

As we engage in oral history, we are often made "uncomfortably aware of the elusive quality of historical truth itself."[35] "Oral sources," as Alessandro Portelli reminds us, "tell us not just what people did, but what they wanted to do, what they believed they were doing, and what they now think they did."[36] In other words, nothing is certain in oral history. It tells us less about events than about their current meanings. Therefore, being objective, neutral, or balanced is next to impossible when it comes to doing oral history. And, rest assured, this is a good thing! In this instance, I not only built subjective links to our interviewees, but also to Baba. Although our decision to share authority was a difficult one to make and to work out in practice, it was absolutely necessary. A messy process, collaboration was demanding, "requiring an ability – even courage – to deal with people and situations that [were] difficult; a certain tolerance for ambiguity and uncertainty about how [this] project [would] work out; and a willingness to take risks, not follow established protocols, and make decisions based on the logic of the work itself."[37] Sharing authority, especially with family members who act as both interviewees and interviewers, necessitates dialogue at every stage of a project. Conflict and consensus will result. These are healthy outcomes that allow us to develop relationships and push the boundaries of the discipline.

This book is composed of a number of layers. It reflects on how oral history theory takes shape in practice, and it views Baba's stories with as much scrutiny as I am able and willing to provide. All families, as Annette Kuhn demonstrates, have their deep, dark secrets.[38] Mine is no exception. I have tried to be a considerate and selective storyteller, mindful of the fact that my ethical obligations as a researcher (namely, issues pertaining to consent, mitigation of harm, and right of withdrawal) are difficult to navigate when working with a family member. This narrative is not about airing my family's dirty laundry. Rather, it is about trying to understand the stories that I have heard throughout my life and why they are important to Baba and to me. They are central to her identity, and they speak to who she is as a Ukrainian Catholic woman, mother, and grandmother. They are also important because they provide a lens through which we can engage with the history of Sudbury's Ukrainian community and understand its complicated dynamics. Ordinary folks, like Baba, can be extraordinary history-makers, and consequently they must be given more space in our work.

Organized both chronologically and thematically, Chapters 1 through 4 each begin with one of Baba's tales, pieced together through our ongoing conversations inside and outside the interview space. Following this, the stories are subjected to a deep analysis, and her memories are connected to the themes that arose during interviews. Chapter 5 employs a spatial analysis to bring together Baba's memories of community. Drawing on my field notes, I reconstruct some of our interviews, providing a sense of their undercurrents and how they affected what people told us. I have used our interviewees' names throughout, unless someone requested anonymity. When this occurred, I created a pseudonym and enclosed it in quotation marks. Oral historians frequently debate and discuss the need to "protect" interviewees through the use of pseudonyms, especially when unflattering and/or controversial remarks are made during an interview. There are two instances in this book where I used pseudonyms for this reason. Sudbury is a relatively small community, so my need to "protect" was great.[39]

Although I tried to provide a balanced account of the community's history, most of our interviewees were Catholics, limiting the tale I could tell in these pages. Baba's lifelong involvement at St. Mary's Ukrainian Catholic Church and the fact that the church remains vibrant explain my choice. Sudbury's Orthodox, progressive, and nationalist Ukrainian communities have largely disbanded, so locating willing interviewees was difficult. Another factor that informed my writing is the way in which Baba and I directed remembering during interviews. We adhered to a questionnaire that contained many closed-ended questions (to view it, see the Appendix). Instead of asking someone to tell us about her childhood, for instance, we focused on particular parts of her experiences, leaving little room for her to remember on her own terms. Our approach, and the learning that resulted, is something that I have tried to be honest about here. Explorations into the deeper meanings inherent in stories rarely occur in single interviews, even when trust exists. Instead, we concentrated on mapping the details of interviewees' lives, and unfortunately this left little time for sustained reflection. That said, insights that may have been lacking in interviews were central to my conversations with Baba. This book revolves around her story, an approach that makes the most sense for me, given who I am, my connection to this history, and my decision to include Baba in this project.

The result is a highly personal and collectively constructed social history of Sudbury's Ukrainian community that privileges the stories I heard rather than the records I found in the archive. It uses Baba's gendered memories about home and identity, as well as those shared by interviewees, to demonstrate how the community and its polarized sub-communities developed, paying attention to the impact that social networks and power relations had on evolution over time. This book is set in a period of change for Sudbury's Ukrainians, the region, and the country more broadly. It begins in 1901, a year that marks the onset of Ukrainian settlement in the area, and ends in 1939, a date that symbolizes the conclusion of a distinct phase in both our interviewees' lives, when most became adolescents, and in the community's formation, when the Second World War and subsequent immigration affected its structure. Although this study explores how the community shifted over time and through experience, it also offers new narratives about the First World War, the so-called Roaring Twenties, and the Depression.[40] Furthermore, this book is the first of its kind to thoroughly examine the Ukrainian Canadian experience outside of Western Canada, departing from the narrow elitist and organizational agendas that typically characterize the literature.[41]

Communities must be problematized if we wish to gain a sound understanding of them. Rather than taking a "common sense" approach to community, a view that limits its scope to "the ideas of a shared place and a static, self-contained entity," we must consider it as an imagined reality, a social interaction, and a process.[42] Only through the adoption of a fluid model can we begin to understand the varying ways that Baba and our interviewees envisioned their communities. These meanings largely depend upon the social networks to which they belonged and the gendered and politicized experiences they had within them. Catholic, Orthodox, nationalist, and progressive Ukrainian men and women imagined, negotiated, and experienced their communities in distinct ways. An ongoing and ever-evolving process, community was mediated through a range of conflicting and converging factors that changed over time, over space, and over generations.

Social networks, and the gendered identities that people assumed as a result of them, played major roles in creating the contours of this immigrant community and the sub-communities therein. Specifically, they took root in St. Mary's Ukrainian Catholic Church, St. Volodymyr's Ukrainian Greek Orthodox Church, the ULFTA Hall, and the UNF Hall, and they largely determined who did and did not belong to the local community as well as to the region and the nation. Places such as these, as Lynne Marks notes, define community, enabling those who functioned both within and outside of it to negotiate membership, respectability, and loyalty.[43]

Power relations also shaped notions pertaining to respectability and loyalty. The Sudbury area was dominated by mining companies, their long and powerful reach stretching into the public and private lives of each and every resident.[44] Consequently, those affiliated with St. Mary's, St. Volodymyr's, and the UNF Hall, which cooperated with the companies, were respected and valued members of the larger community, vastly different from the ever-reviled progressives, who challenged the mining companies' hold on citizens. Community was therefore "an exercise in power, of authority, legitimacy, and resistance," acting to include, exclude, nurture, and alienate.[45]

This book is a journey into my imagined Ukrainian community, Baba's Ukrainian community, and the communities that other Ukrainians in the Sudbury region hold dear. True to its nature, the project has continued to evolve over time. Although the book enables me to discuss the choices I made about process and outcomes, I wanted to create a space where Baba and our interviewees could also share their perspectives. A website, www.sudburyukrainians.ca, holds the potential for this kind of inter-action.[46] As you read this book, you can visit the website and listen to the stories that lie at the heart of its narrative. In some of the audio clips, you will hear how Baba and I interacted during interviews. The website also enables Baba to articulate her views on the project, by authoring in sound. The digital revolution makes it possible to continue sharing authority with Baba and interviewees long after our conversations ended.[47] This is my attempt to extend the conversations and to initiate further community engagement.

Ironically, it took me eighty-two single life story interviews with men and women, and a couple of years spent away from the project, to realize that I was having a deep, textured, meaningful, and ongoing dialogue about the past with Baba; it began in my youth and continues to this day. I had to learn a little bit about each person in order to learn a lot about my own grandmother. When we were interviewing, I passively listened and relistened to her stories but took them for granted. I was too busy fighting for control to realize that this repetitiveness mattered. She told the stories for a reason, and they either encouraged people to go on or silenced them completely. Since I did not spend much time with inter-viewees, I cannot offer a thorough analysis of their stories and the reasons why, from their perspectives, these dynamics affected their telling. Rather, my focus is on the themes that intersect with those inherent in Baba's tales and how we used the dominant threads within them to piece together a collective narrative about the history of Sudbury's Ukrainian community.

CHAPTER ONE

Building

Recreating Home and Community

EVERY TIME BABA DELVED into the past, speaking to me both on and off the record, she began by recalling the circumstances that led her parents, Peter and Annie Zyma, to Sudbury. This tale often varied, especially when it came to dates, details, intonation, body language, and emotion. Some dates were inconsistent, others were always the same. Parts of the story, when told on one occasion, were vague, but sometimes they were incredibly detailed. The pace and tone quickened or slowed or halted, and her voice rose and fell as she imitated those whom she remembered. As Baba waved her hands in the air, shuffled in her seat, shed a tear, giggled, or stood up to act out a part of the story, her memories conveyed a range of emotions: excitement, anger, joy, frustration, curiosity, and sadness.

Whenever we saw each other, Baba and I tried to piece together a tale that made sense to both of us. This was a fragmented history, based mostly on memories that Baba's parents had shared with her rather than on her own experiences; we constantly negotiated and renegotiated its form, content, and meaning. Whereas I attempted to get the story "straight," reiterating it and asking new questions, Baba reminded me of the parts I had overlooked or had gotten wrong and proceeded to share new memories that allowed us to gain a deeper understanding of the reasons why Peter and Annie found themselves in this northern mining town during the early 1920s and how they set about recreating home and building community.

According to Baba, Peter was one of seven children. He was born in 1896 in a small village near Ternopol in Austria-Hungary; at this time Ukraine ceased to exist as either a separate entity or a distinct province within Austria-Hungary or Russia.[1] Shortly after Peter turned twelve, his

FIGURE 1.1   The Zyma family, c. 1928. Every year, Peter ensured that the family, dressed in Sunday best, posed for portraits like this one, which he sent to his family in Austria-Hungary. Back row, from left to right, are Peter, Barbara, Annie; second row, from left to right, are Steve and Baba. Mike is seated on the floor. *Courtesy of Olga Zembrzycki*

father died and life became difficult for the family. A few years later, Peter decided to come to Canada, where he would work and save his earnings before returning home to support his mother and siblings. Baba emphasized that Peter always intended to go back home, but he never did; instead, he sent photographs, taken annually, of his family.

In 1912, at age sixteen, Peter came to Espanola, Ontario, with his brother Stephan, joining his sister Magdalena, who had immigrated a few years before. In Espanola, a small company town about seventy kilometres west of Sudbury, Peter and Stephan worked for the Spanish River Pulp and Paper Company, cutting down trees in the surrounding bush. Although Baba was unclear about the details of this part of Peter's life, she thought that he spent the next eight years moving between Espanola and Port Arthur, present-day Thunder Bay, going wherever he could find a job; Stephan returned home during this period because he had a wife and family there. I asked Baba how the First World War affected Peter. Although she did not remember her father speaking about the war, she stressed that he always downplayed his Austro-Hungarian identity: "[He] didn't admit it because during the war they were putting them in concentration camps." "You mean internment camps," I responded. "Whatever," Baba declared. She added that Peter refused to apply for Canadian citizenship until 1967, when Barbara, Baba's sister, forced him to get it so that he could collect his old age pension. Baba said nothing more about this part of the story and returned to her previous thought. By early 1921, when Peter turned twenty-five, he had had enough of his transient lifestyle. He decided that it was time to put down roots, so he began to look for a wife.

Annie Sydor was born on a homestead in 1904 in Winnipegosis, Manitoba, to poor Ukrainian immigrants who had come to Canada during the late 1890s. The second of eleven children, she completed grade two and then spent much of her childhood tending to her siblings and helping her parents with chores. When Peter arrived in Winnipegosis in 1921, Annie was working in a local market, scaling fish that had been caught in Lake Winnipegosis; her meagre salary helped her parents make ends meet. Baba told this part of the story in bits and pieces. Annie did not speak much about her early life, and in return, Baba said that she herself did not ask many questions.

When Peter began his search for a wife, friends encouraged him to "go west," where he would find plenty of "nice, strong girls"; the assumption, according to Baba, was that a man needed a strong woman to farm and run a household. I reminded her that there were probably few available Ukrainian women in the towns where he worked. She paused, nodded, and continued, explaining that Peter took the advice of his friends, boarded a train, and travelled to Winnipeg, Dauphin, and then Winnipegosis. Reaching the village in early February 1921, he stated his purpose to a local resident who led him to the Sydor farm. I asked Baba who this person was and why Peter had been taken to this particular farm. She brushed my questions aside and went on with the story; she did not have an answer. As Peter approached the farm he spotted Annie, then sixteen and a half years old. Although Baba was unclear about whether "it was love at first sight," she laughed and declared that it did not matter. "This arrangement had absolutely nothing to do with love," I told Baba. "Peter wanted a wife and he had found one." "They grew to love one another," she insisted. I had heard this story many times before; it was a favourite that Baba frequently invoked from her repertoire. We moved on.

Peter wasted no time. A strong-willed and determined individual, he asked Mrs. Sydor if he could marry Annie. After granting him permission – Baba noted that the mother was only too happy to rid herself of the responsibility of caring for this child – Peter walked up to Annie and asked her whether she wanted to marry him. Annie told her children this story many times, and Baba remembered that it always made them laugh. In a quiet, hesitant, and timid voice, she imitated her mother. Standing with her arms crossed and her eyes focused on the floor, she said, "I don't know. I guess so." "What did she know at sixteen?" Baba proclaimed. "She was like a mail-order bride!"

Within three weeks, Peter and Annie were married. They took up a homestead not far from the Sydor farm, but this arrangement turned out to be quite temporary. Peter "was never a farmer," explained Baba, "he was a gentleman." After the birth of their first two children, Barbara in 1922 and Mike in 1923, Peter moved his growing family to Espanola, where he went back to work for the mill. A few years later he heard that the Mond Nickel Company (MNC) was hiring men at its mine in

Worthington, a company town about forty-five kilometres west of Sudbury. Peter got a job at the mine, and while he boarded in Worthington, Annie and her two children remained in Espanola, living with Magdalena and her family. Shortly thereafter, Peter transferred to the MNC's Frood Mine and moved his family to a rented house on Montague Avenue in the Donovan, a Sudbury neighbourhood that was within walking distance of the mine; in time the International Nickel Company (INCO) would become Peter's employer. Here Annie gave birth to their third and fourth children, Steve in 1925 and Baba in 1927; Peter Junior, the last child, would come later, in 1940.

I thought about this story for a long time and wondered how Annie must have felt during this period. Baba's response, that she rarely discussed this part of her life, did not satisfy me. How could she not talk about these formative years? As Baba and I went through the story for the umpteenth time, I declared that Annie must have been very lonely. Being away from her husband, family, friends, and community, and living in desolate, rugged, industrial towns with young children would have been a challenging and difficult experience. Baba sat quietly and let me ramble on before announcing, "Of course she was lonely! She cried every day!" In fact, it got so bad that one day, when Baba was six, Peter came home from work and told Annie to get on a train and go home, so she packed up Baba and boarded a train to Winnipegosis. Although Baba's memory of this trip was choppy, she vividly recalled that her mother cried the whole time they were away. As Baba looked out the train window, her mother cried. And, while visiting the Sydor homestead, her mother cried. Within a week, Baba and Annie were back on a train bound for Sudbury. When I asked Baba to tell me more, she just said that the trip made her mother realize that she belonged in Sudbury; home was where she made it. She had a husband and three children waiting for her – she missed them terribly – and she had begun to establish a social network there. In her depression, Annie turned to a neighbourhood group of Ukrainian women for support. She and Peter also became extremely active in St. Mary's Ukrainian Catholic Church after it was built in 1928; her father, Baba emphasized, played an instrumental role in the church, as a builder, member, and cantor.[2]

This version of the story became Baba's dominant narrative as she told it to me over time and in various settings. Composed of her memories and those of her parents, some parts were romanticized, silenced, and embellished.[3] She was comfortable recalling the past in this way. Her polished account swept aside any and all inherent complications and complexities, of which there were many. Baba's father was its leading figure; she idolized Peter and referred to him frequently, underscoring his importance in both her family and Sudbury's Ukrainian community. A quiet but serious authoritarian figure, Peter was not home much; he was either working or attending church functions. As a result, Baba spent most of her time with her mother. Annie was a good storyteller, and Baba came to understand her father's frequent absences through her glorified tales about him. Peter's elusiveness provided fodder for stories that were worthy of Annie's telling and Baba's retelling. On the other hand, Annie's life was mundane. Her seemingly ordinary experiences, of raising children and managing a household, which included a boarding business, were largely absent from Baba's account. When we spoke about these "problems," a subject to which we returned often, I asked more questions to push her to go deeper, but she always set limits when it came to how she recalled the past and what she wanted to say about it. This particular narrative gave Baba a sense of where she came from, and its degree of comfort was an integral part of her remembering. It was her story and her history, and most importantly, it situated her in a past that was of her own making.

Family stories can act as powerful personal truths. Based on layers of remembering, forgetting, and retelling, this anecdotal and intimate narrative ordered and validated Baba's experiences.[4] It also allowed us to place community and identity at the centre of our study. For Peter and Annie, a sense of community took time to develop and was rooted in their gendered experiences in their informal networks; power relations between Peter and the companies that employed him also affected how they lived their lives. As a single man and then a breadwinning father, Peter moved between company towns in northern Ontario because he was dependent on the wages that he earned in the lumber and mining industries. His social world was composed of his siblings, people he met while he boarded and worked, and eventually his immediate family members. Well aware of the politics of his identity – Ukrainian men were labelled as enemy aliens during the First World War – he refused to become a Canadian citizen until he knew that his Austro-Hungarian extraction would not limit him; he feared that he would lose his job, or worse, be deported, if he wore his ethnicity on his sleeve. He chose instead to emphasize his Catholic identity; local mining companies, as Chapter 3 demonstrates, favoured Catholic workers over those who held socialist beliefs. The dictates of Peter's employers were never far from his mind. Annie's place, on the other hand, was in the home, caring for her children and managing the household. Whereas Peter interacted with others on the job, and later in church, Annie's initial social network was smaller and more intimate because it was confined to her neighbourhood.

Baba's story about the conditions that led her parents to settle in the Sudbury region mirrors many that were recounted by the men and women whom we interviewed. We drew on this web of stories, on Peter's and Annie's experiences, as well as Baba's, to direct the conversations and make sense of what we were hearing. Through these connections, our interviewees, like Baba, shared fascinating stories about community, recalling the informal social networks to which their parents belonged (before the building of formal community institutions), making links between identity, gender, and politics, and describing how the area's mining companies affected their parents' lives and, ultimately, the polarized communities they built.

Sudbury began as a Canadian Pacific Railway (CPR) construction camp and was also the centre of a seasonal but prosperous lumber industry. Because it was a junction point, marking the intersection of the Algoma Eastern Railway (AER) and the main CPR lines, company officials believed that it would be short-lived. This might have been the case had ore not been discovered there in the summer of 1883.

The creation of the Canadian Copper Company (CCC) in 1886 was an important development that helped to assure the future of mining in the region. Founded by Samuel Ritchie, an American entrepreneur, the CCC situated its main site of operation at Copper Cliff Mine, about ten kilometres west of Sudbury. However, initial blasting at the site proved disappointing because it revealed that the ore was of a low grade and that it

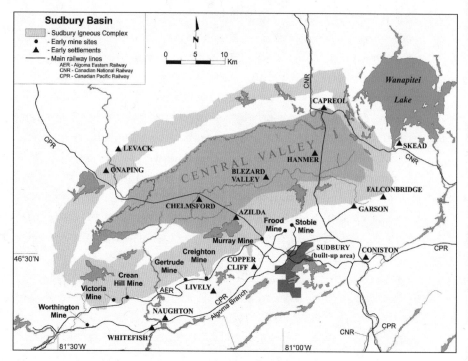

FIGURE 1.2　The Sudbury Basin. *Map by Léo L. Larivière*

contained nickel, an element that was expensive to refine and that lacked an international market. As a result, work slowed until officials realized its potential: when combined with steel, nickel was the best material for military armour. With this discovery, the small mining camp around Copper Cliff Mine quickly turned into the village of Copper Cliff in 1890.[5]

The CCC provided housing to its British workers, an exclusionary policy that forced its other employees to settle in small hamlets that sprang up on the outskirts of company property. As the CCC expanded its operations and attracted more workers – most of whom were ethnic men willing to do the dangerous and difficult work involved in mining – these fringe developments became ethno-cultural communities. With the CCC housing located in the middle of Copper Cliff, the Crows Nest settlement, northeast of this area, lodged Italian workers; the Johnson Extension, to the southeast, became a Ukrainian and Polish hamlet; and Finnish and French Canadian workers and their families lived in Shantytown, just south of the village.[6]

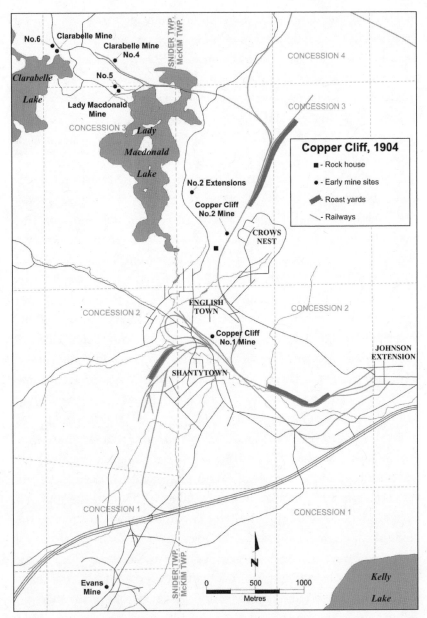

FIGURE 1.3   Copper Cliff, c. 1904. *Map by Léo L. Larivière*

Seeking to improve living conditions, the CCC incorporated the village into the Town of Copper Cliff in 1901, uniting the fringe developments with the company settlement in the centre. It was a stark and desolate place. Sulphur fumes had destroyed most of the natural vegetation, animals roamed freely, outdoor privies lacked proper drainage, garbage was strewn throughout, and many creeks and wells were contaminated. Diseases, especially typhoid fever, posed a constant threat to residents, and the infant mortality rate was among the highest in the country. Despite these circumstances, early improvements were made only in the British section of town. This situation did not change when, in 1902, INCO assumed control of Copper Cliff and the CCC (the INCO trade name was not used until 1919).[7]

Developments in other parts of the region mirrored those in Copper Cliff. Ludwig Mond, the Swiss inventor of a new way of refining nickel, established the Mond Nickel Company (MNC) in 1900 and soon employed three hundred men in his nickel mines.[8] Originally located west of Copper Cliff, the MNC operated its Victoria Mine Smelter there until 1913, when it moved production to Coniston and Levack, small towns located east and northwest of Sudbury. Like the CCC, the MNC was most concerned with accommodating its British workforce, relegating immigrants to the ethnic settlements that developed in and around Coniston. The company housing, known as English Town, was in the centre of Coniston; French Town lay to the east, in Old Coniston. A CPR line further divided the town into linguistic groups, with Italians settling on the north side of the tracks in Italian Town and Ukrainians and Poles calling Polack Town, on the south side of the tracks, home.[9] Housing in Polack Town consisted of unsubsidized, shabby, single-story dwellings that lacked running water, whereas the MNC provided its British workers with homes that had various amenities. Like the CCC, the MNC played a major role in determining the living conditions of its workers and the kinds of communities they were able to create.[10]

The first wave of Ukrainian immigration to Canada began in 1891. Pushed out of Austria-Hungary and Russia by overpopulation, the nobility's control of forest and pasturelands, and the absence of an industrial sector, Ukrainians were pulled to Canada with promises of free land and jobs.[11] Although most went to Western Canada, many settled in northern Ontario, northwestern Quebec, and parts of Eastern Canada between 1900 and 1910.[12] During this transformative decade, the CCC and the MNC increased production and opened new mines, leading thousands

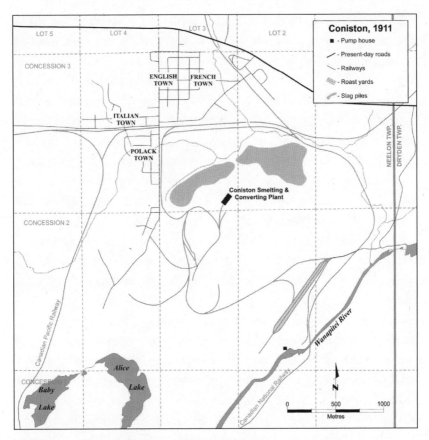

FIGURE 1.4 ·Coniston, c. 1911. *Map by Léo L. Larivière*

of immigrants to flock to the Sudbury region's predominantly British and French Canadian mining towns. In particular, Ukrainians formed small, masculine, transient communities in Coniston, Copper Cliff, Creighton, Garson, Victoria Mine, and Worthington, company towns near Sudbury. Copper Cliff, the area's most established town, had the largest Ukrainian population in 1911, composed of 201 men and 54 women; most came from Galicia, the biggest and most populous province in Austria-Hungary.[13] In these communities, men worked for the CCC or the MNC, labouring sixty to eighty-four hours a week in exchange for fifteen to twenty-five cents an hour. Although a few women worked as domestics, earning about two hundred dollars a year, most ran boarding households that included their own families and up to thirty boarders.

The predominantly male demographic that characterized these communities was typical for the ethnic segments of northern frontier settlements. Mining towns, as Nancy Forestell and Kerry Abel have demonstrated, were often spaces for bachelors well before families moved in. It took time for a sense of community to develop, especially among immigrant men, who had to be convinced that they could achieve prosperity in areas that depended so heavily on boom-or-bust industries.[14] Men, like Baba's father, frequently moved between resource towns, looking for a decent and reliable wage – they were often enumerated in several areas in the Sudbury region – before they married, had children, and effectively stabilized these places.[15]

Community, at this time, was therefore premised on informal social networks and the connections that men and women made to them. Life in the company towns near Sudbury was quite difficult, especially for women. Living in these rugged environments, first with Peter's family in Espanola and then with her husband and four small children in Sudbury, Annie was isolated, lonely, and depressed. In these trying times, she turned to her neighbours. These women, who found themselves in a similar situation, connected with Annie, supporting her and giving her useful advice. In particular, Baba remembered Mrs. Shustra, who lived in a one-room shack in the Donovan. Annie and Baba often visited her. As Baba sat on a trunk in the kitchen and ate candy, Annie and Mrs. Shustra shared their thoughts, worries, fears, hopes, and accomplishments. Although Baba recalled the treats more than the conversations, she stressed the importance of this lifelong friendship and the sense of community that was rooted in Mrs. Shustra's home.[16]

Sophia Parchewski's (née Mateyko) memories about her initial years in the area speak to similar themes. In 1952 when she sat down with her daughter, Mary Hansen, to reflect on her experiences, she emphasized community and how informal social networks facilitated belonging. In 1911, when Sophia was seventeen, she and her uncle left Potocheska, Horodenka, and came to Creighton. Shortly thereafter, she met and married her husband, John, and they moved to Worthington, where he worked for the MNC. John and Sophia came from the same village and were able to share stories about home, but they remained "lonely in this strange new land of forests, hills and sparse settlements." Although they lived in a log cabin with four other families – two French and two Ukrainian – Sophia did not begin to connect with them until the birth and subsequent death of her first child, a son. This was a trying period and Sophia never forgot how her housemates supported her. They also built a coffin and sewed a dress for her son before they drove John to a nearby cemetery for the burial; Sophia was too ill to attend. She forged friendships and gained a sense of community because of this tragedy, realizing that "we all had the same purpose – to make our home in a new land."[17]

Although Annie and Sophia were able to carve a space for themselves in their new surroundings, others were not as fortunate. Maria Zarichny (née Vasiliuk), an orphan from Karashyntsi in Galicia, came to Garson in 1913 at the age of fourteen. She had been in Canada for sixty-four years when Mary Stefura interviewed her, but her memories remained raw and emotional. Maria faced trying circumstances from the moment she set foot in Garson, learning that her older brother, Fred, her only family member in Canada, had been badly injured in a mining accident. A month later, Marko Zarichny, who was much older than Maria, coerced her into marrying him. Marko was an alcoholic and soon after the wedding, he began to regularly beat his young bride. Maria endured ten years of domestic abuse before she and her three children left Marko, eventually settling in Kirkland Lake, a town about three hundred kilometres north of Sudbury.[18] Maria did not speak of friends or family members when recalling this part of her life. She may have blocked them out of her memory, or perhaps she lacked a social network. Place helps to explain some of the isolation she experienced. Garson was a company town, where men outnumbered women by more than two to one, so making meaningful connections with local women would have been difficult for her.[19] Even if Maria had belonged to a social network, like the ones upon which Annie and Sophia relied, it is questionable whether its members would have intervened in her situation. Supporting a woman who was depressed or grieving was very different from interfering in a woman's abusive relationship with her husband.[20]

It was also hard for women to turn to others for help when they experienced sexual abuse. Although Catherine Hawryluk had familial and communal sources of support, she found herself alone when she became pregnant out of wedlock. Catherine was an eighteen-year-old immigrant from Galicia who lived in her uncle's boarding house in Copper Cliff. While there, she fell "victim to the wiles" of a boarder and became pregnant; it is unclear whether she engaged in a consensual relationship or was sexually assaulted. Two months afterward, Catherine married another man, Anton Hawryluk. On 25 July 1914 she was taken into police custody for murdering her newborn twins.[21] After concealing her pregnancy and giving birth, Catherine smothered her babies and buried them about two miles from her home. Courts sentenced her to death for this crime, a penalty that was later commuted to life imprisonment.[22]

Catherine's drastic actions speak to the double standard pertaining to sexual morality at this time. Consensual or not, intercourse with a man outside of marriage confirmed a woman's sexual immorality.[23] Catherine was well aware of this, and her illegitimate pregnancy left her distressed and with few options. Indeed, her fears about her moral standing in Copper Cliff's Ukrainian community eclipsed concerns about her physical well-being and safety. Since she could not turn to others for help, she concocted a desperate plan to save herself from disgrace. Like other young Ukrainian women who came to the Sudbury area during this period, she quickly married because it was a common thing to do and it ensured a degree of financial security. Also, though the sources are silent on this issue, Catherine's uncle may have discovered her pregnancy, "marrying her off" in an attempt to protect her reputation.

The geographic dispersion, masculine character, and transience of the region's Ukrainian population made community building difficult for women. Informal networks developed in homes and on streets in ethnic hamlets, but belonging, as these stories suggest, was not universal. Men also had a diverse set of immigrant experiences, which were largely influenced by their Old World convictions. Whereas some men immigrated as devout Greek Catholics, others, such as those who came from Southeastern Galicia, arrived with strong socialist and nationalist beliefs, which they had developed in enlightenment societies and reading clubs.[24] Still others became radicalized in the Canadian mines and forests where they worked, as a result of the harsh and dangerous conditions they faced on a daily basis. These private and public cultures of worshipping and protesting forged the identities of many men, determining where they lived and why some accepted their unsafe working conditions, whereas others challenged them.[25]

Living in predominantly male boarding houses constituted a large part of the masculine immigrant experience. Depending on who lived in a house, they could be calm and welcoming or rough and rugged. More often than not, they were loud but safe places where boarders cohabited with families and fellow countrymen who maintained similar ideological beliefs. The informal social networks that developed in these spaces reinforced Old World convictions and served as a subtle form of social control – most men acted accordingly, out of fear that unflattering news would get back to loved ones at home. However, alcohol and heated debates about work, women, or the Old World could quickly turn boarding houses into politicized and even dangerous spots. Although most debates were resolved through bantering or even a simple fistfight, some, like the one between Dmytro Wandesko and a Mr. Matura in a Garson boarding house in June 1914, were settled with weapons and resulted in death; following an argument, the cause of which is unknown, Matura stabbed and killed Wandesko.[26] This extreme case of rough boarding house culture reminds us of the complexities of these places; they were not always successful in regulating ethnic behaviour and uniting community members.[27]

Working conditions also divided men. According to Baba, Peter accepted the status quo. A loyal employee, he got up every day, walked to work or took a bus, laboured underground for twelve hours, and then returned home to find Annie and his four children waiting for him to begin dinner. Grateful to have a regular paycheque, Peter never complained about his job or the risks that it posed. Perhaps he prayed for his safety when he went to church.[28]

For others, employment stability was not worth the daily risks to life and limb. In silent protest, some quit their jobs and simply found work elsewhere, never voicing their opinions in public. When Baba and I interviewed Pauline Kruk (née Mykoluk), she was forthcoming and humble. Baba had known Pauline most of her life; the parents of both were founding members of St. Mary's Ukrainian Catholic Church, and

Pauline was Barbara's (Baba's sister) sister-in-law. This felt like a comfortable meeting between old friends. We sat in Pauline's living room, surrounded by images of her family and enough seating for a small army; Pauline is a devout Roman Catholic who, at the time of our interview, had eight children, twenty-six grandchildren, and six great-grandchildren, so it was not surprising that family and religion dominated our conversation. After Pauline and Baba shared news and I introduced the project, Pauline began to tell us about her parents' voyage to Canada and how they met on a train bound for Port Arthur. Pauline never hesitated to speak, because she trusted us; Baba's presence put her at ease. She went on to tell us about her ten siblings, listing them and noting when and where they were born, before sharing some early but poignant memories about the deaths of her younger brother Peter and her older sister Olga. Although she did not know why Peter died about a month after his birth, she vividly recalled his tiny body lying on a table in her home and how a priest had arrived to baptize him; this was an important ritual for her parents, Malanka and Jacob. Olga's death, she emphasized, was harder on the family. Olga was twelve when she passed away after being hospitalized for two weeks with an unknown illness. Pauline said that she could still see her parents crying; they never recovered from the loss. These memories were defining features in her familial narrative. As she paused for a moment to reflect, Baba recalled Olga's funeral. Her words offered Pauline support and spoke to the fact that this was a shared memory. The conversation shifted. They discussed impersonal memories, reminiscing about where the funeral home had been located. Pauline did not return to her story, as Baba's comment led her to transition back to her parents' history. This interruption frustrated me, but no one else seemed to realize what had happened. For Pauline and Baba, the comment was just a natural part of the conversation and actually served to defuse a sad, tense, difficult moment. I had to come to terms with the fact that Baba's presence in the interview space had benefits and drawbacks. Pauline continued to speak about her parents, explaining their move from Port Arthur to Copper Cliff. I asked whether Jacob worked at the mine, assuming that this would be the case and that we would quickly move on to the next question. He did, she said, but he later chose to work at Sudbury Steam, a local dry-cleaning business, instead. Surprised, I asked why he quit working for the company. Pauline declared that it was too dangerous for him. During a shift, he had spilled acid on his clothes, and it burned through to his skin. The risks were clear; I did not have to ask another question. Jacob had a wife and a large family to support. They depended on him. The family had also experienced enough death.[29]

Men who openly challenged mining conditions did so in the pages of *Robochyi narod* (*The working people*), the newspaper representing Ukrainian Social Democrats in Canada and the United States between May 1909 and September 1918, and at Copper Cliff's Finnish Hall, where they formed a local branch of the Federation of Ukrainian Social Democrats (FUSD) on 16 March 1913.[30] Being aligned with the FUSD, which viewed working conditions as part of a class struggle, had serious implications for miners.

Baba and I spent two full days conducting interviews with Ukrainian men and women who lived in Coniston, about a fifteen-minute drive east of Sudbury. Although she had met some of these people at various church and communal functions, others, such as Steve Buchowski, were strangers to both of us. As we approached Steve's house, Baba and I discussed our "plan of attack" and agreed that I would act as the primary interviewer, and she would remain silent. Interviews, however, seldom go as planned. Nor is sharing authority something that can be staged. Collaboration works best when it happens naturally, evolving from the flow of the conversation and the relationships that we develop with interviewees. This was definitely made more difficult because of the triangulated dynamics in the interviews that Baba and I conducted. In this case, Baba and I worked hard to share authority ourselves and with Steve. Baba quickly struck up a conversation with him as he opened his door and welcomed us into his home. Whereas I was shy, she was outgoing, noting that they had probably seen each other at various church functions throughout the years. She tried her best to make a connection to him and put him at ease. After we settled into the chairs around Steve's kitchen table, I began to ask him about his parents. He knew little about their background and quickly produced a copy of *The Coniston Story*, a community history with brief biographical sketches about the town's pioneering families.[31] Instead of abandoning my interview guide and asking Steve questions that he could answer, I glanced at the book's entry for the Buchowski family and continued to inquire about his parents. As Steve pieced together some semblance of a narrative, to satisfy my disconnected queries, Baba continued to try to relate to him by speaking about people whom they both knew. Soon, the interview devolved into an informal conversation; the three of us interrupted each other and spoke over top of one another as we tried to make sense of the few statements that Steve made with certainty. This was far from a perfect interview, but in some strange way it worked. Long before I did, Baba realized that my questions were futile, and she took the lead to steer the meeting in a more productive direction. After this rough and, at times, uncomfortable start, our friendly bantering seemed to take the pressure off Steve, and he proceeded to tell an important story about his father's early experiences.

He told us that his father, John, came to Copper Cliff around 1908 because his uncle, Wasyl Buchowski, owned a general store there. A hardworking man who attended Mass at St. Stanislaus Kostka Church, John was employed in the store alongside his relatives until he got a job at the CCC. Steve was quick to point out that he did not remain there for long, because he "got blackballed" as a communist and lost his job. I asked Steve whether his father was involved in attempts to unionize workers. He simply stated that John did something that got him fired. "Did he ever talk about this?" I replied. "I never asked him," he said. Steve emphasized that the loss of his job left John angry and bitter for most of his life. In blacklisting his name, company officials barred him from ever working for another mining company in the area; the town of Coniston eventually employed him as a janitor.[32] Unlike the details of his parents' history, this narrative was etched in Steve's memory. Having worked for INCO for forty years and lived in Coniston all his life, he was well aware of the politics of mining and the enormous reach of the company.

Old World ideological beliefs and the harsh working conditions they encountered on a daily basis continued to complicate the experiences of Ukrainian men during the First World War. In August 1914, the Canadian government passed the War Measures Act, identifying all unnaturalized immigrants from Austria-Hungary, Bulgaria, Germany, and Turkey as enemy aliens, subjecting them to arrest, detention, exclusion, and deportation, and denying them the rights of bail and *habeas corpus*. The enemy alien label applied to about 60,000 Ukrainians, and between 1914 and

1919, 5,954 of them were incarcerated in twenty-six internment camps.[33] Although this initial act applied solely to unnaturalized immigrants, the Wartime Elections Act of 1917 went farther, disenfranchising immigrants from enemy countries who had been naturalized after 31 March 1902. By blurring the boundary between unnaturalized and naturalized immigrants, this act referred to both real and imagined enemies, and "led many Anglo Canadians to see all 'foreigners' and 'aliens' as a single, hostile 'enemy' bloc."[34]

Canada-wide patterns indicate that the federal government instituted these wartime measures, and internment in particular, to address deep-seated Anglo-Canadian fears about immigrants rather than any real threats that they posed to national security.[35] Nativist depictions of the uncultured, inferior, and morally and sexually dangerous foreigner were well established before the war.[36] Prior to 1917, municipal governments used internment to purge their towns of unemployed immigrant men.[37] Following the Russian Revolution and the subsequent emergence of an international socialist subculture, an upsurge in labour militancy, and increased cooperation between Anglo-Canadian and foreign-born labour radicals, Ottawa shifted its focus from "enemy aliens" to "radical aliens," harassing, arresting, and interning unnaturalized Ukrainians who had ties to the Ukrainian Social Democratic Party (USDP), the FUSD's successor.[38] Some of these national patterns speak to the regionalized but nuanced experiences of Sudbury's Ukrainians.

Baba was the only person who specifically referred to the war's impact on her father. The transience and instability of the region's Ukrainian residents partially explain this silence. Although all unnaturalized immigrants were identified as enemy aliens and required to register and regularly report to their local magistrate's office – this label probably fed Peter's fears – disenfranchisement did not have a major impact on residents, because few were naturalized citizens who owned property; boarding houses and company homes dominated their landscape. Despite these regionalized experiences, there was a link between socialism and internment after 1917. The War Measures Act gave mining companies the means to punish socialist agitators. In 1918, after months of surveillance, a company judge sentenced three of the CCC's Ukrainian employees to internment for possessing seditious socialist literature. This small but significant number of internees also reveals why the community now lacks a collective narrative about this period.

Although the immediate pre-war years were prosperous ones for the CCC and the MNC, an international recession in the winter of 1914 forced the companies to slow production and lay off a major portion of their workforces.[39] The international nickel market was slow to recover during the early years of the war, and most men were not rehired until 1916, when a shortage of labourers forced the companies to offer some men their previous jobs.[40] These difficult circumstances surely affected Ukrainian men – immigrants were often among the first to be fired – but available sources contain few reports about them. This absence suggests that their daily rhythms continued to follow well-established patterns: men stayed in the area as long as they were employed, and when they lost their jobs, they sought work in the next resource town.

Those who remained in the Sudbury region continued to reside in Coniston, Copper Cliff, and Creighton. In addition to determining where employees lived and the conditions in which they worked, the CCC and the MNC administered justice in these towns, hiring police officers, operating jails, and appointing judges. As such, they were responsible for enforcing the federal government's wartime measures.

Although the USDP operated in these company towns during the war, Ottawa's enemy alien measures and mining company layoffs seriously affected its membership: in 1913 it had forty-three committed members, and in 1918 there were ten.[41] As a result, members organized few activities until they established a Prosvita Hall in May 1918; this cultural community centre had an amateur group that performed popular but instructional plays to raise both money and awareness for socialist causes.[42] The USDP may have had only a handful of members, but its social events at the hall were well attended by Ukrainians; limited leisure opportunities led many, regardless of their political persuasions, to frequent them.[43] The revenues generated by *The Murderers,* a play about the tragic consequences of alcoholism and illiteracy that was performed in Copper Cliff and Creighton Mine during the summer of 1918, demonstrate the appeal of these activities: it brought in $243.00, a large sum at this time, and the resulting profit was $41.55.[44]

Members planned to send the cash to Winnipeg to support the building of the Ukrainian Labour Temple, but this changed in late August 1918, when CCC police officers arrested eight USDP members; a portion of the money paid their legal fees, and the rest went to Anastazya Mikhnievych, the wife of one of the men. The arrestees possessed seditious socialist literature, which officers confiscated and sent to Ottawa for translation.[45] In the end, one man was sentenced to two years in jail or a $2,000 fine, Mikhnievych's husband was sentenced to three years in prison or a $3,000 fine, Y. Harsymovych, P. Stefaniuk, and N. Yavny were interned, and three others were released under the condition that they moved to Creighton and refrained from participating in socialist causes.[46] Although the activities of these men led the CCC to put them under surveillance for a number of months prior to their arrest, it is important to stress that they were not tried and convicted because they were socialists.[47] They were punished because they were guilty of a criminal act: possessing seditious literature.[48] Internment was a drastic response to this crime, but Ottawa's wartime measures made it a feasible option for the CCC judge, a man who had been a company miner for twenty-five years before undertaking this role.[49] It also suggests that the CCC was trying to send a clear and powerful message to its subversive employees.[50]

Anastazya Mikhnievych was outraged by the arrest of her husband. Left with two sons, poor health, and no source of income, she wrote a letter to *Robochyi narod,* explaining that her husband had been an active member of the socialist movement in Austria-Hungary and had merely brought his beliefs to Canada. Given his commitment to the socialist movement, she appealed to those with a "raised consciousness" to send her money so that she could pay her husband's fine.[51] Although it is unclear how socialists responded on a national level, we know that Anastazya relied on the generosity of her husband's local contemporaries because they gave her a portion of *The Murderers* profit; Copper Cliff's socialist community was alive and well in these formative years. The Buchowski General Store also helped women like Anastazya. Wasyl Buchowski extended credit to families who lacked a stable breadwinner, a mark of goodwill that, as we shall see, ultimately contributed to the collapse of his business.

FIGURE 1.5   Buchowski General Store, c. 1916. The group at the left, *from left to right,* includes Eugene Buchowski, Olena Buchowski, Harry Buchowski, unknown nurse, Wasyl Buchowski, Walter Buchowski, and Nadzia Buchowski. The group at the right includes the store employees. John Rozinski, second from the right, married Nadzia in 1915. This store was one of the few public communal spaces for Ukrainians who lived in Copper Cliff to gather and chat about import- ant issues. Additionally, as the photo demonstrates, it was a private space where kinship networks, as viewed through Nadzia and John's marriage, functioned. The possible division of its space is also interesting: the Buchowski family is on one side of the shot, whereas the employees are on the other. Nadzia is practically in the middle, seemingly acting as a bridge between the two groups. *Courtesy of Greater Sudbury Historical Database, http://webcat.sudbury.library.on.ca*

Mary Anne Buchowski and I spent the better part of a sunny day in her Ottawa living room, discussing her family's history and its con- nection to Sudbury; we "found" each other through a local Ukrainian genealogy group.[52] Although we had met only once before, we had no problems connecting; she was committed to my project and excited to see how her stories "fit" with my research. From the moment she greeted me at her door, our conversation was intense and emotional.

Having just sold her family's last piece of property in Sudbury, she was desperate to hold on to something that would connect her to the town. The past served this purpose. I conducted a life story interview with Mary Anne, but our discussion constantly returned to her grandfather Wasyl Buchowski, his general store, and the difficult conditions that led to its demise. Since Wasyl died before Mary Anne was born, her stories regarding him had been passed down through her family. The contents in a tattered file folder – family letters and documents, photographs, and her grandfather's obituary – told another tale, revealing a series of desperate and horrific events in Wasyl's life. As Mary Anne spoke about her grandfather, she struggled to weave together a narrative that reflected his experiences.

According to Mary Anne, Wasyl came to Canada from the village of Serafyntsi in 1904 and settled in Copper Cliff, where, by the time his wife and children arrived in 1910, he had established the first Ukrainian general store in the region; this was a place where immigrants shared news about the Old World and discussed local happenstance and politics while they shopped for necessities.[53] Although most immigrants arrived with little more than the clothes on their backs, Mary Anne explained that Wasyl had married into a wealthy family whose members provided the money to build the store. She showed me a number of photographs, attesting to the family's affluence. Figure 1.5 shows that Wasyl employed a significant number of men and women as well as a nanny who cared for his children. Another photograph depicts Wasyl's wife, Olena, being driven to Sunday Mass in a horse-drawn sleigh, an uncommon occurrence given that Copper Cliff was small, and most immigrants could not afford such a luxury.

Within ten minutes of starting our conversation, Mary Anne was in tears. As she pulled a handwritten letter from her file folder, she told me that Wasyl's good fortune ended in 1917. When Ukrainian men started to lose their jobs at the CCC, he extended credit to them. This was an easy decision for Wasyl, Mary Anne asserted, because he "was a good-hearted man who cared about people and did not want to see them go without."[54] In normal circumstances, this system would have worked itself out eventually, as customers tended to pay their balances every other week, when the company issued its paycheques. However, since the CCC had laid off a portion of its workforce, there was often no wage on which to rely. By November 1917, Wasyl found himself in a difficult situation: he had issued too much credit and was unable to pay for his stock and meet his mortgage payments. Mary Anne then passed me the letter that she had been holding. Written by Wasyl's bookkeeper, it was a detailed summary of the store's history. Wasyl, it stated, was confident that he could eventually recover from his losses. At that point, however, he needed more stock, so he asked a wealthy local merchant, who held the store's mortgage, to give it to him on credit. The merchant refused, advising Wasyl to burn down the store so that he could recover his losses by collecting the insurance money.[55] Mary Anne was quick to declare that this was not an option for her grandfather: it was dishonest and it was irrational, since his building and inventory were worth more than his insurance policy would pay him.

On 19 November 1917, a fire destroyed the store. Mary Anne returned to her file folder and pulled out another handwritten letter, which, in her opinion, resembled a suicide note that revealed the "truth." It connected the local merchant with the fire and outlined how this person had tried to blackmail her grandfather.[56] Mary Anne insisted that Wasyl had resolved all the issues pertaining to the fire in a legitimate manner. After losing the store, he slowly paid off his debt and moved his family to a farm he owned in Long Lake, just south of Sudbury. In 1928 he left Olena and their three youngest sons to settle in Sudbury, where he became heavily involved in the local socialist movement; it is unclear whether he was connected to the USDP while he lived in Copper Cliff or became politicized later. Wasyl died in 1934 and, as Mary Anne stressed, never recovered from the fire. In her mind, it was a major turning point for him, destroying his family and his mental and physical health.[57] The Buchowski General Store was directly affected by the economic circumstances of the First World War. Like the USDP members who helped Anastazya, Wasyl and his family made significant sacrifices to ease the troubles of those who lost their jobs. By extending credit, the store served as a vital resource for Ukrainian immigrants who lived in Copper Cliff.

Fearing that there would not be enough jobs for returning soldiers, INCO, the CCC's successor, dismissed 2,200 of its 3,200 employees in early 1919. Massive layoffs like this one, coupled with concerns about the status of Canada's "alien" workers, led to the appointment of the Royal Commission on Industrial Relations later that year; the commission held meetings in twenty-eight industrial centres, including Sudbury.[58] Testimonies provided by company officials and workers clearly speak to the complex power relations that structured Ukrainians' daily lives and the communities they were struggling to establish in company towns. They also attest to the ways that politics continued to affect identities and thereby complicate belonging in the postwar period.

When C.V. Corless, an MNC mining engineer, was asked to reflect on employee living conditions in Coniston, his remarks were vague, brief, and calculated. According to him, the company's housing was in good condition, and the men typically worked eight-hour days and were paid sixty to seventy cents an hour. Corless said nothing about the dangers of the job or the miserable conditions in Polack Town. Although he mentioned the recent layoffs, he pointed out that no strikes had occurred, because the men were "happier than they would have been had they been highly organized and had outside interference."[59] D.J. Fortin, a structural ironworker, was unable to remain silent, declaring, "I see some of these employers claim that they are not antagonistic to organized labour and I know the reverse to be the fact. I know that immediately [when] a man takes an active part in labour organizing he is immediately discharged from his position."[60] Fortin's remarks, like the story about John Buchowski's blacklisting, demonstrate how mining companies regulated the activities of their workers. There were no strikes, because the companies ensured that they did not occur.

Michael Balandaski's frank testimony picks up on a thread in this discussion. A Ukrainian machinist's helper, he had little to lose when it came to criticizing INCO because the company had blacklisted him for carrying a union card while on the job. As he described how the layoffs affected his contemporaries, he noted one way that INCO was trying to exploit the men. Three days after dismissing 1,400 workers, INCO announced that it would re-hire 100 of them. However, their wage would be diminished by seven cents an hour for the same work.[61] A socialist at heart, Balandaski argued that Ukrainians were not recognized for their vital contribution to the Allied victory. The layoffs and the hourly wage reductions were disrespectful measures, given that these men had "[produced] nickel and all the necessary things with which to fight the German and Austrian militarism."[62] Surely, they had earned the right to call themselves Canadians. Balandaski gave voice to their unease; they were no longer called enemy aliens, but this label and the outsider status that it connoted lingered with men, even Catholics like Peter, for many years, affecting how they negotiated their place in both the region and the nation.

WHEN THE WAR ENDED, Ukrainians were expected to go back to living as they had prior to 1914. This was an impossible expectation. Whereas some withdrew from Canadian society – changing their names to conceal their ethnicity and refusing to apply for Canadian citizenship, open bank accounts, or buy insurance – others became politicized by their enemy alien status as well as the treatment they received from mining companies. Adjusting to these varied circumstances led many to establish formal ethnic spaces: small, polarized enclaves within the larger community, where their voices would be heard and their opinions could be shared.

CHAPTER TWO

Solidifying
Organized Ukrainian Life

AT ONE POINT OR ANOTHER, my conversations with Baba typically led to St. Mary's Ukrainian Catholic Church. I rarely had to bring it up because it was always there, looming large in her narrative about the past as well as in discussions of her everyday experiences. Baba's rich and vast repertoire of stories about her parents, family members and friends, and memorable events and social functions revolved around the church. As the centre of her social world, it effectively structured her identity and rooted her in Sudbury's Ukrainian Catholic community.

It is difficult to condense our many exchanges about the church into a single and cohesive tale. Baba's connection to it was forged through her experiences within it. Dominant memories of them, rehearsed, told, and retold for years, came up in our formal interviews and were frequently repeated when we spent time together; fleeting ones emerged in all kinds of situations. For instance, a chance encounter with friends whom Baba had not seen in a long time would prompt her to tell me a story about a ·dance that she had attended in the church basement, or the sight of a building would remind her of a parish priest who had spent many holiday dinners at her family's table. Indeed, at first glance, there seemed to be little logic when it came to these random but important reminiscences. As Baba divulged new stories and repeated variations on old ones, I gained a better understanding of the central role that St. Mary's played in her life.

Baba's identity and sense of belonging to this space no doubt originated with her father, who viewed himself as "Catholic first, Ukrainian second, and Canadian last." Whenever the church came up in our conversations, Baba frequently reiterated a short story about the role that Peter played in its founding. After moving his family to Sudbury, he

49

approached International Nickel Company (INCO) officials and asked them to donate money toward the construction of a church. They agreed and St. Mary's was built in 1928. Although this was the gist of the story, Baba sometimes added to it, emphasizing that her parents, along with other parishioners, were also involved in numerous fundraising drives to pay off the building's debt. The Priemski family's boarding house in the Donovan, for example, was the site of many memorable parties, where Baba loved to sit and watch the grown-ups dance the night away as they collected money for the church.

The last time that Baba mentioned her father's early involvement in St. Mary's, I asked who had told her the story. This question surprised her. Although I had heard it on many occasions, this was the first time that I had asked her to expand on her rehearsed narrative. In a defensive tone, Baba declared that she had just heard it as a child: "No one told me the story." Perhaps, she surmised, she had overheard a conversation at the church between parishioners, or maybe it had come up at home. "Did your mother or father tell you the story?" I prodded. "No," she said. Since Baba did not know the exact details, she encouraged me to omit the narrative. "Why?" I asked. Instead of answering, Baba changed the subject. Her request bothered me. As I pondered the ethics of respecting it, I thought about the ways in which she had comfortably embraced the story over the years. Why had my simple query led her to doubt the legitimacy of something she had always held to be true? Were my questions, and the ways I asked them, the problem, or was it the fact that her experiential authority was coming to blows with my scholarly expertise? Unable to let the issue go, I mentioned it a couple of weeks later in a phone conversation. My questions, she insisted, had little to do with her feelings about the story. Rather, she had just read the "official" history of St. Mary's, a new publication to mark the church's centennial, and her father's name was not listed among those who had secured the INCO grant.[1] This absence led her to contemplate the validity of the story. She had always been firm and clear about it, so I was disappointed to hear that the "authority" of the book negated her understanding of it. In response, I stressed that her personal truth did not require verification.

Baba may have been uncertain about the details of the anecdote, but those that referred to Peter's faith and his commitment to St. Mary's were unwavering. Her father, she stressed, spent all his spare time at the church. As the cantor and "right-hand man" of the parish's many priests, he assisted with daily Masses and other ceremonies, such as baptisms and funerals. He did whatever the priests asked of him and never, Baba emphasized, accepted money for his services: "He wanted to build St. Mary's, not take from it." The church men's league, choir, and drama club, along with executive positions on the parish council, also kept Peter busy. Not surprisingly, his daily routine – of working long shifts underground and participating in most church activities – limited the encounters that Baba had with him. She remembered him as a quiet but stern and imposing figure, and she shared few intimate details about him. For Baba, family time spent at the dinner table was therefore quite precious. It was here that everyone would share stories before Peter walked out the door, dressed in a clean, pressed suit and his Stetson hat. When I questioned Baba about his absence from her childhood, she made light of my remarks, stressing that she was grateful to have had him as a father because he played a large role in determining the kind of person she became. Had her father not insisted on speaking Ukrainian at home, she would not be fluent in the language. Without his insistence on her regular attendance at Mass and her participation in parish activities, she would have no faith. And, had he not insisted on ritualized holiday behaviours, such as the blessing of food baskets at Easter, she would have little connection to her culture. Peter may not have been an ideal father, but he was her father and she loved him nevertheless. This was as far as Baba was willing to go when it came to remembering this commanding figure.

As in the courtship story that opened Chapter 1, Annie's place in Baba's memories about the church was quite limited. What, I wondered, was her relationship to the place that meant so much to her husband? Did she resent the time that Peter gave to it? If there were tensions about the church between her parents, Baba did not address them. Instead, she explained that Annie was also very religious. She sang in the choir and participated in the drama club. As part of the women's league, she cooked for church fundraisers, organized parish dinners, and decorated the hall for special events. Women, Baba declared, were "the backbone of the church." Peter may have played an important role in the parish, but, Baba insisted, "there would be no church without the women." If this were the

FIGURE 2.1   The pioneers of St. Mary's Ukrainian Catholic Church gather on the steps of Christ the King, an English Roman Catholic church next door to St. Mary's, for a celebratory mass, c. 1951. Peter is in the front row, at the far right. Annie stands beside him, on the left. *Courtesy of St. Mary's Ukrainian Catholic Church, Sudbury, Ontario*

case, why did she rarely mention her mother when speaking about the church? Baba did not hesitate when answering this question, explaining that Annie had to "make time" for it. Her responsibilities, of managing a boarding household and raising five children, left her little spare time. If she could convince a boarder or her daughter Barbara to babysit, she got dressed in her Sunday best and went to the church with Peter. If she couldn't get away, her involvement was limited to weekly Masses, until her children were old enough to care for themselves or participate in the many church activities. Over time, St. Mary's became a major part of Annie's community. Like her neighbourhood, it was a place where she forged lasting relationships with those who shared similar beliefs and experiences.

FIGURE 2.2   Baba's first communion, c. 1934.
Courtesy of Olga Zembrzycki

Brought up in the church, Baba emulated her parents and made St. Mary's her own. Given her parents' commitment to the church, most of her childhood, adolescence, and adult years were spent there. In addition to attending weekly Masses, she went to Ukrainian language school every Monday, Wednesday, and Friday, and on Saturdays she had catechism lessons. When she turned fifteen, she joined the Ukrainian youth league and spent hours cleaning the church, bookkeeping for the priest, and organizing dances for her peers. These dances hold a special place in her memories. Having grown up watching her parents participate in these kinds of events, she relished the opportunity to raise money for the church while having fun. At one dance in particular, she remembered that the priest had worried about her decision to hire a twelve-piece orchestra, warning her that she would be lucky to break even. Viewing this as a challenge, Baba went to work selling tickets – a task she happily did throughout her involvement at St. Mary's – and managed to cover the cost of the orchestra and contribute to the church bank account. "I proved him wrong," she smirked. Naturally, when Baba became too old for the youth league, she joined the women's league, proudly declaring that she gave it sixty-one years of active service. Like her mother, she cooked for church dinners and worked in fundraising ventures, playing a crucial role in building and sustaining the parish.[2]

Most of the men and women whom Baba and I interviewed were Ukrainian Catholics who had some connection to St. Mary's; a minority belonged to the Ukrainian Labour Farmer Temple Association (ULFTA), St. Volodymyr's Ukrainian Greek Orthodox Church, or the Ukrainian National Federation (UNF). Given this common bond between Baba and those to whom we spoke – her lifelong friends – the church often dominated our conversations. Sharing authority, with both Baba and the interviewees, proved to be a difficult goal because Baba's stories about her father's founding role and her parents' contribution to the church largely directed the remembering. Our interviewees frequently shared their memories of Peter and Annie before relaying details about the history of St. Mary's and telling stories about the experiences that they and their parents had there. They recalled Peter's presence at the church, the fact that he could always be heard singing there, and Annie's role in its kitchen as one of the many cooks for fundraising and social events. Peter and Annie were good people, they repeatedly stressed. Although these comments were nice to hear, these spaces were also incredibly difficult for me to navigate, especially as I tried to untangle Baba's memories and those of interviewees. More often than not, Baba insisted on having a forum for her stories before others could recount their own memories. Given these complications, they tended to replicate patterns that were inherent in her stories. In particular, they emphasized the important, tangible, and gendered ways that they and their parents had built a community within the church. Men undertook leadership roles, on building and parish committees, whereas women were relegated to support positions – cooking, cleaning, and fundraising – that held less authority and power than those accorded to men; male chauvinism and prescribed gender roles limited women's opportunities. Gender, however, did not figure in interviewees' memories of their childhood selves. Instead, ethnicity and age dominated their tales. Those who grew up and grew old in the Ukrainian progressive, Orthodox, and nationalist communities shared similar recollections, outlining the ways that their churches and halls heavily influenced their identities, the communities to which they belonged, and their own understanding of themselves and their place in society.[3] If community took root in the informal social networks within which Ukrainians forged relationships among neighbours and co-workers who shared similar struggles as well as Old World convictions, it was solidified in the social organizations and politically exclusive ethnic spaces that they began to build shortly after settling in the region and well into the 1920s.

The geographic dispersion and transience of Sudbury's Ukrainian population made networking and the establishment of ethnic communal spaces difficult. However, the residents of Copper Cliff overcame these challenges by constructing the area's first Ukrainian institution and the province's first Ukrainian church: St. Nicholas Greek Catholic Church. Networking depended, at least in some ways, on numbers; this company town had the area's largest Ukrainian settlement until the 1920s.

Between 1900 and 1907, Copper Cliff Ukrainians attended Mass at St. Stanislaus Kostka Church. French-speaking Jesuit priests operated the church, conducting its services and sacraments in French according to the Roman Rite. These ceremonial procedures were foreign and even suspect to Ukrainians, and they led a group of men to organize a church building committee. Their efforts resulted in the construction of a simple wooden structure that was consecrated as St. Nicholas Greek Catholic Church by Pastor Reverend Timothy Wasylewych on 12 February 1909; there, Wasylewych offered Masses in Ukrainian, administered sacraments, and counselled his parishioners.[4] Building a church signified the community's desire for permanence, stability, and continuity in a changing environment.[5]

St. Nicholas's popularity and existence were short-lived. By 1914, parishioners had neither the time nor the means to raise funds or donate money to cover the church mortgage and subsequent expenses, a debt that amounted to $7,500. The transient nature of the community and the federal government's wartime measures probably played a role in the church's decline as well. St. Nicholas operated until 1920, when a fire destroyed its interior and its records.[6] Due to dwindling interest and a shutdown at the Copper Cliff Smelter that year, parishioners decided not to resurrect the church. In fact, most Ukrainian families moved from Copper Cliff to Coniston, Levack, and Sudbury at this time, where they formed small communities of between two and three hundred people that continued to be dominated by single, transient men.[7] With the addition of streetcar and bus services, men could easily commute to work and put their earnings toward buying a home of their own.

In the latter part of the 1920s, after INCO recovered from a severe downturn in the international nickel market and merged with the MNC, it undertook a number of major construction projects. The building of a smelter and a copper refinery in Copper Cliff led the company to hire 2,865 men temporarily and 3,100 permanently at its Frood and Copper Cliff operations; Frood Mine was located in the northwest corner of Sudbury.[8] INCO chose not to build more company houses, so many new and old workers settled in Sudbury, where residential construction boomed and neighbourhoods were transformed almost overnight.

Gatchell, a neighbourhood located to the west of Sudbury's Downtown, was home to many Italians; the Flour Mill, northeast of Downtown and informally referred to as French Town, was dominated by French Canadians; the Donovan, which was northwest of Downtown and within walking distance of INCO's Frood Mine, was a mixed immigrant neighbourhood that was home to families, including Baba's, with breadwinners who laboured at this mine; and lastly, the East End was a transient Slavic part of town, populated by employed and unemployed single men. "Sudbury," according to A.D. Gilbert, "was beginning to take on the appearance of a cluster of communities, each with a distinctive ethnic, religious, and occupational atmosphere." "Nevertheless, there was," he states, "surprisingly little evidence of animosity between the various groups of which the town was composed."[9]

The history of Sudbury's Ukrainian community speaks to a different reality. There may not have been much animosity between other ethnic

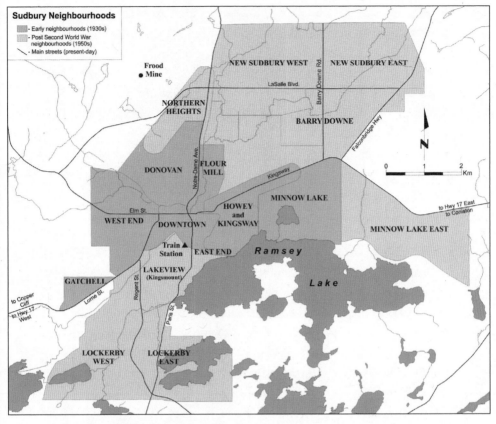

FIGURE 2.3   Sudbury neighbourhoods. *Map by Léo L. Larivière*

groups, but there was certainly a great deal of tension between the two very divided communities in the Ukrainian population. Ukrainian Catholic and progressive men, women, and children lived in the same neighbourhoods, shopped at the same stores, and attended the same schools, but their political and religious beliefs, rooted largely in their Old World convictions, set them apart. They established organizations that were in opposition to one another, and INCO threw its support behind the Catholic community, severely limiting the opportunities available to those who identified with the progressive movement.

Although Ukrainian Catholics were the first to build a communal space, progressives began meeting informally in Copper Cliff during 1913; they called themselves the Federation of Ukrainian Social Democrats

(FUSD), then the Ukrainian Social Democratic Party (USDP) in 1914, the Ukrainian Labour Temple Association (ULTA) in 1918, and finally, the Ukrainian Labour Farmer Temple Association (ULFTA) in 1924.[10] Forming enlightenment societies in many local mining communities, progressives discussed the merits of Bolshevism and communism, criticized the local labour situation and mining company policies, and ranted about the inadequacies of Catholicism. In their opinion, parishioners who paid priests to churn out "fairytales" about life were wasting their money since Catholicism brought nothing but "backwardness" to Ukrainians.[11] It was imperative that all men become members of "one large labour family."[12]

In April 1924, after many years of meeting in homes, Ivan Pereima and thirty-nine other men established a local branch of the ULFTA in Coniston.[13] This was a risky venture in an MNC town, where citizens were always under surveillance, monitored by a small force of company policemen, and one wrong move could result in the loss of both a job and a place to live; men were routinely fired for fighting, drinking, and causing disturbances during their leisure time.[14] I suspect that the company knew very little about the organization in these early years. During the same period, Coniston's Ukrainian Catholics built a Prosvita Hall in 1926 and added a chapel to it in 1928. Calling the structure St. Michael's Ukrainian Catholic Church, they worshipped there until a fire destroyed the building in 1934; parishioners did not construct and open a new church until 1952.[15] Textual and oral records say little about the fierce battles that took place between the two groups.[16]

Prior to the 23 November 1924 opening of their new building, Coniston progressives organized a series of politically charged events to raise money for it. Concerts, plays, and lectures – speakers were often Communist Party of Canada members – focused on the class struggle.[17] They also established a children's school so that their children could learn the Ukrainian language and culture, and become acquainted with the aims of the international communist movement.[18] Ironically, a women's section, which would have socially enlightened and educated the mothers of these progressive children, was not established until May 1925. Like other ULFTA branches – the name change occurred in February 1924 – this was a masculine organization, run by men, for men.[19] Its members believed that they had an important role to play in building the progressive community. As Rhonda Hinther argues, they were "determined to preserve and celebrate their sense of identity as Ukrainians while at the same time improving their circumstances as workers and farmers."[20] Education was the means through which they would achieve these goals.

On 6 January 1921, twenty-five men formed a Sudbury branch of the ULTA. Although membership fluctuated in the early 1920s because of layoffs at INCO and the MNC, members eventually purchased a plot of land on Spruce Street in Sudbury's West End neighbourhood, and on 1 November 1925 they held their first Ukrainian concert in their new hall.[21] Working together on a variety of ventures, the Sudbury and Coniston ULFTA branches staged plays and concerts, shared a children's schoolteacher, invited key figures in the movement to speak to their members, and held joint picnics, socials, bazaars, and dances to raise money to pay off their building debts. In addition, they organized functions with progressive Finns, who also had a hall on Spruce Street, celebrating events such as Lenin's birthday, May Day, and International Women's Day as a united political entity.[22] Working-class solidarity was central to the success of the local progressive movement.

Progressive men spent the bulk of their spare time at these halls, discussing politics and devising strategies to ensure that their movement would build and sustain their community. They assumed the branches' leadership roles, using politics and anti-Catholic sentiment to define their masculinity.[23] Belonging was no longer just a gendered experience, but a political one as well.

Progressives adopted the Soviet belief that men and women were free and equal but did not practise this principle in the movement. "[Equality]," as Frances Swyripa stresses, "often remained an elusive and contentious ideal."[24] As men took on leadership roles, women were relegated to subordinate positions that not only reinforced male chauvinism, but also mirrored the traditional European gender roles that structured their Canadian households.[25] "These differences," according to Swyripa, "gave men and women separate spheres, and they exploited so-called 'female' qualities to place homemaking and motherhood above community work and to dictate the form that community work took."[26] Progressive women built their community by adhering to this submissive stereotype.

Women were drawn into the ULFTA for a variety of reasons. Like the men, some had cultivated a strong predisposition to radical politics in their peasant villages prior to coming to Canada. "For others," the working conditions they saw and experienced "were sufficient to underscore the inequality inherent in the capitalist system and Canadian society." Anti-clerical sentiments, which they developed either in Canada or in their peasant Ukrainian villages, and the encouragement of friends and family members, also led some women to the movement.[27] For them, the ULFTA Hall was a social space that shaped their identities while they built and solidified their community.

Women did not assume a formal role in the Coniston ULFTA branch at the outset, but they were present nevertheless, cleaning and decorating the hall and sewing costumes for the various plays performed throughout the region. On 24 May 1925, seven women finally decided to change the situation, joining the men's section to "gain experience and have their consciousness raised" before they formed their own section.[28] Men made these women feel insecure, constantly stressing that they were backward, illiterate, and uneducated.[29] "Why," some asked, "[do women] need an organization; [they need] only to be able to cook."[30] Undoubtedly, household duties limited the time that women could give to the organization too. Over the next few months, more women joined the men's section, and a few even undertook some of the formal masculine roles – chairing and seconding motions – involved in holding a general meeting.[31] After four months, with this experience in hand, they created their own section, electing an executive and announcing that they would donate eighty-eight dollars to pay off the branch's building debt.[32]

Women in the Sudbury ULFTA branch did not hesitate when organizing their own section. On 14 December 1925, a month after the building opened, six women formed a section and four more joined a week later.[33] They immediately undertook supporting roles, cleaning the hall, cooking for socials and picnics, collecting donations to pay the branch debt, and ensuring that there were items to auction at the bazaars.[34] Motherhood also moulded their roles in the ULFTA.[35] They helped to establish the youth section and the children's school, and did not hesitate to file formal complaints when they noticed problems with teachers.[36] Women were kept quite busy, putting in long hours at the hall; men's fears that their wives might not have enough time for their households were often well founded. Community building, it seems, could not have taken place without all the unpaid work that women did behind the scenes, work that brought men's directives to life. Politics, prescribed gender roles, and motherhood shaped their femininity and the ways that they contributed to the life of their community.[37]

Since the involvement of boys and girls was vital to the ULFTA's future, the national executive organized children's schools and youth sections in local branches throughout the country in 1924. The hope was that exposing children to Ukrainian culture, traditions, and language as well as communist ideals would produce devoted adult members of the movement, who would continue to build the community that their parents had worked so hard to establish. Although childhood experiences were diverse, boys and girls undertook similar roles in the branches, since their activities were not segregated by sex. They played together, sang together, laughed together, performed together, and learned together, and thus gender was less important in the construction of their identities.[38] Unlike their adult counterparts, whose roles were defined by gender, progressive boys and girls were encouraged to come together in a common class struggle.[39] A united and youthful voice would help the community grow.

Mary Brydges (née Ladyk) grew up in the Sudbury ULFTA branch, and she was the first person whom Baba and I interviewed. Insisting on visiting her "old friend from the Donovan," Baba told me stories about Mary as we drove to her house in Sudbury's West End. Baba explained that she had grown up down the street from the Ladyks, and as a teenager she had worked at Macks' General Store, which was owned and operated by Mary's brother-in-law. Mary's family, she stressed, especially her mother and sister Annie, had also played founding roles in the ULFTA Hall, or as Baba referred to it, the "Spruce Street Hall." As we pulled into the driveway and approached the back steps of Mary's large two-story home, I was nervous and excited to conduct my first "real" interview. All my planning had finally paid off, but I did not know what to expect. I also worried about how Baba would affect the exchange; her storytelling left little time for us to discuss how the interview would work. As Mary opened the door and invited us in, Baba and I glanced at each other before we stepped inside. Over time, we would come to rely on these glances, using them to communicate with each other in interviews.

Baba immediately took control, hugging Mary and introducing me as her granddaughter; the fact that I was doing research was secondary. A shy but warm woman, Mary invited us into her living room and insisted on making both of us comfortable before she sat down on the sofa next to Baba. She had to sit close, she explained, because she had difficulty hearing and seeing. When Baba made a witty comment about growing old, Mary responded in a serious tone, telling us that her days in her home were numbered because she would soon be moving to Pioneer Manor, a nursing home where her sister Annie lived. Having just turned ninety, she needed assistance with day-to-day tasks. Baba fell silent and Mary turned to me.

When I remember this experience, I immediately think of the energy I felt in the room: you could cut the tension with a knife. Mary was a private person and I felt overwhelmed. I struggled to initiate a conversation and began by asking Mary to tell us about her parents. Her response was short and to the point; she knew little about their history. "That was too long ago," she declared. I encouraged her to go on, telling her that not having answers to my questions was perfectly acceptable. Baba and I looked at each other, and then she smiled at Mary. Mary proceeded to tell us about how her Canadian-born father, John, had travelled to Austria-Hungary to find a wife. There he met and married her mother, Barbara, who was eighteen years old. John and Barbara came back to Canada and settled in Port Arthur, where Mary was born; they had three other children: Peter, Katie, and Annie. Barbara and the girls later came to Creighton and then Sudbury. "And your father came with all of you?" I asked. "No, no, they were separated," Mary said, "'cause she [Barbara] was so young, you know." It took me a moment to register what Mary had said. I tried to clarify her statement and go a bit deeper but soon gave up, sensing that she was uncomfortable. Shifting the conversation to her childhood memories, Mary immediately mentioned the ULFTA Hall. She could not remember where it was located. To help her, Baba asked whether she was thinking of Spruce Street. "No," she said. Mary thought for a moment and blurted out "Oak Street." With this detail out of the way, she explained the importance that her mother placed on the hall children's school. Barbara never learned to read or write. She considered herself "stupid" and did not want her children to "be like her."[40] She thus insisted that they attend Ukrainian school. As a result, Mary, who proudly beamed while she spoke, told us that she learned to read and write in Ukrainian and to play the mandolin. This educational experience was a central part of her childhood. Later in our interview, I returned to the ULFTA, asking Mary if she would tell us more about her involvement in the "communist hall." Mary became defensive, making it clear that she disliked my label. Although Baba tried to fix my error, by referring to it as the Spruce Street Hall, the damage was done. With two words, I had effectively shut down the conversation and could not get Mary to elaborate on how the hall had affected her life. I never used the "c" word again, unless interviewees employed it themselves. By engaging in the process, I was learning how to be a compassionate and thoughtful interviewer as Baba tried to right my wrongs and carve a space for herself as a co-interviewer. Thrown into the deep end, we quickly developed a collaborative style that sometimes worked well but had mixed results in other instances. As soon as we changed topics, the tone shifted. Mary reminisced about growing up in a large boarding house and about her experiences as a "miner's wife," mentioning that she had left the ULFTA Hall when she married an Englishman. She seemed to derive comfort from Baba's nods and positive affirmations. In these moments I saw that Baba could act as an important mediator between interviewees and me, and was not just a liability. Mary also tried to take the focus off herself, often attempting to draw Baba into the conversation by posing questions that typically started with "Do you remember?" For her part, Baba resisted these calls until I turned off the recorder. At that point, the conversation became light, informal, and lively. I sat on the other side of the room, listening and observing.[41]

Educational experiences, like the one described by Mary, along with participation in events such as plays and concerts, gave progressive children confidence and a sense of pride in their heritage. They were thrilled to be able to read books in another language and to receive standing ovations and chocolates after a performance; audience members frequently threw chocolate bars onto the stage at the end of a play to signify

that they had enjoyed it.[42] Most children joined the Coniston and Sudbury ULFTA youth sections to have fun and meet other children, not to
actively participate in the class struggle.[43] Although they sang the
"Internationale" and performed communist plays and music, they do not
seem to have taken the movement's political aims seriously, much to the
chagrin of their teachers and parents. At times the branches struggled to
hold their attention. Although youth sections consisted of between twenty
and sixty children, few came to rehearsals, classes, or organized lectures
on a regular basis, and those who did tended to be late and disruptive.[44]

Children were not as devoted to the ULFTA as their parents. If activities
did not interest them, they spent their spare time elsewhere, engaged in
pastimes that they deemed more enjoyable. Youngsters, as Hinther argues,
"exercised agency and power by complaining or voting with their feet
when activities arose that they did not enjoy."[45] They had more options
than their parents when it came to networking and community building.
Age and ethnicity, more than gender and politics, shaped their experiences in this exclusive ethnic space.[46] Born and/or raised in Canada and
able to speak both English and Ukrainian, they were not limited to spending their free time there.

After Copper Cliff's St. Nicholas Greek Catholic Church burnt down
in 1920, Ukrainians celebrated Masses and sacraments in English- and
French-language Catholic churches and, informally, in private resi-
dences until 1923, when eleven families met with Father Mykola Shumsky
to begin fundraising for a new Ukrainian church. The absence of a church
was problematic for many Ukrainians, including Mary Dudowich (née
Kuchira). Unfortunately, Mary died just a couple of weeks before her
hundredth birthday, while I was waiting for ethics clearance to begin my
interviews. Although I did not have an opportunity to sit down and speak
to her, Baba and I did spend an afternoon with "Taciana," remembering
Mary and the experiences she shared with her. One tale, in particular,
intimately speaks to this transitional stage in the church's history. Soon
after coming to Creighton at age sixteen, Mary attended a wedding in
Garson, a joyous and spirited celebration. She was taken aback by the
fact that the wedding guests outnumbered her entire village in Ukraine.
There she met Metro, who was twenty-three years her senior, and they
danced the night away. Shortly thereafter, Metro proposed to her. After

some hesitation, Mary accepted his offer, but because she desired stability, Metro had to prove that he was gainfully employed at INCO before she said yes. Since there was no Ukrainian church in Creighton, the couple travelled to Coniston, where a French priest at Our Lady of Mercy Church married them. Although there was a translator present, Mary often joked about the ceremony: since she had not understood her vows, perhaps she and Metro had never married.[47] Mary, it seems, was quite a character!

A group of Catholic men, including Baba's father, Peter, organized a parish council to overcome obstacles like the one Mary mocked. They spent five years raising money to build a church of their own, where they could worship in their own language and embrace their own traditions. Founding parishioners, both men and women, performed plays, organized picnics, and held bazaars to raise money for this cause. By the time Father Joseph Bala purchased a lot at 78 Beech Street, in Sudbury's Downtown, the young church had raised about four thousand dollars. INCO also contributed by donating twenty thousand dollars, but its generosity was driven by an ulterior motive. The sum gave the company power within the church, enabling it to continue to regulate its workforce and distinguish between its good Catholic and bad progressive employees.

INCO needed foreigners to perform the difficult and dangerous underground labour that Anglo-Canadian and British men refused to do. To attract a stable workforce to the nickel capital – men with families were considered more reliable than single men, often referred to as sojourners – INCO invested in Sudbury's infrastructure. It viewed baseball diamonds, hockey rinks, and churches as appropriate social outlets for employees.[48] A Ukrainian Catholic church served two purposes: it encouraged men to put down roots and to oppose both communism and union activity. Parish priests were instrumental in monitoring the company's Ukrainian employees.

Although the letter reproduced in Figure 2.4 is quite short, it nevertheless demonstrates the relationship that INCO forged with priests at St. Mary's. A parishioner, such as George Boluk, would ask the priest for a reference. If the priest believed that he was a committed member of the church and deserved a job, he would write a subtle letter like this one, indicating that the man was indeed a member of the church and not the ULFTA.[49] St. Mary's, it must be noted, was not the only church to

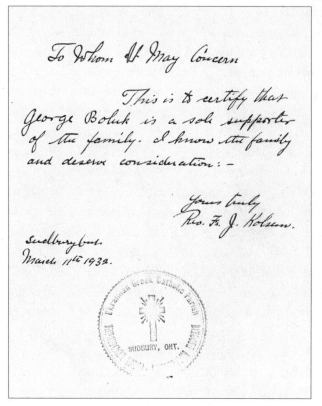

FIGURE 2.4   Father John Kolsun vouches for a Ukrainian
Catholic man. *INCO or Canadian Copper Employment Records,*
1912-39, Ukrainians in Sudbury Collection, in author's possession

take a public stand against communism. A number of French and English
Catholic churches also aligned with INCO to fight the "reds."[50]

Baba's father, Peter, was quite close to many of the priests who served
St. Mary's, developing spiritual and personal relationships with them.
Baba grew up hearing stories about the infamous visits that the company
shift bosses paid to the priests, to ask about parishioners' activities. She
also remembered many late-night dinners, when Peter returned home
from work with his shift bosses in tow. Annie would have to get up and
cook for them, as they drank, ate, and discussed politics into the early
hours of the morning. Although Baba never spoke in depth about these
episodes, her eavesdropping and their stressful nature led her to declare,
"Ukrainian Catholics never had a problem getting a job at INCO."

FIGURE 2.5   Sudbury's anti-communist Catholic churches, no date. Spruce
Street, the location of the Finnish and Ukrainian progressive halls, was a progressive stronghold, whereas Beech Street, in Sudbury's Downtown, was an anti-
communist bastion. The churches, from the foreground to the background,
include St. Mary's Ukrainian Catholic Church, St. Anne's French Catholic Church,
and St. Joseph's Roman Catholic Church, renamed Christ the King in 1935.
Courtesy of Ray Thoms, Ray Thoms and Kathy Pearsall, Sudbury *(Toronto: Stoddart, 1994), 107*

Whenever I asked her to elaborate on this point, she just said, "Leave it
at that, Stacey!" For her, the issue was still delicate, and even illicit, and
she did not want to make comments that she could not prove. Additionally, it did not fit with her romanticized version of the past and the myth
she attached to the memory of her father, a subject discussed in the following chapter.[51] St. Mary's quickly adopted some of INCO's objectives,
condemning communism, identifying communist supporters, and con-
verting them to Catholicism whenever possible.[52] The relationship established by INCO's large donation benefited both partners: the church grew,
its pews were filled with a working and thus financially supportive congregation, and INCO created a trustworthy, employable, and essential
foreign labour force.

Despite differences, Ukrainian Catholics espoused the community-building strategies of their progressive foes, assuming gendered and generational roles within the church. Catholic men acted as parish leaders. They established a building committee, and along with the parish priests, they planned a number of fundraising campaigns that were implemented by female members. Many of the men also belonged to the Sudbury branch of the Canadian Sitch Organization (CSO).[53] The CSO, renamed the United Hetman Organization (UHO) in 1934, was "a Ukrainian athletic association that had been founded on secular ... principles, and persuaded its members to reject the trappings of democracy and to recognize Hetman Pavlo Skoropadsky as Ukraine's only legitimate and hereditary ruler." It was committed to Catholicism, and "its repudiation of democracy and popular sovereignty, its militant anti-communism, and its goal of forming cadres of disciplined Ukrainian state-builders won the church's enthusiastic support."[54] Priding itself on obedience, discipline, order, and respect for religion, the CSO propelled men into leadership positions in the church.

Whereas progressive women were required to be class-conscious mothers and wives, Catholic women were expected to be good Christians, good companions to their husbands, good mothers, good parishioners, and good daughters of the church and its people.[55] Like their progressive adversaries, whose ideals sometimes overlapped their own, Catholic women contributed to their community by shouldering the small but important tasks involved in the upkeep of the church. Through their efforts, they also made friendships that helped them expand their social networks.

When St. Mary's opened its doors in October 1928, women established a league of their own and got to work organizing a series of weekly tea parties to raise money to decorate the building and complete the altar furnishings.[56] Teas were not part of Ukrainian peasant culture, so women essentially "Ukrainianized" the activity to suit their needs. In a fascinating example of how culture becomes hybrid over time, women, as Swyripa explains, "served their teas on cross-stitched tablecloths, sold Ukrainian handicrafts instead of crocheted potholders at their bazaars, and replaced the chicken supper with the pyrohy supper."[57] Additionally, women cleaned the church, organized fundraising dances and balls, cooked for functions and weddings, and formed an immigration and traveller's aid committee that welcomed new female Catholic immigrants to the region and united those who were married with their husbands.[58] As mothers of the next generation of Catholics, they were also instrumental in convincing, and sometimes forcing, children to attend Mass and participate in the church children's school.[59]

Eugenia Maizuk's mother (née Kureluik), Stephania, was one of the many women who devoted their lives to ensuring that the region's Ukrainian Catholic churches ran smoothly. Baba and I met with Eugenia and her husband, Joe, on a cold but sunny day in January 2005. We sat in a bright room that overlooked their glistening snow-covered backyard, and Jenny offered us hot drinks as Joe spoke with Baba about happenstance at St. Mary's. When Jenny returned from the kitchen, she made herself comfortable and began to tell us about her parents, Vasil and Stephania, and her memories of growing up in Coniston's Polack Town. Joe and Baba jumped in from time to time, helping her remember people, places, and dates, but these intrusions seemed to make little difference to the form and content of Jenny's narrative; she took control of the interview space, directing the conversation and staying on track throughout. Whenever I asked her questions, to clarify or elaborate, she responded briefly and returned to her story. Education was an important thread throughout this exchange, allowing her to make sense of her parents' choices and how they affected her life.

Shortly after Vasil arrived in Canada, he enrolled in English-language classes for immigrants in Toronto, where he held several jobs before going west to work on a farm. Much like Baba's father, Vasil did not like farming, so when he heard that the MNC was hiring, he left the farm, got a job with the company, and lived in a Coniston boarding house. Stephania's sister, who ran this business, managed to save enough money to bring Stephania to Coniston, where she had "her pick of husbands." There she met and married Vasil, and together they had six children. Since Vasil was devoted to education – "he didn't want his children just to be nobodies, to be serfs" – he put money aside to ensure that they would not spend their working lives inhaling sulphur fumes, as he had. Like many immigrants, Vasil and Stephania ran a tight household, stressing homework and chores over leisure time with friends.

While raising her children and attending to the needs of her boarders, Stephania was also a founding member of St. Michael's Ukrainian Catholic Church in Coniston. She made constant visits to the church during the winter, feeding the stove with wood to keep it warm, and she went door-to-door in Polack Town, collecting money for the construction and maintenance of the church. Stephania also took charge of hosting teas at St. Michael's. Like the women discussed by Swyripa, she had to learn about this activity before she could make it her own. She not only frequented Anglican teas to see how they set their tables, she also bought a tea set to "practise" pouring tea properly. Concerned with doing things well, Stephania, who served as president and vice-president of St. Michael's Ukrainian Catholic Women's League, also sat in on women's league meetings at St. Mary's. There she continued to learn, adopting and avoiding best and worst practices. The church was the centre of Stephania's community and the place where she gained an education.

After attending high school, Jenny enrolled in the Toronto School of Dress Design. Few Ukrainian girls her age completed high school let alone post-secondary education. Lifelong learners who strived to achieve the typical immigrant dream, Vasil and Stephania wanted their children's lives to be better than theirs. Without their insistence on education, Jenny's life, she recognized, would have been very different.[60] She would not have had the luxury of taking her love of sewing and clothing design to a professional level.

Although women assumed supporting roles in both Catholic and progressive institutions, their efforts may be viewed as subtle forms of leadership and initiative. As Lynne Marks discusses, there was power in domesticating and feminizing church interiors, a process that allowed women to manage some of the money that they worked hard to raise.[61] Women in both camps also had complete control over church and hall kitchens, which were free of male scrutiny.[62] There they exercised and exerted power among and between themselves, forming cliques and hierarchies that were rooted in internal politics, personality clashes, and gossip.[63] Labour was one issue that divided women. Those who donated their time and rolled up their sleeves resented the "fina panis" who sat on the sidelines and took credit for their achievements.[64] Building community

was a complicated process, requiring women to negotiate power relations on many levels.

The tensions and battles between women in these spaces continued to
animate some interviewees. A topic of much gossip, these conflicts were
often a starting point for getting people to talk about their community
engagement.[65] Since Baba had spent a lot of time in the church kitchen,
she and our interviewees knew many of the same people and could relate
to each other. Before we arrived at "Elena's" house on a blustery winter
day, Baba gave me a sense of what to expect. Elena, she said, loved to talk.
I would have no problem getting her to open up. Really, our problem
would be leaving. "Expect to be here most of the day," Baba laughed. By
now, we had conducted over thirty interviews together and had established our ground rules – the interviewee and I would speak about the
past, and Baba would abstain from asking her own questions until I was
finished. We had also worked out our non-verbal signs of communication; she quickly got to know my "dirty looks," as she called them, and
my calls for help. I had no reason to believe that this interview would
differ from the rest. I was wrong.

Elena was pleasant and welcoming as she greeted us at the door of her
small but cozy house, hung up our jackets, and seated us at her kitchen
table. She lit a cigarette and introduced us to her husband, "Peter." A
seventy-five-year-old man of Eastern European descent who came to
Canada in the 1950s, Peter spoke little English and proceeded to make
himself comfortable on the couch in the next room, where an unopened
bottle of whisky and a shot glass sat on the table in front of him. Was he
planning on drinking that now, I wondered. He reached for the bottle,
broke the seal, poured himself a shot, gulped it down, and sat back on
the couch. Moments later, he repeated the process several times and
eventually passed out. Trying to focus on the task at hand, I turned on
my recorder and asked Elena to take me back to the beginning, to speak
about her parents and her childhood. In a few moments, she was telling
us about an abusive experience she had had in a Western Canadian
classroom. An Irish teacher hit her over the head because she spoke
Ukrainian in class. "This was how the Irish, Scotch, and English treated
the Ukrainians," she said. The incident was not her fault, she explained,

as Ukrainian was the sole language spoken in her home: "I just didn't know better."

After many years of struggling to put food on the table, Elena's parents moved their family to Sudbury in the late 1930s. "I never thought I'd stay in Sudbury this long," she mumbled. Her father failed to find work at INCO, so the family continued to have difficulty making ends meet. "These were hard times," she said. Baba weighed in: "Well, you managed." Elena's parents could not afford a place of their own, so they lived with two other families until her father abandoned them. This was probably for the best. Elena alluded to more abuse: "Some of us didn't have nice fathers ... [On the outside] it was a mask. You always did as you were told." I didn't have the courage to ask her to elaborate. Elena moved to Toronto to get away from her troubled family, and while recounting this time in her life she spoke more in depth about her father, explaining that his drinking and womanizing were "cultural things." That was as far as she would go when discussing the abuse she endured. In the background, Peter cursed in his sleep, and Elena yelled at him to be quiet. I jumped; I am not usually a nervous person. Sadly, she had returned to the situation she tried to flee many years before.

Ukrainian communal spaces were Elena's escape from domestic abuse. When she spoke about them, she came alive; she gave all her energy to them, and in turn, she derived her energy from them. The five years she spent in Toronto were filled with good memories about participating in organizational life. While there, she "learned how to be a Ukrainian," baking bread and learning how to paint *pysanka* (Easter eggs). Baba once again joined the conversation, complimenting her on her bread and mentioning two other women who were known for their baking skills. Elena digressed and she and Baba spoke about some of the friends they shared. Frustrated, I tried to get the conversation back on track, so that Elena could elaborate on her communal involvement before Peter awoke. Soon, Elena returned to a chronological narration of her story, explaining that upon her return to Sudbury, she threw herself into volunteer work, undertaking executive roles and spending as much time as possible in the kitchen, making perogies and cabbage rolls to raise money. "It was up to the women," she stressed.

Elena created close relationships with many women in the organizations in which she was involved but was quick to differentiate between those who did and did not have money. She mentioned both class and the deep divisions that frequently surfaced over labour issues. "[Unlike others] I can stand proud for the work I did," she said. She and Baba proceeded to gossip about those who shirked their responsibilities. Every time a woman's name was mentioned, they got riled up. Their tones changed and their voices grew louder. They also spoke about their parents, debating the influence they had in their respective organizations and trying to make distinctions that were futile to me but central to how they defined themselves in relation to their communities. I did not manage to get the interview back on track. Peter woke up shortly thereafter, disoriented and yelling at Elena. I looked at Baba and signalled that it was time to go. Elena tried to get us to stay longer. We quickly grabbed our coats, managed an awkward goodbye, and rushed out the door. Elena stood in the background, offering us jars of borscht while she held her husband back. I was shaken up when I got in the car. "She's had a hard life," Baba said, unmoved. I did not have the energy to respond. We drove home in silence. Elena had spent the better part of her life negotiating power dynamics and trying to build a supportive community. About a year after our interview, Peter died. Elena sold her house, packed her bags, and returned to southern Ontario, leaving her beloved community behind.[66]

Catholic children also participated in the organizational life that consumed their immigrant parents. They attended Mass, took language, catechism, and dance lessons, sang in the church choir, learned to play a variety of musical instruments, and staged plays that had religious connotations. Although reaching adolescence meant that boys and girls joined the separate junior men's and women's leagues, in which gendered tasks were central to their experiences and prepared them for their adult responsibilities, children were taught in an environment that was relatively free of gender constraints.[67]

About a month after St. Mary's opened, Father Nicholas Bartman established a children's school that was committed to "[counteracting] the effect, as much as possible, of Communistic doctrines." It enrolled twenty to forty children and offered an intensive program in which classes took place four days a week, from five to eight o'clock in the evening.[68] Like progressive children, some Catholic boys and girls enjoyed this educational experience more than others did. If catechism did not appeal to them, they walked past the church and into places like the local movie theatre, where they spent the money that their parents had given them for school. Ultimately, Baba and her peers defined community on their own terms. The church was the centre of Baba's social world, but she also spent a lot of time on the streets of the Donovan, playing with an ethnically mixed group of children. Although children did not take their community obligations seriously, most maintained a connection to St. Mary's through adolescence and adulthood. As they grew older, their faith and their commitment to the church strengthened. The cultural- and language-based generation gap between progressive children and their parents as well as Cold War politics and INCO's aversion to the ULFTA explain why the same cannot be said for that movement.

ALTHOUGH TENSIONS between progressives and Catholics were minimal during the 1920s, the opening of St. Mary's Ukrainian Catholic Church in October 1928 intensified divisions among Sudbury's Ukrainians. As they worked out their competing notions of community, they took to the streets and publicly declared their differences in a series of physical and sometimes violent clashes.

CHAPTER THREE

Contesting
Confrontational Identities

BABA WAS BORN in a small house in the Donovan on 21 February 1927. She was Peter and Annie's fourth child, and her birth coincided with an important transitional stage in the history of Sudbury's Ukrainian community. Grounding their identities in ethnic spaces, Catholics were hard at work raising money to build a church, whereas the progressives, a smaller group, were actively engaged in a variety of activities in their two new Ukrainian Labour Farmer Temple Association (ULFTA) Halls. As founding members of St. Mary's Ukrainian Catholic Church, Peter and Annie put themselves, as well as their children, in the middle of the differences polarizing Sudbury's Ukrainians. The Zymas' place in the community was further complicated by the fact that Peter was extremely active in the parish. He regarded himself as a servant of the church and participated in its politics. He made both friends and enemies as a result of his fervent religious beliefs, and therefore it is not surprising that one of Baba's earliest memories focused on a violent clash between her father and a number of progressive men. This confrontation marked the end of Baba's childhood innocence, establishing her place in the community and teaching her the importance of recognizing difference.

Whenever Baba spoke about the 1930s, she told me two stories. One, which will be examined in the following chapter, dealt with her family's struggles during the Depression; the other recounted a "communist attack" on her home. Although she was only six at the time, this latter tale was deeply embedded in her memory. During one sunny afternoon, about twelve men congregated outside Baba's house on Frood Road and proceeded to throw rocks through the porch windows while they called Peter names. "My father, mother, sister, and I were in the house, and it was definitely during the day," Baba remembered. "It happened right in the middle of the day! Father might have just gotten home from work. I don't know where my brothers were." As a child, Baba focused more on the noises she heard and the fear she felt than on the circumstances that brought the men to the house.[1] "We ran to the back room and hid underneath the bed," she said. "Mother was screaming. She was hysterical. There was lots of yelling." When I asked, "What were people saying?" she replied, "I don't know, there was just lots of noise." Baba emphasized that her parents were helpless. They did not have a telephone to call the police: "Nobody had a phone back then." "Did your father report the incident?" I asked. "I don't know, I don't think so," she answered. When I asked, "Why do you think these men attacked your family?" Baba's reply was straightforward and rehearsed: "We were attacked because we were Catholic. Maybe father had gotten into a dispute with them. He was an easy target because he was a leader in the community. He kept a high profile. We were attacked because we were religious, not because we were Ukrainian." True to form, Baba held the men, not Peter, accountable for the incident. In her opinion, it was a microcosm of the larger divisions between Ukrainian Catholics and progressives that were playing out in Sudbury. She rejected my attempts to problematize the situation. "Maybe your father was acting as an informer for INCO," I surmised. Baba would not consider this possibility. "Father probably knew the men," she stated as she changed the subject. "They were communists, you know."

Although I grew up hearing about this confrontation, it never really occurred to me to ask if there were two sides to the story. Every time I listened to Baba's version, I was always left with the impression that she and her family had been victimized by the "communists from the Spruce Street Hall." As her granddaughter, I wanted to believe this account: that my great-grandfather had been wronged, that he had played an important role in the community, and that he had stood up for his beliefs despite the dangers of doing so. As a historian, however, I pushed myself to deconstruct it, recognizing that Baba had fashioned this tale in the minutes, hours, and years following the altercation. I had many questions that went, and continue to go, unanswered. What kept Peter and his shift bosses around the dinner table into the wee hours of the morning? When he saw priests welcome INCO officials into the church, did he engage with them as well? What did he say? Surely, they did not want to discuss religion. Baba emphasized that Peter was a vocal and proud man. He was not capable of sitting idly by and listening to people denounce Catholicism. When he condemned the progressive movement, he thought he was doing the right thing. "Communists" were bad people in his eyes. There was no room for an alternative interpretation. By controlling the telling of this story and refusing to relinquish any authority, Baba continued to adhere to this view while she protected her family's legacy and her father's mythic role in it. She clung to the narrative because it was the basis upon which her understanding of herself and "others" relied. Picking apart its complex layers threatened to expose the cracks, uncertainties, and contradictions in its foundation. Peter had to be the "good guy" in the story; the silences surrounding him inhabited the safe borderlands of Baba's memory and thus did not figure in her personal truth.[2]

Had I been able to interview the progressives who threw rocks at the house that day, it is quite likely that their stories would have been very different from Baba's. Perhaps they would have implicated Peter in the confrontation, telling me that they had acted in revenge for losing their jobs. The reasons behind this attack, however, are less important than what they say about Baba's identity as a Ukrainian Catholic. As she hid under the bed, shaking in fear and listening to the sounds of breaking glass and yelling, she was faced with a striking depiction of the "other." This public airing of differences allowed her to understand her place in the community. The church had always been a part of her life, but Baba became a Ukrainian Catholic that day, assuming the identity that played a central role in her parents' lives. At the time, she lacked the conceptual and contextual knowledge needed to arrive at this conclusion, but it both consciously and unconsciously shaped who she is.[3]

Given Baba's upbringing and the ways she depicted and labelled progressive Ukrainians, I tried to place limits on how we would share authority with them. When I interviewed progressives, I often left Baba at home. I made this decision without giving much thought to the implications. Perhaps I was trying to protect and shelter her from them, or them from her. In hindsight, I know that much of the decision had to do with power. I was trying to create a safe and open space that was free of Baba's narrative as well as her judgments and perspectives. I didn't want her baggage to affect how progressives told me their stories and articulated their views about the differences between Sudbury Ukrainians. It has taken me many years to embrace Baba's story and the role that she played in this project, and I also think that part of me was trying to retain control. From time to time, I wanted to have the freedom to negotiate the interviewer-interviewee relationship on my own. That said, Baba had many friends in the Ukrainian community, some of whom happened to be progressives. She attended interviews with the progressives whom she knew, and these encounters ended up being vibrant spaces, often providing lots of room to grapple with and debate the "good Catholic" and "bad communist" labels of Baba's youth. Her relationships with progressives were often more subtle and less black-and-white than I realized. By trying to manage how we would share authority, perhaps I missed out on some valuable exchanges. I do, however, stand by my decision. Solo interviews gave me some respite from the intense and often difficult dynamics of authority that Baba and I worked hard to negotiate. Most importantly, the contrast they provided allowed me to see the value of her participation in the project.

Whether Baba was present or not, politics structured the memories of progressives, just as they did for the Catholic, Orthodox, and nationalist Ukrainians to whom we spoke. Baba's story was by no means unique. They too experienced the differences that polarized the community, using their ethnic halls and churches to root, construct, and reinforce their distinct identities. They also worked out these identities, and their definitions of the Other, in Sudbury's streets, schoolyards, playgrounds, and alleys; like Baba's front yard, these were hotly contested sites of conflict, where tempers flared and bodies clashed. The parades, demonstrations, public ceremonies, and habitual taunting, gossiping, and name calling that occurred there enabled them to assert and maintain their differences while they negotiated the boundaries of their communities. Organizational growth also complicated identity making during this period. Whereas progressives remained united, Catholics divided into a number of factions, building more politically and socially exclusive communal spaces. Through a public culture of confrontation, Ukrainians contested community and demonstrated who were and were not respectable citizens.[4]

Although the building of St. Mary's Ukrainian Catholic Church in 1928 and the ULFTA Halls in Coniston in 1924 and Sudbury in 1925 gave Ukrainians a public face and enticed some men and their families to relocate to the region, the promise of a decent and reliable job in the mining sector remained the crucial attraction. INCO and Falconbridge Nickel Mines Limited, which opened its doors in 1928 just east of Sudbury, recorded peak levels of nickel production in the late 1920s and early 1930s, and thus expanded their workforces, leading to a period of sustained growth.[5] Sudbury's population more than doubled in a ten-year period. Ukrainians comprised roughly 5 percent of this population in 1931, about 760 people, becoming the third-largest ethnic group in the city, behind those of British and French descent.[6] This growth is significant, given that the country was in the middle of an international recession.[7] The 1929 stock market crash crippled the economies of most Canadian towns and cities, but Sudbury remained relatively untouched by the crisis. In this "mecca" for the country's unemployed, men laboured underground and earned wages that were impossible to attain in other locales.[8]

However, not all Ukrainian men were guaranteed jobs at the local mines. INCO and Falconbridge used ordinary Ukrainians and priests from St. Mary's as informers, to determine who would and would not be hired. Informing was a lucrative business for priests, who received "generous financial assistance" from the companies and who collected an eighteen- to twenty-dollar fee from each man for whom they found work.[9] Those who shared information, on the other hand, could rest assured that their jobs were secure. Men who were lucky enough to obtain work in these circumstances constantly struggled to keep it. Progressive ties, in particular, were sufficient grounds for firing, blacklisting, and indefinite suspension.[10]

ULFTA members believed that a union would help them combat these unfair hiring and dismissal practices, and also advocate for better working conditions, a five-day work week, and a seven-hour work day. To this end, they organized a large May Day rally, with progressive Finns, in 1930.[11] At this well-attended event, police arrested and charged three women and fifteen men for disturbing the peace.[12] Although it accomplished little, the rally helped progressives begin to define themselves publicly against Ukrainian Catholics, as a group that would not tolerate the exploitative measures of the mining companies.

Parishioners at St. Mary's tried to disassociate themselves from these Ukrainians by showing their commitment to democratic ideals. In addition to composing a young and thriving church that was "engaged in combat" with local progressives, they established a branch of the Canadian Sitch Organization (CSO) and a League of Christian Workers.[13] The League, in particular, aimed to "counteract the effects of Communistic propaganda and to spread the ideals of the Canadian constitution" so as to "unite Ukrainian workers in this district into a law abiding brotherhood."[14] Unlike progressives, they would not take to the streets and threaten Sudbury's social order.

Following this reasoning, seventeen veterans of the Ukrainian National Army formed Branch Ten of the Ukrainian War Veterans Association (UWVA) on 9 February 1930.[15] A precursor to the Ukrainian National Federation (UNF), a Canadian branch of the Organization of Ukrainian Nationalists (OUN), this group cooperated with St. Mary's, joining the League of Christian Workers and holding meetings in the church basement to devise strategies for "rescuing" those "who'd fallen into the clutches of the Bolsheviks."[16] However, the relationship between the UWVA and St. Mary's was short-lived.[17] A group of parishioners, who were also CSO members, opposed the UWVA and convinced the priest to revoke its hall privileges.[18] After losing their meeting space, UWVA members met at the Royal Canadian Legion, where they worked hard to identify themselves as "law abiding residents of [Sudbury] and as supporters of the government of Canada."[19]

The region's economy collapsed in the latter half of 1931. As the mining companies reduced their workforces, "bankruptcies, and default of mortgage payments and taxes became commonplace," leading unemployed men to wander through Sudbury's streets begging for work, shelter, and food.[20] Father Nicholas Bartman, the parish priest at St. Mary's between 1928 and 1931, told his parishioners that their woes were the result of poor choices: "the workers and the unemployed don't pray enough, don't attend church, and don't go to confession." Progressives shot back, declaring that Catholics were often among the poorest because they

Progressive Ukrainians
- Ukrainian Labour Farmer Temple Association (ULFTA) in Coniston and Sudbury
- Men's, women's, and youth sections

Catholic Ukrainians
- St. Mary's Ukrainian Catholic Church
- Men's, women's, and youth leagues

Canadian Sitch Organization (CSO)/United Hetman Organization (UHO)
- Catholic male monarchist members who opposed the UWVA

Ukrainian War Veterans Association (UWVA)
- Catholic and Orthodox male nationalist members who opposed the CSO/UHO
- Secular Canadian branch of the Organization of Ukranian Nationalists (OUN)

Orthodox Ukrainians
- St. Volodymyr's Ukrainian Greek Orthodox Church
- Men's, women's, and youth leagues
- Nationalist members

Ukrainian National Federation (UNF)
- Ukrainian National Federation Hall
- Men's, women's, and youth organizations
- Secular but composed of Catholic and Orthodox nationalist members
- Endorsed the OUN and opposed the CSO/UHO

Ukrainian Self-Reliance League (USRL)
- Lay arm of the Ukrainian Greek Orthodox Church
- Opposed the UNF because it endorsed the OUN
- CSO/UHO aligned with the USRL in 1939

FIGURE 3.1   Ukrainian organizations in the Sudbury region, 1930-39

"[gave] their last penny to the priest."[21] Church membership did indeed rest upon a financial obligation. Priests expected their congregation to make a donation every Sunday as they passed baskets through the aisles during Mass. Whereas collection plates were placed at the entrances of ULFTA Halls so that members could give anonymously, St. Mary's parishioners engaged in a public display of giving. And, as Nellie Kozak's (née Tataryn) story reveals, when it came to making this contribution, there were certain expectations, even in difficult times.

Nellie was a close friend of Baba's sister, Barbara. She and her husband, John, often visited my Aunt Barbara and Uncle Tony, spending their afternoons engaged in intense card games. Unable to have children of her own, my endearing aunt, or "Chachi," as I fondly called her, spoiled me rotten, doting over me as I sat on her lap and watched the adults interact. Sadly, Chachi and Uncle Tony died in a tragic car accident when I was five. Our family was devastated. John and Nellie rarely visited after they died. When Nellie opened the door and saw me standing beside Baba, she could not believe how much I had changed. For my part, I remembered neither her nor the time we had shared together. I smiled and followed Baba into her apartment. This was the final interview that Baba and I conducted. By this time, we had settled most of our differences, learning to compromise and communicate. That said, we still struggled to share authority when we met with close family friends. The details of our lives seemed to get in the way, creating an intimate and animated starting point for remembering the past but also leading us in directions that had little to do with the stories being told. Or so I thought. This was a space where interviewees and Baba worked out their memories, by gossiping and exploring tangents that spoke to the larger themes dominating their narratives.

A warm, friendly, and outspoken individual, Nellie immediately began to tell us about her parents, Mary and Michael. She often mentioned them, recalling stories about the dangers her father faced underground and the central role her mother played in their large boarding house. Within minutes, we were on the edge of our seats, listening to an intense tale about a mine cave-in "Pops" experienced in 1931. He had been left for dead, but when his co-workers finally pulled him from the ground, they realized that his heart was still beating despite the fact that his chest and legs had been crushed by a rock. He spent two years in INCO's Copper Cliff hospital, recovering from the accident, and he walked with crutches for many years following his release. During this difficult period, Mary assumed responsibility for her six children. She struggled to feed and care for them, and to meet the monthly mortgage payments of $42.25. "I'll never forget that [figure] as long as I live," Nellie uttered. Mary received a cheque from INCO for fifty dollars a month but with little left over, she also ran a boarding house, picked and sold blueberries, and collected and sold coal from the tracks nearby. A strong and dominant individual, Mary had to be ruthless, "ruling with an iron fist," as Nellie put it, adding "she was bossy right until the end!" As I listened to Nellie speak, I couldn't help but think about the similarities between her and her mother, especially when Baba tried to get a word in and she would cut her off. Although they spent some time reminiscing about the past and the people they knew, Nellie was very clear about the ground she wanted to cover in the interview. She fixated on her Depression-era experiences and on her mother's ability to make ends meet. "We were poor," she stressed, "but we never went hungry."

To get through these difficult times, Mary and Michael derived strength from their faith in God and the community they created at St. Mary's. Like others, they gave their time and money to the church, even when both were in short supply. This was a constant balancing act. Nellie remembered one Sunday, in particular, when "Mamma had eleven cents in her pocket and that was all the money she had in the world." Intending to place her last dime in the collection plate, Mary accidentally donated the penny instead. Much to her embarrassment, this did not go unnoticed by the priest. He approached Mary at the end of the Mass and berated her, saying, "If you haven't got any money to put in the collection plate, don't put in a penny, because it is an insult to God." "You remember him, Olga?" Nellie added. "Mmm hmm," Baba replied. Although she had just eleven cents left until Michael's next paycheque, Mary left the building that day in shame, feeling that she had let down her beloved church. This story was the first that Nellie told us when she spoke about St. Mary's. It was prominent in her memory, and she seemed to cringe as she shared it with us, perhaps mimicking how she felt as she watched the priest scold her mother. She quickly changed the subject, remembering the parties that her parents hosted in their home to raise money for the church, as a way to make up for their insufficient donations. "We didn't have anything," she emphasized, "but my parents were very much for the church." Baba nodded in agreement.[22]

The progressives opened their hall to help Ukrainians get through the Depression, using it as a community centre, a hostel, and a soup kitchen; the church did not follow suit.[23] Demanding "work or relief" from the "capitalist class," progressives continued to take to the streets, organizing a large march on city hall on 25 February 1931.[24] Unlike the May Day rally of the year before, this event quickly turned into a violent confrontation when the group, composed of progressive Ukrainians and Finns, reached its destination. After some men tried to cross the police line, they were "beaten over the heads with iron bars," and their placards, which were inscribed with revolutionary slogans, were broken by police.[25] Nine "Reds" were arrested and charged with vagrancy and unlawful assembly.[26] Viewed as disloyal Canadians who "[transgressed] the hospitality of this country," the men were sentenced by a Sudbury judge to a term of imprisonment and warned about the possibility of deportation.[27] The municipal government also condemned the demonstration, refusing to hire anyone who had participated in the clash.[28] Progressives were very different from the "loyal" and "law-abiding" Ukrainians who belonged to St. Mary's and the UWVA.

Despite this news, progressive Ukrainians and Finns organized another march in late April 1931, and it too turned violent. They hurled rocks as policemen and firemen used their clubs and hoses to control the crowd. When the battle ended two hours later, police arrested nine men and one Ukrainian woman, Anna Ivoniuk, and charged them with assault; Anna assaulted a police officer and was badly beaten as a result.[29] Dissatisfied with the economy and the municipality's response to the state of affairs, progressives used city streets to air their discontent.

Also in April 1931, Ukrainian Catholics endured a brief period of turmoil, which was both unexpected and swiftly resolved – St. Mary's temporarily closed its doors because of "internal dissension" and a "lack of funds and co-operation from the church authorities."[30] When the church reopened three days later, parishioners learned that Father Nicholas Bartman had been replaced by Father John Kolsun.[31] Neither Baba nor the other Ukrainian Catholic interviewees recalled a time when the church had been closed. According to them, it was always a successful and thriving ethnic space. An interview with Anne Matschke (née Kuchmey), however, provided some useful information about this forgotten moment in the community's history. Had it not been for Baba's presence, and the gossiping between her and Anne, the colourful story surrounding the closure of the church as well as the deeper meanings of Anne's narrative would have been lost.

Although Baba arranged this interview, she was diffident about accompanying me because she did not know Anne personally. "You just go ahead without me," she said. I persisted, arguing that her presence was needed for the sake of consistency: "You came to most of the others, Baba." Eventually, Baba relented and reluctantly agreed to come with me. I suspected that she would know Anne once she saw her, since she lived in the Ukrainian Seniors' Centre apartment building that Baba sometimes visited. The first half of the interview was relatively unmemorable, but it changed when Baba realized that she grew up with Anne and simply had not recognized her married name. The two women quickly returned to their youth, reminiscing about the people they knew and the places they patronized, and these shared memories quickly led to an interesting gossip session. I let them reconnect and my ears pricked up when I heard Father Bartman's name.

Anne did not remember the church closure per se, but she did recall the scandal that engulfed Father Bartman. One particular Sunday Mass stood out in her memory. As she sat with her family in the front of the church, waiting for Father Bartman to begin his weekly sermon, a woman ran into the building with a baby, screaming, "It's his! It's his!" She placed the baby on the altar and ran out again, shouting, "Don't listen to him, he's a liar!" Although Anne declared that this had been a "communist prank," she added that, nonetheless, Father Bartman did have a child and that when this news became public, he was reduced to a lay state and subsequently became a lawyer.[32]

Parishioners were dissatisfied with Father Bartman's leadership because he neglected the church, mismanaged its finances, and collected money for services that he never performed – St. Mary's had an $1,800 surplus when he arrived and a $4,000 debt when he departed.[33] Letters exchanged between Father Bartman and Bishop Basil Ladyka indicate that he was taking advantage of his position, paying himself a generous salary and collecting money from the local mining companies.[34] When Ladyka transferred Bartman to Sydney, Nova Scotia, Bartman launched a lawsuit against the Ruthenian Greek Catholic Episcopal Corporation, claiming that it owed him $6,929.50 in promissory notes signed by the preceding bishop.[35] His duties at his new parish were also complicated by an illicit relationship that may have begun in Sudbury. Shortly after arriving in Sydney, his "wife" gave birth to a daughter, which set off a highly contentious scandal among parishioners.[36] Perhaps Anne's story of a baby indicates that Sudbury's progressives learned about Bartman's affair well before Bishop Ladyka did. Bartman went to great lengths to condemn the "evil Bolsheviks" while in Sudbury. So, if he did have a child while serving there, it is quite possible that progressives tried to exact revenge by turning his illicit relationship into a public spectacle.

Like the battle that occurred on Baba's front steps, the details of Anne's story are less important than their meanings. Anne was raised by devout Ukrainian Catholic parents who condemned communism and ensured that their children had little connection with the ULFTA Hall. During her interview, Anne demonized progressives, recalling that they often lobbed tomatoes and eggs at her and her friends when they left church events. These "other" Ukrainians were "bad" people, and the prank at the church simply reinforced this idea. Although it shamed Father Bartman, it also helped solidify Anne's identity as a Ukrainian Catholic, providing a personal point of reference for delineating difference.[37]

After the church's temporary closure, the local economy grew worse. Workers were laid off on a daily basis, and those who retained their jobs were compelled to boost their output to compensate for the shortage of men. Overworked miners routinely collapsed in the hot temperatures underground and thus found it hard to meet their new quotas. To add insult to injury, INCO required its employees to accept a 10 percent salary reduction in November 1931.[38]

Despite the desperation of the times, mass demonstrations were kept to a minimum until 1 May 1932, when progressives launched their most explosive protest. Ironically, May Day coincided with Easter – Ukrainian Catholics follow the Julian calendar – so this date marked notable holidays for both segments of the community. Led by Myron Kostaniuk, a prominent progressive, six hundred demonstrators marched down Sudbury's streets, bearing the "red flag of the worker's revolution." Although a local bylaw required them to carry the Union Jack at the head of their parade, they refused to do so, rejecting the "flag of the bosses."[39] Since they had broken the bylaw, police "fell upon the marchers like wild dogs ... beating them brutally on their heads."[40] Shortly thereafter, a number of concerned citizens, who regarded the incident as a "fight for the Union Jack," also began to beat and round up progressives; it is unclear whether any of them were Ukrainian Catholics. Mayor Peter Fenton, a police officer, and nearly all the eighteen Ukrainian and Finnish men and women who were arrested were injured during the confrontation. Later that evening, police raided the Finnish Liberty Hall and the Sudbury ULFTA Hall, and seized their records.[41] According to Chief David Louden, local progressives had "flouted the law and offended the loyalty of Canadians." In his opinion, the time had come to "stop being lenient" and to "combat communism."[42] Some Sudburians agreed and made a point of delineating between "Red" Ukrainians and others.[43] By refusing to carry the Union Jack, progressives had violated "an informal code of respectable public performance" and thus cast aspersions on their own citizenship.[44] Unforgettable displays of identity, such protests directly affected belonging.

As parade leader, Myron Kostaniuk was given the toughest sentence, serving seven months of hard labour in the Burwash prison.[45] Writing about this event many years later, his daughter, Mary, explained why this "black day became well fixed in [her] memory." Seeing police beat her father and haul him to jail served as a vivid reminder of why she became a progressive:

> My political convictions, which I formed in my home and within the organization, assumed their final shape at this time. I was able to see with my own eyes the great injustice that was being perpetrated against ordinary people by the capitalist system and I came to the conclusion that workers and farmers [could] put an end to this sort of exploitation of mankind and the consequent suffering only by replacing that system with a socialist order, one in which there is no exploitation of man by man, no private profit, and where common people enjoy the benefits accruing from the wealth of the nation. The Soviet Union, I saw, was a shining example of this.[46]

Like Baba and Anne, Mary used this experience to understand her place in a heavily divided community.

Being a progressive was not, however, always a straightforward decision. Nick Evanshen's story speaks to the complications of assuming this identity. Nick and his wife, Jackie, greeted Baba and me at the door of their bungalow with excitement and warmth; still very much in love, they had been married for fifty-seven years. Baba and Nick spoke briefly about their mothers, Annie and Mary, and their subsequent friendship, and then Baba made her way up the stairs with Jackie and I went downstairs with Nick. As Baba and Jackie disappeared into the kitchen, I overheard Baba telling her about the project and how she did not need to listen to another interview, because she had "heard it all." Why had she come, I wondered. Due to the open-concept design of their home, I struggled to focus on Nick's remarks while Baba and Jackie carried on above us; their muffled conversation can be heard on the recording.

When I started my recorder, Nick told me about his father, Steve. Coming to Canada in 1913, just before the war, he eventually "rode the rails" to Sudbury because he heard, through the "Ukrainian grapevine," that there were lots of jobs to be had there. He found work at the Copper Cliff Smelter and then met and married a girl from his hometown; together they had four children, two boys and two girls. "And that was your mom?" I asked Nick. "No, that was someone else," he replied. Sadly, Steve's first wife died of pneumonia a few years after she gave birth to their children. This marriage, Nick explained, was a "deep, dark secret." He did not even know the name of the woman, adding, "My dad never talked about it."

I cringe every time I listen to this interview. Instead of letting Nick guide me, I asked a lot of irrelevant, closed-ended questions. Although they provided me with rich details, they had little to do with the story that Nick was trying to tell me. I suppose all oral historians squirm when they revisit their interviews, hearing the paths left untaken and the interruptions that led people in different directions. Oral history is an imperfect practice, and I had problems finding my own voice and style when Baba was absent. I tended to sit on the sidelines when she was there and was overbearing when she was not. Despite my intrusions, Nick forged on, happy to have an engaged listener seated across from him.

While Steve worked "seven days a week, twelve hours a day, for twenty-five cents an hour," to support his family, the neighbours looked after his children. Distraught, he wrote a letter home, asking if there were a girl who would come to Canada, marry him, and raise the children. Steve's brother sent Mary, Nick's mother. With a photograph of Steve and a passport that he had arranged for her, Mary arrived in Montreal in 1923. She felt awkward and strange, Nick explained, having spent the two-week

Atlantic crossing worrying about the situation in which she would soon find herself. Shortly thereafter, Mary married Steve. "Did they get along?" I inquired. "They had to get along," he continued, "it was survival for both of them, really." Within a year, Nick was born: "[Mother] had come over and married a stranger with four strange kids, and she just wanted one of her own." The family of seven lived in a small house on Whittaker Street, in Sudbury's West End, until Steve built a large boarding house near the train station. The family struggled financially until Mary took in thirty boarders.

As a rule, Ukrainians who were not ULFTA members tended to stay off the streets on May Day, silently protesting against the holiday while ensuring that they would not be branded as communists. Nick's parents issued an annual warning to him, demanding that he too avoid the May Day celebrations. Despite this order, Nick often hid behind the buildings lining the parade route, "watching all the fights and celebrations" that took place on that day. As a spectator, he defied his parents and became aware of the "other" Ukrainians who lived in the region. He explained that Steve had been a member of the ULFTA when he arrived in Sudbury, but when he realized "how political it was he quit the hall and never joined any other organizations, washing his hands of everything." When I asked why Steve had left the organization, Nick repeated one of his father's lines: "I am in Canada now and I am a Canadian citizen." He did not attempt to explain this statement. Well aware of the heavy cost of carrying the progressive label, Steve withdrew from the movement so that he could keep his job at INCO.[47]

INCO closed its mines in Coniston, Creighton, and Garson in 1932 for a three-month period and continued to lay off men at Copper Cliff and Frood; by July 1932 its workforce numbered 2,000, down from 8,839 in 1930. At the same time, Falconbridge employed only 250 men in its mines.[48] These difficult circumstances directly affected the UWVA. Faced with a declining membership and lacking a hall of their own, members of this fledgling organization staged a comeback in July 1933. After listening to a speech given by Vasyl Hultay, leader of the nationalist movement in Canada, thirty-seven Ukrainian Catholic and Orthodox men and women formed a local branch of the UNF, "in order to encompass a broader sphere of the Ukrainian community." The UNF fought against "communism" – like St. Mary's, the local mining companies recognized it as an ally – and waged a fierce battle against the CSO.[49] Although the UWVA had lost its right to meet in St. Mary's basement in 1930, Catholic members continued to attend events at the church nevertheless. Not surprisingly, politics paralyzed the parish council, which included members of the CSO and the UNF, during this period.[50] Father John Kolsun, Bartman's replacement, tried to remain neutral when it came to the CSO-UNF division, but Catholic members of the UNF regarded his neutrality as CSO favouritism and attempted to sabotage many of his efforts.[51] Ideologically, the UNF was critical of the church, viewing it as not only deficient in Ukrainian patriotism but also responsible for dividing Catholic and Orthodox Ukrainians.[52] A competition for committed members, it must be noted, also led to conflicts between the CSO and the UNF.

Unemployed nationalist men began to construct a building shortly after members elected an all-male building committee. With just $20.29 in the UNF bank account, they spent their days volunteering on-site while nationalist women established a communal kitchen at the Voronchak home, where they took turns cooking for the men; UNF gender roles were consistent with those discussed in the previous chapter. About six months later, on 14 January 1934, nationalists – there were fifty-four official members at this point – held their first meeting in their new hall on Frood Road in the Donovan.[53] Father Peter Kamenetsky, who was transferred to St. Mary's in November 1933, personally supported the UNF and even asked Bishop Ladyka for permission to bless this secular space.[54] Not surprisingly, his request infuriated the Catholic men who belonged to the CSO and had enjoyed the support of past priests. They, including Baba's father, Peter, wrote to the bishop to report Kamenetsky's nationalist leanings and to request a new parish priest.[55] In truth, Kamenetsky had no choice but to cater to the needs of nationalists. When the UNF Hall opened, about sixty families stopped attending Mass, leaving him with just six families and thus little money to augment parish revenues.[56] Had Kamenetsky not sided with the nationalists and enticed them to return to the church, St. Mary's would have been forced to close its doors permanently.[57]

The UNF Hall also served as a place of worship for Greek Orthodox Ukrainians until they built their own church, St. Volodymyr's Ukrainian Greek Orthodox Church, in 1940; INCO supported this move because it "neutralized Bolshevik influences among its workers."[58] The Ukrainian Greek Orthodox Church of Canada was established in July 1918 by a group of nationalist-minded intelligentsia who believed in democracy and placed "Ukrainianism first and religious upbringing second," a move that signified "a conscious and patriotic return to the faith of their ancestors, who had been obliged to renounce Orthodoxy and unite with Rome in 1596."[59] These nationalists, who differed from the Catholic members of the UNF, regarded themselves as "'born again' Orthodox because to them Ukrainian Orthodoxy now represented their national identity and their cultural heritage."[60] Refusing to recognize the sovereignty of the pope, most "Ukrainian Greek Orthodox priests [thereby] regarded the inculcation of Ukrainian nationalism and patriotism as part of their pastoral work."[61] The UNF Hall was an interfaith, and to a certain degree, politically varied ethnic communal space where Catholic and Orthodox Ukrainians mingled. Despite their differences, they came together to support upward mobility and integration, to preserve the Ukrainian language and culture, and to emphasize the need for an independent, non-communist Ukrainian state in Europe.[62] However, this accord did not necessitate cooperation between the Catholic and Orthodox Churches. Nationally, the Ukrainian Catholic clergy "regarded the 'schismatic' church ... as much too secular, too concerned with mundane ideologies and politics and too out of touch with the sacred and everlasting."[63] Locally, priests at St. Mary's viewed the emerging Orthodox community as another movement that was taking away its members.[64] Although they came to blows from time to time, Orthodox nationalists and their Catholic counterparts who were not CSO members recognized that they had to unite to fight the "evil" element within the larger Ukrainian community. They condemned progressives almost immediately, making it clear that they were prepared to wage a public "war against communism" if need be.[65]

Sudbury's economy began to make steady improvements as this newest battle gained momentum. By June 1933, responding to international nickel shortages, INCO had reopened Creighton Mine, expanded Frood Mine, and refired the Coniston Smelter; production rose by 275 percent.[66] Perceiving this shift as heralding an impending war, progressives initiated a membership drive, compelling workers to unite against the "fascist forces" behind it.[67] In response, nationalists declared that the ULFTA was on the verge of closing because many progressives had defected to their camp. Although there is little truth to this claim, some men did trade one movement for the other. Spying and other instances of betrayal became commonplace during this period, especially as progressives tried to establish a local branch of the Mine Workers' Union of Canada.[68] Sudbury was filled with willing company informers. Nationalist, Catholic, and Orthodox Ukrainians as well as members of the CSO, renamed the United Hetman Organization (UHO) in 1934, happily betrayed their progressive counterparts if it secured their jobs and weakened the local branch of the ULFTA. Unlike other communities, which were inundated with Royal Canadian Mounted Police (RCMP) officers, Sudbury regulated itself.[69]

Nationalists continued to chip away at the progressive movement, organizing a mass anti-communist rally in November 1936. As they marched through city streets with Union Jacks in hand, they demanded that Ukrainians choose between their cause or communism, arguing that improved living conditions as well as Christian morals and ethics were the "foundation for unity against Bolshevism."[70] Using the local English-language newspaper, the *Sudbury Star,* to wage a media campaign, nationalists went to great lengths to show Sudburians that they were different from "other" Ukrainians. They invited reporters to photograph ethnic celebrations, and a strategically placed Union Jack often appeared somewhere in the resulting images.[71] Perceiving them as Ukrainians who were capable of preserving their heritage and respecting their citizenship, Sudbury welcomed their peaceful public spectacles.

Hetman Danylo Skoropadsky's visit to the Sudbury UHO branch in December 1937 also hindered the efforts of progressives.[72] However, as Skoropadsky condemned the "Bolsheviks because they [tried] to destroy a sound Ukrainian nationalism," his movement was slowly unravelling.[73] According to Orest Martynowych, nationally, the alliance between the Ukrainian Catholic Church and the Hetmanite movement was coming to an end because UHO members "placed partisan, political, and organizational interests above those of the Catholic Church, used religion for political ends, and undermined the Church's authority."[74] Locally, the UHO troubled Father Kamenetsky because its "members promoted the slogan 'Sitch [CSO] first, the Church second,' failed to attend Easter confession, demanded a pastor who was a Hetmanite, refused to pay parish dues until that demand was met, and impeded efforts to pay off the parish debt."[75] There is no doubt that Kamenetsky's favourable relationship with members of the UNF had a major impact on this situation as well. Skoropadsky's visit to Sudbury thus marked the beginning of the end for the local UHO branch itself. By the winter of 1939, the UHO had severed its ties with the church, choosing instead to align with the Ukrainian Self-Reliance League (USRL), the lay arm of the Ukrainian Greek Orthodox Church.[76]

The USRL deeply divided right-wing Ukrainians.[77] While its members valued Ukrainian nationalism, Canadian patriotism, and democratic ideals, they condemned the OUN tactics endorsed by those who belonged to the UNF; the USRL's link to the Orthodox Church also made many nationalists, the bulk of whom were Catholic, extremely uncomfortable. Despite these significant differences, USRL members met in the UNF Hall until April 1938, when a fight broke out between the two groups of men. They were committed to breaking down the progressive movement but could not reach consensus about the best way of establishing an independent Ukrainian state.[78] Progressives had an absolute field day with this incident, using it as an opportunity to point out that they composed a strong and united front.[79]

Members of the UNF and the USRL continued to bicker until nationalists learned that the leader of the OUN, Evhen Konovalets, had been assassinated by a Soviet agent. Shifting their focus back to progressives because they were looking for "revenge on Moscow," they went to the ULFTA Hall on 12 June 1938, where progressives were holding a meeting to discuss Konovalets's death, to confront those who supported the Soviet Union. They seated themselves among the crowd of about two hundred Ukrainians, and just as the meeting was about to begin, they rose and sang the Ukrainian national anthem. Evidently, this was a signal "for the fireworks to start." Within minutes a large-scale fist fight had erupted in the hall. As one woman "hurled salt into the eyes of the milling crowd," men punched each other, hit each other's heads and shoulders with chairs, threw rocks through the hall windows, and even tossed a sharp chisel into the crowd. Although the police arrived in a few minutes to disperse the group, twenty-five chairs had been smashed and all the windows had been broken; four men were sent to the hospital to receive medical attention for their injuries.[80] Progressives condemned the violent actions of Sudbury's nationalists, arguing that the clash demonstrated UNF support of fascism and fascist tactics.[81] This statement was not far from the truth, given that the UNF, as the Canadian branch of the OUN, endorsed its views. In particular, the OUN "praised Hitler's strong leadership in turning Germany into an industrial and military power," and it "admired the growth of German militarism and of positive German interest in Ukraine."[82]

Like the "communist attack" on Baba's home, this battle left a lasting impression on Oryst Sawchuk, a lifelong member of the ULFTA, and John Stefura, a Ukrainian Catholic nationalist. I interviewed Oryst and John without Baba; I asked her to stay home when I met Oryst, and she had a conflicting appointment when I sat down with John. I was thrilled to land interviews with these two men. Oryst had played a prominent role in the progressive movement and was still trying to keep the local branch of the Association of United Ukrainian Canadians afloat and its remaining members together; John had grown up and grown old in both St. Mary's and the UNF Hall. John's wife, Mary, had also been an important figure in the community, acting as its unofficial historian and collecting oral histories, on behalf of the Multicultural History Society of Ontario, in the late 1980s and early 1990s.

On a cold January day, I ran up the walkway and knocked on the door of Oryst's office; it was connected to his house and located just around the corner from the old Spruce Street Hall. No one answered the door. I pushed it open, walked into the cozy studio, and yelled "Hello!" "I'll be down in a minute," a voice called from above. A small radio on the front desk, tuned to CBC Radio 2, played a lovely classical number. I took off my coat and looked around. I was surrounded by a beautiful collection of artwork, and many of the paintings and drawings depicted local scenes. Oryst came down the creaky stairs moments later, introducing himself and offering me a seat in the next room. "Is this your work?" I asked. "Yes, it is," he beamed.

My initial exchanges with Oryst were incredibly positive. He was warm and honest, and I could not help noting that he did not live up to Baba's demonized depictions of the "communist." I also found myself thinking about my great-grandfather, Peter, and how much he would have disapproved of this meeting; he had, for instance, disciplined Baba and her sister for merely attending a dance at the ULFTA Hall. As we made ourselves comfortable, Oryst began to tell me about his parents, explaining that his father "wasn't the kind of a guy that would sit down with you and talk; he would never share. Mother gave me more information ... than he did ... I think he was a product of his time." Given this and the close relationship between Oryst and his mother, Sophie, she was a dominant figure in his narrative. He went to great lengths to explain her experiences and contemplate her struggles, especially after the 1929 crash. Having lost most of their money, the Sawchuks moved from Winnipeg to Sudbury, where they bought a large house, and Sophie ran a boarding business that accommodated six men. It was there, Oryst stressed, that she learned about the "hard knocks of the working class." Her conversations with boarders "politicized her." "Turned off by the church," she was drawn to the ULFTA; this was where she learned to read and write, engaged in cultural activities, and forged a community. A busy woman, she ran a successful business and still managed to participate in most events at the hall.

Oryst also spent much of his spare time there, going to Ukrainian school and participating in plays and concerts. While Sophie laboured in the kitchen, he learned the Ukrainian alphabet. As he shared his childhood memories with me, politics took centre stage in our conversation. His tone was reflective and, at times, tentative, as he explained how his progressive identity led to his exclusion from the larger community. "I could never understand the resentment," he stated. "I always felt like an outsider." He spoke about how local priests kept tabs on progressive activities, and he recalled the whispered talk he overheard among his parents' peers about spies: "This discrimination was always in the back of my mind, the stigma."[83]

Oryst also remembered the 1938 altercation at the hall. Although he was only ten at the time, he tried to make sense of what had happened while he told me the story. "Someone," he said, "announced that there was going to be a speech given by a man who had just returned from Ukraine ... The hall was packed. There were as many nationalists there as our own people." In the middle of the speech, there was a clash. "Someone started something," he remarked. The nationalists had brought baseball bats and salt, and he remembered his mother telling him that one of the leaders was John's father, Alec (Illia) Stefura.[84]

I had interviewed John two days before meeting with Oryst, and although he mentioned the battle, he said nothing about his father's participation in it. Born in Saskatoon, John came to Sudbury with his parents, Alec and Emilia, in 1929, when he was nine months old, because "INCO was hiring for twenty-five cents an hour, and you could work ... seven days a week if you wanted." Like Baba, he grew up in the Donovan. He proudly declared that its multicultural nature led him to speak Ukrainian and French before he started school. John added that Alec was a cofounder of the UNF Hall and that, as a carpenter, he helped build it in 1933. "Why did your father get involved in that?" I asked. In reply, John shared an interesting story about his parents' connection with St. Mary's. Although INCO had provided money to build the church, it lacked pews when it opened in October 1928. Parishioners set about raising money to remedy this, and after they purchased the necessary material, they discovered that Labarge Lumber had actually donated it. Frustrated and upset, Alec "had the gall to stand up [at a parish meeting] and ask what happened to the seven hundred dollars." "The next day," John explained, "he was fired from INCO." As a result, the family spent most of the Depression on relief, though Alec did odd jobs for the city whenever possible, to get through this difficult period. John used this story to explain the divisions between the UNF and the church. The differences were both ideological and deeply personal. Since the church was the only place where these Ukrainians felt comfortable meeting, and people like John's father were not welcome there, they decided to build their own hall.

The tale about the 1938 altercation came up much later, when I asked John whether he had any memories of communism in Sudbury. Like Oryst, he was a young boy at the time and recalled being at the UNF Hall when the group of men went to the ULFTA Hall and got into a fight. Although he shared few details about the incident, he did remember that the adults had tried to keep it from him and his friends. "We knew something was up," he noted. "There was a lot of ... excitement." "So it was the fathers?" I asked. "Yup," he replied. According to John, a communist rally was taking place at the hall, and the nationalists "claimed that they were going over there to ask questions ... but got into a fisticuffs" and wrecked the place. I shifted the conversation and asked, "I take it you weren't allowed to go to the communist hall?" "No, no," said John as he grew quiet. "We'd never think of it, even now." He laughed and looked contemplatively into the distance.[85]

When Oryst mentioned John's father in our interview, I wanted to kick myself. I had not asked John the right questions or pushed him to elaborate on his tale. I quickly realized that our interview was full of missed opportunities. The meanings behind some of his stories became clearer as Oryst and I continued to talk. "Begin with that notion of doubt everything," he warned. "Whatever you hear, even what I say, doubt it." Knee deep in the community's politics but trying to phrase my remarks diplomatically, I jumped into the conversation and stated that people had different perspectives regarding events. To this Oryst declared, "I think there is a truth, [though]; there are things that have happened; you can document them." I pointed out that his view of the incident at the hall was very different from John's. "Yes, of course," he said. "I saw it as a benign event and he saw it as a very hostile one. The question is why? What was it? It was ideology, I guess." Oryst elaborated on this statement: "The intersection of Birch and Spruce [Streets] [the location of the ULFTA Hall] was like a gateway to hell for many, for many Ukrainians. To others, it was a salvation, a way of achieving some sense of tranquility in their lives. I think it's essentially ignorance that has caused this contradiction." Over eighty people participated in this project, and no one explained the community's divisions as eloquently as Oryst did here. His remarks left me speechless.[86]

In the end, the role played by John's father in this battle is irrelevant. However, the reasons why Oryst and John told these stories as they did were quite important. Enabling them to assert their identities and construct their images of Ukrainians, these memories served as a means through which they could understand their places in a polarized community. Like Baba's, their narratives were about "us" and "them," and they spoke to the high stakes in participating in the organized life of the community. Ironically, John and Oryst both became architects and had long and successful careers in Sudbury. Although they were members of this small and exclusive group, their paths rarely crossed, and when they did, they had little to discuss. According to Oryst, this silence was the result of their organizational affiliations.[87]

When the Second World War broke out, nationalists busied themselves with patriotic activities to sustain the home front, staging major fundraising events for the Canadian war effort on their own and in conjunction with the Red Cross. Nonetheless, progressives continued to think of them as fascists.[88] A rumour, which can be neither confirmed nor denied, about nationalists sending a gold watch to Hitler in support of his efforts in Germany did nothing but reinforce this particular depiction.[89] It was "better to be a fascist than a red," one of our interviewees proclaimed when speaking about this period.[90] Many progressives clung to this belief because it helped them understand why the Canadian government outlawed the ULFTA in June 1940.[91] Left without a public space in which to congregate, they organized informal meetings in their homes, where they discussed their status in the community, devised strategies to regain control of their hall, and continued to reinforce their definitions of "other" Ukrainians. Although the ULFTA Hall reopened in October 1943, progressives never recovered from its closure; their support of the Soviet Union and the local movement to unionize workers led to further isolation in the postwar period.[92]

As Ukrainians flocked to Sudbury in search of jobs during the Depression, they built more politically and socially exclusive spaces. No longer divided along just Catholic and progressive lines, they formed Orthodox and nationalist camps as well. Ukrainians were pulled in four often conflicting directions and, as a result, identity and belonging were hotly contested issues within and outside all these communities. Personal and localized feuds and debates about the future of Ukraine complicated the relationships that Catholic, Orthodox, and nationalist Ukrainians forged with each other. At times, they could not get along with either their friends or their enemies. Whereas progressives, on the other hand, were a united group, the mining companies and a local barrage of Ukrainian attacks, set off by St. Mary's and sustained by the UNF, relegated them to the margins of society. Viewed as "evil" and "unrespectable" Ukrainians, they faced constant bouts of discrimination during this period and well into the postwar era. By publicly airing their differences, Ukrainians made and remade their identities and determined who did and did not belong to the region and the nation. As Catholic, Orthodox, and nationalist Ukrainians clung to the rhetoric of citizenship to demonstrate their loyalty to Canada, progressives took to the streets and proclaimed their devotion to the Soviet Union and an international working class. The resulting clashes deeply divided Sudbury Ukrainians, leading them to constantly negotiate the boundaries of their distinct communities.

These confrontations profoundly affected children, shaping identities that they maintained throughout their lives. Baba defined herself in opposition to the "communist" Ukrainians who wreaked havoc on her home during that one fateful and highly memorable afternoon in the early 1930s. She also used this frightening experience to understand the differences that polarized her community. She and her parents, Peter and Annie, were Ukrainian Catholics who were devoted to St. Mary's because of incidents like the one she witnessed. This powerful story cropped up almost every time that Baba and I conducted an interview together. As we sat with interviewees and chatted (or gossiped) about community politics, they used her experiences to explain their own. Given that most of them were Catholics, they had a shared and straightforward understanding of the community's dynamics and their places within it. As they peered around a crowd to glimpse a parade or a demonstration, ducked rocks and flying tomatoes, or called other Ukrainians names, they made public connections to the complicated personal identities they assumed. These experiences, rather than the religious, ideological, or political roots in which they were grounded, enabled men and women to understand who they were and why they associated with a particular community.

Interviewing without Baba, it must be noted, made for a different experience, especially when I sat down with Oryst. In many respects, I never left home without Baba, using her anecdotal story about the confrontation to generate dialogue and, in this case, to get Oryst thinking about the deeper meanings behind it. Although he thought that her presence would have made for an interesting conversation, I doubt that we would have managed to get past the "us" and "them" framework that tended to dominate when she attended interviews. She did not necessarily silence people, but she definitely directed remembering and how they formulated and shared their thoughts. There were always limits to what could and could not be said; feelings and friendships were at stake. Without Baba, Oryst and I were able to contemplate the issues that lay beyond the surface of her story. We did not arrive at any concrete conclusions, but we had room to debate and discuss why Oryst – not Baba – saw himself and his community as he did.

As UKRAINIANS WENT head-to-head on Sudbury streets, they engaged in a working-class struggle to survive. The Depression was a historical event that did not pick sides. Organizational affiliations were of little importance in this regard, given that everyone had to find ways to house, clothe, and feed their families.

CHAPTER FOUR

Cultivating

Depression-Era Households

NICKEL MADE SUDBURY a safe destination for Ukrainians until the market collapsed in 1931, around Baba's fourth birthday. By this time, Peter had become a stable breadwinner for his family, coming a long way since lining up outside the gates at INCO's Frood Mine, where he stood among large groups of men, begging, "Mister Boss, please give me job." While renting the Montague Avenue home where Baba was born, Peter managed to save enough money to purchase a lot on Kathleen Street, in the Donovan, where he built an eight-room house. When construction was complete, his family as well as six boarders moved into it. While raising four children, Annie cared for these men, cooking and cleaning for them and collecting their boarding fees. Since this initiative covered the monthly mortgage, Peter decided to purchase another lot on Frood Road, also in the Donovan, where he built another home that he rented to a French couple with twelve children: the Lachances. Baba laughed when she remembered this family, recalling that "they were chopping wood on my mother's kitchen floor [in the new house], because there was a wood stove in there, and my mother was having a fit, you know! What could she do?" She explained, "They were getting twelve dollars a month rent, and that was big money during the Depression. People worked in the bush for five dollars a month; twelve dollars in rent was keeping that mortgage going." Life was good for the Zymas. Their hard work and sacrifices seemed to be paying off.

Peter and Annie had no problem meeting the mortgage payments on these two homes and paying their weekly grocery bill at the Perkovich neighbourhood store until Peter's shifts were cut back from six to three a week when the nickel market collapsed. "Tell me what happened," I asked. Baba said, "We lost the house on Kathleen ... He didn't have no money, four kids, my mother had this boarding house and my father had all his old friends living with us." She continued,

> When the mines slowed down and some of them got laid off, they moved [and] they left my father holding the bag. My mother had that account at the grocery store, and she couldn't pay it. [The boarders] said, "When we go back, we'll pay you for your room and board" because they owed us a lot of money ... They left and they never even wrote back, they never sent us the money. So he lost that house.

Frustrated, Baba told me that a man by the name of McWhitey repossessed the house. He gave "all the Ukrainians a mortgage because he had money," but when they could not pay their bills, he evicted them. "Luckily, when my father lost his house we had another one to go to, Frood Road," Baba declared. Others were not as fortunate. She remembered seeing her neighbours being evicted from their homes: "Women and their children were crying, asking 'Where am I going to go?'" She felt helpless.

Parts of this story came up many times during my formal interviews and informal encounters with Baba. They were deeply ingrained in her narrative, and she always told them either before or after she spoke about the "communist attack" that opened the previous chapter. At a formative time in her life, these experiences interrupted Baba's childhood and had long-standing effects on her. Together, they shaped her identity and made her keenly aware of her place in the world. Whereas one served as a reminder of her Ukrainian Catholic identity, the other spoke to her working-class roots, a reality over which she had little control. This realization was disconcerting for a perceptive young child.

Baba constantly brought up the Lachance family when I asked her about the Depression. "I'll never forget them," she told me. She felt guilty, realizing that they were forced out so that she would have a place to live. The image of Mrs. Lachance and her twelve children standing on the street in front of her Frood Road home still haunted her. However, she believed that this was an important experience, teaching her the value of a dollar and shaping the way she lived her life. She proudly declared that, except for her homes, she never bought anything if she couldn't pay for it outright.

Credit was not an option. As a member of the "generation that has it all," I am constantly amazed at Baba's thriftiness. She wastes nothing and uses and reuses things until they can no longer serve their purpose. I suppose she is, in this regard, not much different from others who faced similar Depression-era struggles.

In addition to feeling responsible for the fate of the Lachance family, Baba experienced anxiety as a child. When Peter lost his shifts at Frood Mine, she constantly worried whether her family would make ends meet. Peter did little to ease her fears. After he lost his home and his INCO shifts, he felt overwhelmed and depressed.[1] Sometimes, Baba told me, he just sat at the kitchen table and stared into the distance. Insecurity was always an integral part of her story.

Instead of pondering whether her parents took on too much by assuming two mortgages, Baba also felt angry and betrayed by the boarders who left without paying their bills. By shifting the blame to people outside of her family unit – one of her consistent storytelling mechanisms – her narrative kept silent on a number of fronts. For instance, she did not tell me how these circumstances affected Peter and Annie. "Did your parents talk about what was happening? How did they cope?" I asked. "I don't know," she said. I continue to ponder how this crisis changed their relationship; did it draw them together or force them apart? A young woman, Annie was still dealing with her own depression and loneliness at this time, struggling to remake her home and community. In rooting her narrative in an economic structure, Baba avoided addressing these difficult and messy issues. This particular take on the past enabled her to draw on selective memories that protected the integrity of her family, never considering whether other dimensions might better explain why events transpired as they did.

Since "people *are* their stories," we must listen closely to their tales and the personal truths they attach to them so that we may reveal their contradictions and complexities. Analyzing the layers of a narrative help us understand how these socially and culturally constructed communicative tools enable people to convey something essential about themselves while they make connections with others.[2] In this instance, Baba's stories gave her a means through which to understand the difficult and troubling memories that marked the early years of her childhood. They provided her with a framework for contextualizing her working-class identity and her place in the community.

Annie continued to keep a number of boarders in the Frood Road home after INCO reduced Peter's hours. Confronted with an uncertain future, she supplemented his erratic paycheques, ensuring some degree of survival for her family; her work paid for the mortgage and the groceries when his could not. According to Baba, some boarders became "like family."[3] "Uncle" Paul, for instance, a friend from Peter's village, moved into the house and never left. His wife and children were in the Old Country, but he never made it back, sending a steady stream of money in his place. Paul drank to ease his loneliness and guilt, and Annie looked after him until his untimely death in 1975. For the Zymas, community began in the home, where Peter, Annie, Baba, and her siblings were surrounded by a network of extended family and friends.

Although Baba told me few details about her mother, Annie lurked in the depths of her narrative. This was a notable silence. Annie played a major role in Baba's life whether she chose to emphasize it or not. Replicating the gendered roles that women assumed at St. Mary's Ukrainian Catholic Church, Annie rolled up her sleeves, dealt with the day-to-day challenges of life, and got the family through this difficult period. A strong woman, she submitted to Peter but held most of the power in the home, managing the family income, running a business, and raising and disciplining her children. "She would let father say something and then do the opposite," Baba told me. Given Peter's frequent absences, Annie was thrust into this position. She learned by doing and gained confidence as she aged. Baba's tales about her mother may not have been as dramatic or as glamorous as those about her father, but they were important nonetheless. They exemplified the seemingly ordinary but vital role she played in Baba's life.[4]

Interviewees often spoke about their mothers. Having come of age during the Depression, most of them stressed that it was like any other time in their childhoods – difficult – and that their mothers developed and heavily relied upon various coping strategies to get them through each day. As recent immigrants of humble and poor rural backgrounds, they were accustomed to subsistence living and penny capitalism, so the

Depression was just one more challenge in a series of hurdles and tough breaks.[5] Everyone, whether Catholic, Orthodox, progressive, or nationalist, was engaged in a similar working-class struggle to put food on the table. While interviewees' fathers worked, or searched for work, their mothers boarded men, bootlegged, and gardened. Boys and girls were frequently called upon to help their mothers, taking on some of the gendered roles that structured their households.

Unlike Baba, interviewees recognized that their mothers' labour mattered. Mothers were central characters in their narratives, and they spent little time speaking about their fathers. Since fathers were rarely at home, children had few opportunities to develop relationships with them. Instead of assigning them a glorified or romanticized role, as Baba frequently did, they simply left them out of their stories. Some, especially men, recalled boarders when we asked about their fathers. Notions of family and community were constantly shifting in their homes, as these men nurtured, supported, and mentored them when their own fathers were absent.

Interviewees took us deep into the intimate details of their homes, telling us about their hard-working mothers and the sweat and tears they shed to house, clothe, and feed them. Some were more successful than others. Those who did not have the space to open their homes to strange men, the courage to break the law and make moonshine, or the land to plant produce or graze cows were forced to accept relief. This degrading experience left lasting impressions on some individuals. As Baba listened to these difficult stories, she tried to link them with her own: "We lost a house, you know." "My father's shifts were cut back too." "My mother was also boarding men to pay the bills." By highlighting these shared experiences and refusing to give up her experiential authority – her family was hard done by even if it was luckier than others – Baba reduced the past to a nostalgic and simple collective narrative. "Everyone," in her mind, "was in the same boat," and even though "times" were tough, they "were better because everyone helped each other." These one-dimensional statements about the Depression-era community in which Baba participated and later re-created in her imagination, bridged the complexities of experience that people shared with us. Her selectivity, when it came to both remembering and listening, enabled her to make sense of the past, even if it blurred reality. No one seemed to mind. "Everyone was in the same boat," they concurred. Certainly, our ability to share authority with them depended upon this problematic but prevalent understanding of the Depression.[6]

Ukrainian men who were employed at a local mine during the 1930s worked twelve-hour shifts, seven days a week, taking Sundays off only when there was no overtime to be had. They alternated between day, afternoon, and graveyard shifts, and thus they spent most of their waking hours at the mines and, for those who participated in organized Ukrainian life, in the churches or halls that they built. In Sudbury, a man's character hinged on his ability to earn a dependable wage. Ironically, this left little time for family. Although mining was a relatively stable enterprise because it ensured a regular paycheque, it was one of the most dangerous, laborious, and undesirable jobs a man could have. Despite these conditions, many fathers encouraged their sons to become miners. Peter persuaded Baba's brothers, Mike and Steve, to work underground because it was the highest-paying job they could obtain in the region; its pension plan and health benefits were also attractive.[7]

Nick Evanshen's father, Steve, was different. As Nick and I spoke about the past – and Baba and his wife, Jackie, reminisced in another room upstairs – he told me stories about his parents. Although he mentioned his father from time to time, often to contextualize his memories, he focused largely on his mother, Mary. Nick was distant when he spoke "of" his father and engaging and intimate when he recalled his mother. Given that he was Mary's only child, and well aware that Steve's four children from his first marriage resented her and made their relationship difficult, they were incredibly close. He grew up at her feet, as she cooked, cleaned, and made lunch pails for her thirty boarders. "My job was to stay out of the way!" he said. Her labours, he stressed, made a huge difference in his life. Before she began to take in boarders, Mary "went for days with very little food so she could scrape up enough to feed all five children." "It wasn't very pleasant during the [early days of the] Depression," Nick declared, but the boarding fees "helped the family income, [and] improved the situation." "We always had enough food when we lived on Drinkwater [Street]," where the Evanshens' home was located.

FIGURE 4.1 Nick Evanshen plays the mandolin on the back steps of his family's boarding house, c. 1934. This photograph demonstrates one of the ways that Nick entertained himself while his mother attended to the needs of her thirty boarders. Although his mother, Mary, looks through the window at her son and his dancing dog, she was often too busy to attend to him, so he spent much of his time with John and Peter Buyarski, two brothers who lived with the Evanshens for many years.
Courtesy of Nick Evanshen

Nick shared few details about his father because he was never home. Instead, he told me about John and Peter Buyarski, two brothers who "stayed for years and became like family." When they were not working at the nearby East End Bakery, a job that took them away from home in the morning, John and Peter babysat Nick, taking him swimming in the summer and skating in the winter. "Did you see them more often than your father?" I asked. "Probably did," he replied.

Despite Steve's absence from Nick's life, he impressed upon him the importance of education. He did not want his son to work in the mines for a variety of reasons: it was political, the absence of unions meant that there was little job security, and above all, it was dangerous. Steve renounced his ULFTA membership so as to secure and keep his job at INCO's Copper Cliff Smelter; others anglicized their foreign surnames to hold onto their jobs. He also harboured deep resentment toward the company because he believed that he was wrongfully fired. Nick explained that his father was working with a summer student in 1938 and told him not to touch anything while he ran to the washroom. While he was away, the student "played with a bunch of buttons and there was a series of explosions." Blamed for the accident, Steve was fired immediately. When Nick became old enough to work, his father pulled strings with a friend so that he could make him aware of the hard knocks of working underground:

> Father was sharp and didn't want me working at INCO. One of my hockey coaches was an important guy [there], and Dad sent me to get a job at INCO from him. Dad told me to get a job at the rock house, and then the next summer Dad told me to get a job in the smelter, in the converter building. These were terrible jobs to show me that working at INCO was not the ideal job.[8]

Unlike Baba's father, Steve viewed mining as just one of the many employment opportunities that were open to his son.

Nickel market fluctuations and the frequent and often unpredictable production cutbacks and mine closures discussed in the previous chapter took a toll on men and their families. The dangerous and deadly nature of the work was never far from their minds, either.[9] Luckily, Nellie Kozak's (née Tataryn) father, Michael, was pulled from the rubble in time to save his life. He spent many years recovering but still managed to return to work and be a father to his children.[10] Steve Balon's progressive father, Dmytro, was not as fortunate.

When Baba and I arrived at Helen Smilanich's house on a sunny day in April 2005, we were surprised to find Steve and his wife, Tillie, seated at her kitchen table. Up to this point, Baba and I had managed to secure only a few interviews with progressives, so she was proud to have arranged our meeting with this long-time member of the Ukrainian left. She wanted to come with me because she had not seen Helen for some time. "It'll be nice to catch up and see how she is doing," Baba told me. Baba knew Helen through her sister, Barbara, because they had worked together at LaFrance Furs. Since they were friends, I did not see any harm in having her there. Baba's eyes lit up as we entered the room, and she immediately went to the table and hugged Steve, Tillie, and Helen; she had met Steve at many dances over the years, and Tillie had been a teller at her bank. I stood behind her, stunned. Was this the same Steve whom I planned to interview the following week? Yes, it was. "I just figured I would get the interview over with," he declared. Interviewing members of the progressive community with Baba was quite different from what I had envisioned.

Steve wanted to go first. The five of us moved into the living room and made ourselves comfortable. Steve seemed nervous; his remarks were brief and to the point. Helen and Tillie jumped in from time to time while Baba and I listened. Most of his interview was impersonal. He told us stories about other people, and I could not keep him focused on his own experiences. This was very different from the first ten minutes of our conversation, which were intensely intimate. After I turned on the recorder, Steve told us that he knew little about his parents, Dmytro and Anastasia. He knew where and when they were born, that they met somewhere in Canada, and that they married in Copper Cliff. He also said that Dmytro died when he was ten years old. In his next breath, he began to share his few memories of Dmytro: "Father was a miner in Timmins, working at the McIntyre Mine. He contracted silicosis and died on 17 February 1936." "I never really knew my father," he said, "because he was institutionalized with the sickness." Steve's only contact with his father was from the ground outside of Dmytro's hospital window, where he would stand and wave to his father. The room was silent: what an image! Steve changed the conversation, focusing on his mother, the ULFTA Hall, and the important role that it played in her life. We never returned to his father. Unlike Oryst Sawchuk, we did not contemplate the differences that polarized Sudbury Ukrainians. As Steve spoke about his ULFTA involvement, Baba sat and listened, remaining silent about her views toward the left.[11]

Mining took men away from their families. As breadwinners, they spent much of their time labouring underground, earning enough money to ensure their families' survival. Financial security, however, necessitated a significant amount of politicking and risk. Ethnicity and politics mattered. Ukrainian men constantly worried that they would lose their jobs because of their foreign surnames or how they spent their leisure time. Moreover, men and their families constantly thought about the dangers of mining. The very real possibility of illness, injury, or death added to the many stresses they faced during this period.

Heavily masculine resource communities, like Sudbury, offered women few opportunities for earning incomes, and this affected the gendered family strategies they adopted. The virtual absence of female jobs meant that men were breadwinners and women were housewives who had little choice but to rely on their husbands.[12] Nevertheless, Ukrainian women did create their own economic opportunities at home by taking in boarders, bootlegging, and selling various goods. In doing so, they supplemented their husbands' incomes or obtained financial independence, supporting themselves and their children if their husbands either lost their jobs, abandoned them, or died prematurely. In many cases, these women were the primary breadwinners in their homes.[13]

For Ukrainian families, boarding was a common economic strategy that brought in modest but critical funds.[14] A female ethnic entrepreneurship that kept family economies intact, it was "a business like any other, where services were provided in return for cash."[15] The Depression made this risky endeavour particularly precarious since its success depended on reliable and employed clientele who paid their bills regularly.[16] Boarding either eliminated the effects of the economic crash or, as Baba's story demonstrated, it brought them right into the home, adding yet another challenge for the immigrant family to overcome. Many families took in relatives, such as uncles, grandfathers, and cousins, to ensure stability. This arrangement could be beneficial, easing financial burdens as well as the emotional difficulties that came with immigrating to a new country. Some relatives, however, exploited the situation, believing that their families ought to assume the burden of caring for them. Instead of contributing to the household, they pocketed their money. Tensions ran high in these homes and led to bitter battles between family members. Whereas some overcame their differences, others never recovered, distancing themselves from those who took advantage of them.

If not family members, who, then, were these boarders? In some contrast to Italian immigrants, who came to Canada via family chain migration or through an organized *padrone* system, most Ukrainian men considered Sudbury a last resort, where they could earn a good wage and obtain the standard of living they desired but had failed to achieve elsewhere in Canada.[17] If men had family or friends in the region, they usually stayed with them until they got settled and sent for their wives and children. Men who lacked these personal connections networked upon arriving, asking those they encountered to recommend a boarding house that could accommodate them. These spaces were ethnically, ideologically, politically, and religiously homogeneous; for instance, a progressive Ukrainian would not board with a Catholic family. Boarding house operators always took a chance when they accepted strangers, but they had little choice, given the needs of their families.

Thriftiness was therefore the key to success for these businesses. Women had to prepare enough food for their boarders and their families, and still manage to break even financially. Budgeting was difficult when men could not pay their boarding fees.[18] To meet this challenge head on, Ukrainian women prepared ethnic food. According to Robert Harney, Italian boarding house operators and their boarders used food and language to insulate themselves from cultural change.[19] For Ukrainian women, economics rather than a conscious effort to preserve culture and traditions informed their choices. Like most immigrant women feeding families on tight budgets, they took their role as food providers seriously and drew on customary ways of stretching meals.[20] A pot of borscht or a roast pan of perogies or cabbage rolls fed many hungry mouths and could be made in large quantities for a relatively low price. Ethnic foods were staples, made at least once a week because they fit women's budgetary constraints. Soup was also a cost-efficient way to meet caloric needs and make good use of fresh meat and vegetables. Nothing was wasted, and according to our interviewees, flavour was never compromised. In fact, most were quick to point out that their mothers had been exceptional cooks. Ethnic food may have helped to preserve Ukrainian traditions, but above all, it enabled women to ensure that their families had enough to eat and that their boarding businesses flourished.

Since boarding was a labour-intensive business, many women asked for assistance. Some hired single or married women who wished to make extra money, but most relied on their children, whose labour was free and often readily available, assigning them gendered tasks in and around the house: girls undertook domestic chores and boys ran errands outside the home. Girls made lunches and beds, cleaned, served food, did laundry, and babysat their younger siblings. Few learned to cook from their mothers. Cleaning was a task that children could handle; it was hard to mess up, our interviewees told us. However, cooking was a greater responsibility – men may not have minded coming home to dirty floors and unmade beds, but having no meal waiting for them at the end of a twelve-hour shift was a different matter – so cooking was left up to the older women. Boys, on the other hand, were assigned chores that usually took them outdoors. They cut and split firewood, collected coal, and picked and sold blueberries. Some women also kept animals in their backyards, including cows and chickens, and their sons were often tasked with caring for them and delivering fresh milk and eggs to customers in the neighbourhood.

Ukrainian parents, like other men and women of this generation, had gendered expectations for their children that were influenced by economic realities as well as cultural and ideological beliefs. Daughters were trained to be future wives, and sons emulated their fathers and learned what it meant to be a successful breadwinner. In asking their sons to run errands, parents gave them not only independence, but also financial responsibility, teaching them the value of a dollar at an early age. Ukrainians also brought a distinct peasant culture with them from the Old World, complete with gender roles and stereotypes: "They [women] were essential to the functioning of the family as the basic unit of production and consumption, yet they were regarded as inferior beings subject to the authority of their menfolk."[21] This view, it must be noted, was not limited to Ukrainians or even immigrants more generally. The French Canadian women whom Denyse Baillargeon interviewed in Montreal echoed the comments that Baba and I repeatedly heard: "Little boys were like little kings. Very few homes made the boys work. They couldn't be touched. If there was something to be done, the girls did it."[22] In the wider Anglo-Celtic society, an enduring Victorian ideology of separate spheres, which in practice were never fully separate, was not intended to justify male privilege – ideally, boys and girls were trained for separate but complementary worlds – but it certainly led to a double standard. These gendered roles reflected the interplay of a number of issues, transplanting and reinforcing Old World ideas about what it meant to be a "Ukrainian man" and a "Ukrainian woman."

But accounting for a situation and living it are two different things. The women with whom Baba and I spoke were well aware of the gender divisions that ordered their households: their brothers were valued more than they and were treated accordingly.[23] Indeed, their voices betrayed a great degree of bitterness when they shared their broken dreams and told us about the many limitations that were placed on them. Some were upset that their parents did not encourage them to stay in school, haunted by the memory of their father's oft-repeated rhetorical question: "Why go to school [when] you are going to scrub floors and do housework anyway?" Whenever I encouraged them to express their feelings, however, these women, including Baba, simply changed the subject with one simple phrase: "That was normal." Although I wanted them to consider why their parents made these choices and how they affected their own lives, I had to respect the generation gap that divided my interviewees and me. To avoid creating a "discursive disconnect," I had to abstain from breaking into a twenty-first-century feminist diatribe about equality and recognize that fairness was not central to the ways that their twentieth-century households operated.[24]

Interviewees who grew up with boarders recalled that there were always men in their homes, usually eating or sleeping. Boarding, they recognized, was a means through which their mothers could ensure the family's survival. This was especially true for Paul Behun's Catholic family. Angela Behun (née Bilowus) looked tired when she greeted Baba and me at the front door of her home but cheerfully ushered us inside and led us to the kitchen, where we found Paul seated in his wheelchair. A devoted wife, she had spent the last five years caring for Paul after he suffered a stroke. Paul perked up when he saw us. He slurred his greeting and struggled to convey his thoughts but said that he was thankful and honoured to participate in the project. He would help in any way he could. As was the case for our other Coniston interviewees, Baba did not really know Paul and Angela. She had met them at church functions and recognized that they were long-time Coniston residents, so she thought they would make good interview candidates. Although she agreed to let me direct the conversation, she had difficulty holding back, jumping in from time to time to ask Angela and Paul to clarify their statements and to speak about people she thought they both knew. Angela was also quite dominant throughout our exchanges, recounting the past, helping Paul tell his story, and even speaking for him when he did not respond quickly or when she thought that more details should be added to his remarks. Angela and Paul grew up on the same street and had been married for fifty-four years. As a result, she was very skilled at blending her memories with his. Sometimes it was hard to separate who had experienced what; she seemed to take on his fears, joys, and tragedies. Certainly, the informality of the space created an openness that is usually hard to attain with near strangers.

We asked Paul to tell us about his parents, and within minutes, he and Angela were sharing a difficult story about his father, John. Paul's mother, Anna, had no choice but to take in boarders because her husband had died in a tragic accident at a young age. "I was just a small, little boy. He died when I was five," Paul told us. "He died?" I asked. "He died in '30," Angela declared. "Thirty-two," Paul uttered. "Thirty-two, sorry," Angela repeated. "What happened?" I asked. "It was an accident," Paul began. "At the mine?" I wondered. "No," Paul and Angela said in unison. "He went with his friends to drink, and drinking some moonshine from Montreal, he caught on fire." "Oh God," Baba whispered. Paul fell silent. "Nobody found out who because they put him out on the sidewalk,"

Angela continued. "Nobody knows what happened." "They hushed it up," Paul muttered.

Paul and Angela did not go into more detail about this incident. Rather, Paul told us that John's death enabled Anna to collect $2,500 from an INCO insurance policy. This money paid for groceries and living expenses for about a year, and when there was nothing left, Anna applied for mother's allowance, receiving thirty dollars a month for nine years to cover costs. To supplement this income, she took in three boarders, one for every shift at the nearby INCO Smelter. While one man slept, the second man worked, and the third man remained awake. Anna had to rotate the men, Paul and Angela explained, to prove to officials that she did not have a constant breadwinner in the house.[25] Despite these difficult experiences, Paul and Angela could not help but laugh when they remembered the men and the frozen long johns that hung on Anna's clothesline. Baba also chuckled and the conversation shifted to John's adolescence.

With respect to the family, boarders occupied varying positions. In particular, some interviewees elevated them to the status of "uncles," whereas others could barely remember the names of those with whom they had shared their domestic space.

Although Baba and I conducted many interviews together, it is reasonable to say that we really "connected" with only a handful of people.[26] Delving deeply into the past during a single interview session is virtually impossible, and although Baba's presence helped to create a trusting, familiar, personal, and at times, informal environment, few were willing to transgress the limits they imposed on their narratives. Bill Semenuk seemed different. Although he too was caring for loved ones, he set aside one of his busy mornings to speak candidly about the past. He was a sweet man with warm eyes, and I fell in love with him moments after we sat down at his kitchen table; I have since been unable to forget his difficult story or his positive nature.

For Bill, the interview was a good opportunity to reconnect with an old friend. He and Baba grew up together on the streets of the Donovan, and he spoke endearingly about her father and the solid friendship between the Zymas and his parents, John and Mary. He saw me as a part of this intimate circle. In the car ride to Bill's house, Baba told me a little bit about him and asked me to tread lightly when it came to his mother, who died when he was a child. Given her trepidation, I decided not to bring up the issue unless Bill broached it first, which he did shortly after I began to record our exchange. In fact, he organized his narrative around his mother's death, telling us about life before and after she passed away. He mentioned her constantly, as if this were the first time in many years that he had discussed and remembered her. Her health, he told us, deteriorated quickly; she had passed away within two weeks of contracting a skin infection. Baba asked, "Could it have been a form of cancer like we have today?" "Sure," he answered. "Yeah well, they didn't know at that time," she declared. "No," he said. He sat for a moment and then stated, "Come to mention it, I used to come home early from school, just to see if she wanted water or anything ... It was hard for a while after Mother died ... I was just ten." His tone was both matter-of-fact and emotional, and I sometimes felt that I was looking at a young boy, not an elderly man.

Unlike Nick Evanshen's father, who wrote to family members in the Old Country to request a wife, Bill's dad did not remarry immediately. Since he worked a steady day shift at INCO's Frood Mine, he was able to come home in time to meet Bill and his six siblings when they arrived from school. "I'm still astonished at the amount of work he did and how he raised us on his own!" Bill said. After Mary died, some of John's friends moved into the house. Bill fondly remembered these men and how they looked after him and his brothers and sisters when his father needed a babysitter. They became "like family," he said, providing a support system that gave the Semenuks financial and emotional assistance.[27] Bill told us more about his life, easily switching between good and bad memories. As we ended the encounter, he declared that there were many things he did not want to remember. I nodded and did not push, recognizing that the interview space always has limits, even when deep connections are made.

Boys usually developed close ties with boarders because they had more spare time than girls. Parents also subtly limited the time their daughters spent with these men, monitoring relationships to ensure that they did not become sexual. When describing their households, a number of women told Baba and me that they ate either before or after the boarders did and that their bedrooms were located on separate floors. They viewed these details as descriptions of their households, not as parental attempts to limit interaction. When I listened to the interview tapes, I recognized an underlying tension. For interviewees, boarding houses were safe and pleasant spaces because parents regulated them; no one spoke about whether they dealt with sexually inappropriate boarders. However, I myself am partly to blame for this omission. I did not have the gall to ask these kinds of questions. Sex is a difficult, and even taboo, subject for elderly men and women. I did not bring it up and neither did they. I also think that Baba's presence silenced them. They trusted her with their stories, but sometimes the intimacy that was needed to discuss difficult topics, such as incest, assault, and rape, was just not there.[28] It is often easier to tell these sorts of stories to strangers rather than friends. These tales warranted a different kind of trust as well as assurance that anonymity would be respected, conditions that were hard to meet when Baba, a community insider, was in the room.

Although interviewees did not speak about their own sexuality, they were quite willing to gossip about the relationships that others had with their boarders. They did not mention the dangers articulated by social reformers, but they did provide insight into some of the sexual tensions that dominated these spaces.[29] For instance, they recalled women who viewed their boarders as a pool of potential husbands for their daughters, in some cases making their choices very clear so as to avoid unnecessary competition. They also spoke about "floozies" who left their husbands for boarders; these women were ostracized by the community because they often left their children as well. At least, this was how religious Ukrainians spoke about these issues; progressives did not bring up sexuality. In sharing their memories of "bad" women, Orthodox and Catholic interviewees pointed out that they never returned to church, living on the margins of their old communities. Living *na bushwel*, a negative reference to a common-law arrangement, was not respectable. If a Ukrainian woman married, she had chosen a life partner. Divorce was never an option, even if her husband abused her or their children, drank excessively, or lost his job.[30] Stories such as these reinforce the importance of the silences that crop up in oral narratives. Memories about boarders who became "uncles" need to be read alongside those of men who were cunning or abusive. Boarding houses could be sites of pleasure and danger.[31]

Women also bootlegged to supplement family economies. For many, the profitability of this venture seemed to outweigh its risks of drunken, disorderly men and police raids, fines, and imprisonment.[32] Among miners, drinking was a common pastime that largely defined their masculinity, so women who were willing to forgo notions of respectability and morality could make a fortune.[33] When they were not underground or in their halls or churches, many men could be found in blind pig establishments, places that illegally sold alcohol, or, after 1934, in licensed beer parlours, drinking away their hard-earned money.[34]

Operating a boarding house often went hand-in-hand with bootlegging. Along with demanding good food, men asked for booze, especially when liquor stores and beer parlours closed for the night. Women, like Peter Chitruk's mother, Sophie, willingly broke the law to satisfy her boarders and, in the process, amassed a significant nest egg. Although her business began as a way of earning a little extra money, it quickly grew into a lucrative endeavour. The interview that Baba and I did with Peter was another of our more memorable exchanges. A tall, handsome, and incredibly spry man, he rivalled Baba's storytelling abilities. He had us in stitches and in tears with his fascinating tales for over three hours. His honesty and wit also drew us in, making it particularly hard for Baba to abstain from sharing her opinions. She knew how the interview ought to work, but within minutes she joined the conversation to offer her views. "My father's name was Alec Hitruk, Chitruk," Peter said phonetically. "Hitruk, in Ukrainian," Baba corrected. So, I thought, it was going to be that kind of interview. Angry, I sat there fuming as I listened to Peter and glared at Baba. "This man knows how to pronounce his own name!" I thought. Peter indulged Baba, telling her that when Alec came to Canada, he changed the spelling of his name. "Yeah," Baba replied. "See, ours was supposed to be Z-I-M-A, Zima, but when my father came, immigration spelled it Z-Y-M-A." "Oh," Peter replied. Whom were we interviewing here? I tried to redirect the conversation: "Do you know what years your parents were born in?" With distance, I now realize that Baba's interjections made Peter comfortable. They also affected the way he remembered the past and how he relayed it to us. As he and Baba bantered, they subtly competed with each other. He would tell a story and she would try to top it. Unlike Baba's tales, however, his were incredibly masculine, rooted in a rough and rugged culture. His childhood was "like a Wild West show," and his mother, Sophie, loomed large in his narrative. She was a dominant woman who challenged notions of respectable femininity, and his candid memories of her fit into the machismo story, about womanizing, drinking, and troublemaking, that he told us. Baba had met her match.

Peter grew up surrounded by men in his mother's large boarding house. His father was rarely home. When he was not accompanying his father on moonshine runs, Peter was watching his mother serve booze to patrons. "She was more of a businessman than my father was," he proudly declared. "She ran the business." Sophie was an attentive and hard-working woman. What she lacked in education she made up for in street smarts. "She signed her name with an X, but you couldn't fool her when it came to numbers," or booze. Whenever Sophie bought alcohol, she poured it into a spoon and put a match to it to see if it would light, ensuring that her purchase was authentic. She prided herself on selling quality spirits to her regular customers. Her business, and ultimately her family's well-being, depended on her reputation, especially after Alec died in 1948 and she became the sole breadwinner. "Bootlegging meant the difference between keeping your house or losing it," Peter emphasized. "You had to bootleg." Peter's stories about Sophie stressed her fierce and determined character, as well as her unladylike behaviours. He did not mention the mundane operation of her boarding business, choosing instead to tell us about the times that she defied the law. She went head-to-head with the police on many occasions and always won, a veritable hero in his eyes. Questions about whether she was ever charged or imprisoned for bootlegging always met with a resounding "No!" Although the house was raided a number of times, Sophie defied the officers by stashing her bottles in the snow outside or in the staircase, behind the top step that could slide out from its position. Even when she was caught with a German Luger, she evaded police by getting Peter to tell them that he had found it while playing in the hills behind the house. The raids, he told us, stopped after Sophie had a run-in with a city detective at a local store. After they exchanged some words, she smashed a dozen eggs in his face. "The cops never bothered her about bootlegging again!" Peter chuckled.

Peter did not speak about the darker side of the bootlegging business. Drunken men can be abusive. Did Sophie always have control of her space? "She had regular customers," he repeated. The presumption was that these men, whom Peter regarded "as family," would never harm or disrespect his mother. He would not indulge my interest.[35] Unlike Peter, a few interviewees were unwilling to admit that their mothers bootlegged. That was what "other" women did. They did not want the stigma of illegal activity to tarnish their family legacy. Those who spoke about bootlegging did so with great trepidation, emphasizing that it was a shameful but necessary last resort for their mothers. "No one was bootlegging to make money," Bill Babij told us. "They were just doing it to survive." Bill's father, Michael, was a successful breadwinner in the late 1920s, but when he lost his job at INCO's Coniston Smelter in the early 1930s, his family was forced to accept relief. To supplement this pittance of fourteen dollars a month, Paraska, Bill's mother, began to bootleg. To protect her integrity, Bill emphasized that she had little choice in the matter. Since she lacked the extra space to take in boarders, "there was no other way to make a living ... It was a necessity."[36] Another interviewee was also tentative when speaking about his mother's bootlegging. He was not ashamed of the business per se, but of her alcoholism, which led to her untimely death. She could not just sell and serve booze, he declared; she had to drink it alongside the men too.

Actions always have consequences, but Peter's tales lacked such details. Baba was enthralled by his stories; we stayed longer than we should have because she could not stop engaging with him. Although their experiences were very different, they approached the past similarly. Who they were was largely shaped by their parents, people they deeply respected and whom they believed could do no wrong. Their friendly sparring further complicated the interview. Their spirited exchange led Peter to tell us stories that were in opposition to those shared by Baba. They did not come up organically, as is often the case in oral history interviews. Baba subtly but powerfully directed Peter's remembering, encouraging him to speak about issues that interested her and related to her own experiences. Frustrated, I could not compete with her experiential authority.[37]

Bootlegging was a means through which women could generate extra money, during both difficult and profitable times, for their families. Although children smelled beer fermenting behind locked doors in their basements and watched boarders get drunk, silly, belligerent, and even dangerous at their kitchen tables, they did not actively participate in the business. Mothers, it seems, did not want their children to be involved in this risky venture. For some, the fear of being raided, fined, or imprisoned was paralyzing. For others, it was just part of a normal day in a typical Ukrainian working-class household.

Planting backyard gardens also helped families to live more comfortably. Women purchased items such as sugar and flour from their neighbourhood stores, but they practised as much subsistence farming as possible, making use of northern Ontario's short but valuable growing season. They also kept chickens, pigs, cows, and pigeons to feed those who lived under their roofs. Their sons were often responsible for feeding the animals and cleaning their pens; they also delivered and sold the food that was produced as a result of their labours, bringing another source of income into the home. Although public health bylaws, which were enacted in the late nineteenth and early twentieth centuries, prohibited chickens and pigs from being kept close to homes, many interviewees stated that their mothers simply ignored these rules until the early 1930s. The fact that they could do so reflects the pace of development in the Sudbury area. Whereas large urban centres, such as Montreal and Toronto, created and seriously enforced these sorts of bylaws in the mid-nineteenth century, northern mining communities in and around Sudbury did not follow suit until much later.[38] These were fundamentally different places where concerns for the blurring of rural and urban were less pressing.

Interviewees who shared their memories of food and food production, be it in their mothers' kitchens or backyard gardens, told sensuous tales that were set in a particular time and place.[39] Charlie Rapsky was among those who vividly described the sights and smells of Sudbury when recalling the past. Baba was beside herself when she called to tell me that she had managed to arrange an interview with him: "He's a famous Ukrainian painter, you know!" When we arrived at Charlie's house, his wife, Shirley, greeted us at the door. Charlie followed close behind, bounding down the steps from his studio. After a brief introduction, Shirley ushered Baba into the kitchen: "Let's give them some time to chat." This was not the first time someone had arrived to interview her husband. As they walked down a hallway that was laden with Charlie's work, we got comfortable in the living room. Charlie was almost poetic when he spoke. As he remembered his childhood, he seemed to paint verbal snapshots. Whenever I listen to the interview, I am transported back in time. His attention to detail and his sensuous descriptions were rich and powerful. He had spent a lifetime taking in everything around him so that he could gain an understanding of both himself and his world, and convey it to others through his artistry.

Although he lived with his parents, Karl and Anne, and his sister, Marilyn, on Regent Street in Sudbury's West End, he spent most of his time with his maternal grandparents, the Babijs (the spelling was later changed to Baby). Their house on Frood Road was just down the street from where Baba grew up. "It was Baba's [house], not Gido's!" he proclaimed, before telling us that because he was the first grandchild, his baba Justina spoiled him rotten. They had moved from Coniston to the Donovan, he explained: "It was easy to leave places like that ... They were not the prettiest places ... The devastation was beyond comprehension." Bringing the story back to his own experiences, he recalled that playing in the nearby hills was like playing among skeletons; there were dead trees everywhere. "So devastated by industry, the open smelting ... that's one of the tragic facts of this area," he declared. "Do you remember the sulphur being very bad?" I asked. He replied, "Mostly up to the time I was twenty, and then common sense dictated what these companies did. It became less and less by making taller stacks and dumping it onto other people." Sulphur, which was emitted into the air when ore was smelted, not only burned and eventually killed vegetation, but also created a yellow haze that made breathing difficult. His mother, he remembered, often had to plant and replant her crops because of sulphuric acid's destructive tendencies. They tried to eat whatever survived under these conditions.

FIGURE 4.2   Justina Baby, no date. Charlie Rapsky's
beloved baba takes a break from cooking for the men
in her rooming house; the scar on her right forearm
was a work wound she incurred when taking a hot
dish out of the oven. *Courtesy of Charlie Rapsky*

Charlie's memories began in the Donovan, inside his Baba's rooming
house. He spent his weekends there, and when he was a teenager they
had a Friday lunch date every week: "This was our time together, no one
else's." Charlie's Baba was very special to him, as was the Donovan itself.
The place defined his identity: he was a Donovan boy. His nostalgic tales
hearkened back to a simpler and better time. His memories of the neighbourhood were situated in its back lanes, where he spent most of his time
playing. A landscape dominated by picket fences and sheds, this was
Charlie's oasis and escape from the moonscape that surrounded him. He
compared his experiences there with "walking in the Ukraine ... You could

smell *kapusta* [sauerkraut] wherever you went. Everyone had a long garden as well. They were tillers of the soil when they came, and that stayed with them."

When I asked Charlie to tell me about the Depression, he simply stated that it did not affect his family. His father was a shift boss at INCO, so his job was secure during this period of cutbacks and layoffs. His mother sometimes worked as a seamstress, but her labour was not essential for the family's well-being. "We were relatively comfortable," he stated. "We didn't need the extra income." Nonetheless, the additional money was welcome, enabling Charlie and his sister to have all the things they wanted and needed. It also allowed his family to contribute to the community, helping others who were not as fortunate. Charlie mentioned one small but meaningful experience in particular: "I recall one time my mother giving me a twenty dollar bill, and she said 'Don't you lose this!' because it was big bucks, that was about 1937, and I walked to Gatchell to some friend of hers who was dying from what they called consumption, tuberculosis, to give her it and I walked in the house, and her husband had died, they were so poor." He continued, "It was hard for me to believe that people could be that poor! She had two sons, about my age." "I couldn't believe people could be that poor!" he repeated in a slow and drawn out manner. "That's part of the growing up in our era ... So the community would occasionally bring them money to help them along when things were tough." "Were they a Ukrainian family?" I asked. "Yes," he said. "All I remember about her was her name. Her name was Katarina, Katherine in English. And usually it was the priest who would tell someone like my mother if she had any extra money when things were bad. The church could only give you so much, to each, you know. You had to remember jobs weren't a dime a dozen then." "No, they weren't," I said. This incident had a lasting impression on Charlie, putting his experiences into perspective. Like Baba's story about the Lachance family, it spoke to his identity and served as a reminder of his place in his diverse and tenuous community. Life, he realized, could always change at a moment's notice.

Baba and Shirley entered the room about an hour into my interview with Charlie. The nostalgic longing to return to the heydays of the Donovan continued to dominate the discussion. "This was a place where you could leave your doors unlocked," Charlie stated. "Not any more; it's now a ghetto," Baba declared, as she and Charlie lamented the loss of their beloved community. The neighbourhood was unrecognizable, bleak and crumbling, and most importantly, the people were gone, having either died or moved on to re-create communities elsewhere.[40]

Most interviewees viewed the Depression as a hiccup in an otherwise ongoing struggle to make ends meet; few had dramatic fall-from-grace stories like the one burned into Baba's memory. Their fathers laboured outside the home when they could find work, and their mothers boarded, bootlegged, and farmed to put food on their tables, clothes on their backs, and a roof over their heads. Relief may have been an option, but it was always a last resort, given its association with idleness, unworthiness, and shame.[41] In fact, only three interviewees admitted that their families relied on public help. Others may have been on relief, but, like bootlegging, this was omitted from their narratives.

The Depression was a dark and shameful period for families that found themselves on relief. The dynamics in these homes were fundamentally changed, leaving children anxious and upset. Suddenly, fathers who had rarely been home were there all the time. And they were different. Some were distant and depressed. Others had problems limiting their alcohol consumption. Children also overheard hushed conversations that scared them. Why were their fathers cursing Canada? Would they have to move? The economic crash, according to our interviewees, was hard on all family members, yet they focused on their fathers when they spoke of it. As their mothers coped, their fathers crumbled. Lara Campbell eloquently states that this difficult time "laid bare the unstable association of economic independence and masculinity, and the anxiety contained within that hegemonic definition of manhood."[42] But what did that mean to children?

They experienced major disruptions to their normal routines: they moved; they lost their friends; they changed schools; they skipped meals. These experiences made them sad, resentful, and angry. Others felt humiliated. They did not share these feelings with their parents: "We didn't talk about this stuff back then, we just kept it all inside." Alone, children wrestled with their emotions and tried to make the best of their new circumstances. And life, thankfully, went on. Many often realized that they were not alone. Nick Solski, for instance, remembered standing in line at the neighbourhood grocery store with his mother, Anne. With vouchers in hand, she asked in broken English for jam and syrup. The grocer looked at her and shook his head, explaining that she had already used her jam voucher for the month, but she was welcome to the syrup. She did not understand and grabbed Nick's hand, running out of the store. By the time they got home, she was crying hysterically, whimpering that she would never be able to show her face in the store again. She was ashamed to be on relief, she told him. The next time she needed something, she sent Nick. He quickly realized that most people in the store were also using their relief vouchers to shop. "It was no big deal," he declared. Others were struggling to survive. This revelation went a long way toward helping him deal with the stigmas that paralyzed his mother.[43]

The Depression cut across the ideological, political, and religious lines that divided Sudbury Ukrainians. Catholic girls who were chased down the streets by May Day protesters and progressive girls who were called communists in their schoolyards at recess washed floors, did dishes, and ironed laundry when they went home at night. Progressive boys who learned to speak Ukrainian and play the mandolin at the ULFTA Hall and Catholic boys who spent their Sunday mornings as altar boys ran errands for their mothers and spent their leisure time telling jokes to the men who lived in their homes. Mothers who sang in the church choir or slaved over ULFTA stoves bootlegged and made perogies to satisfy their boarders. Fathers who sat on the church organizing committee or led progressive marches through Sudbury streets worried about whether they could provide for their families. Another challenge for immigrant families to overcome, the Depression affected everyone, in one way or another. Daily life was always difficult. For some, it became unbearable during this period. For others, the communities that they worked hard to cultivate sustained them.

Women's labour mattered. Baba's mother, Annie, worked long days to supplement Peter's meagre earnings, though her daily routine did not differ from the one she clung to before and after the crash. For Baba, she did not seem exceptional. Peter, on the other hand, was different. He was home more often and his moods fluctuated dramatically. Baba's image of him was shaken to its core. This was not the strong and confident man she knew, loved, admired, and romanticized. To make up for his short-comings, she constructed sympathetic stories about him. Annie was lost in the details. The emphasis that our interviewees placed on their mothers did not change Baba's memories of the Depression and by extension, of her father. This would always be a hard time for her family, dominated by memories of the lost house and the boarders that let Peter down. I chose to conduct interviews because I wanted to understand the experiences of Sudbury Ukrainians. By bringing Baba along, I was able to gain deep insight only into her own hopes, fears, dreams, and experiences. Some-times, all roads lead home. As Baba and I shared authority, we paved our course, weaving the yarns we heard in interviews into a collective nar-rative that emanated from her story.

FOR BABA AND THE interviewees, the end of the Depression and the subsequent outbreak of the Second World War signified an important break in this narrative. They became adolescents, and Sudbury's Ukrain-ian community and sub-communities continued to change with and around them. Although they were forever marked by the experiences of their youth, they recalled the freedom that went with growing older and how it enabled them to push and pull at the politicized identities that their immigrant parents had imposed on them. Additionally, Sudbury Ukrainians entered a new phase of development during this period. The conflict raging in Europe gave them another set of issues upon which to base their divisions, and the Canadian government's decision to outlaw the ULFTA between June 1940 and October 1943 simply compounded the situation. The progressive community bounced back from this set-back and managed to participate in a fierce battle that eventually led to the unionization of miners, but ultimately Cold War politics and the fear of being blacklisted by the mining companies and the community more generally drove Baba's generation, and those that followed, away from the ULFTA. Postwar immigrants, who came to Sudbury in droves, also altered the makeup of the community. No longer splintered solely along political lines, it became increasingly fragmented by each new wave of Ukrainian immigration. A study of this fascinating period remains to be written.

CHAPTER FIVE

Remembering
Baba's Sudbury

TWO WEEKS AFTER BABA and I conducted our final interview together,
we sat down in her living room to reflect on our experiences in the field.
I wanted to bring a sense of closure to the project and to discuss the very
particular circumstances in which the interviews took place. I did not
prepare any formal questions, encouraging a reflective conversation about
our process and its outcomes instead. This would be an opportunity for
the two of us to share our interview stories.[1]

Although I tried to keep my questions as broad as possible, Baba rooted
her answers in specific examples that were related to her own experiences.

Stacey: Was there one particular thing that stands out in your mind, that
you learned, that you were surprised about? Or anything about human
nature or how memory works?

Baba: Who, me? Well, my memory goes back far.

Stacey: No, but when you were sitting there listening to other people, did
anything surprise you? Did you learn anything from them? Or, we did
so many [interviews] that it is hard to really ...

Baba: No, because I knew most of their backgrounds; I didn't go to strangers. Sometimes I spoke for you, which I wasn't supposed to. But for
me it was just automatically getting in the conversation, you know.
Then I'd get that look from you and I knew. I promise! I promise!

Stacey: Would you say that, because obviously you could say something,
like you would have said something during an interview and someone
else would have said something that would have conflicted?

Baba: The conversation continues.

Stacey: Well, or let's say that you had an opinion about something, like
let's say something that happened at the church and then you know

how somebody could see an accident and five different people could say five different things.

Baba: Five different stories.

Stacey: So really do you think that there is anything like a fact when it comes to this project, do you know what I mean, because people have different views about, say, the communists, that's one thing, because people remember them differently, right? Like some people remember being persecuted on May Day; you have the memory of having stones thrown at you. Everyone has a different view, like other people think that they were just great, not a problem.

Baba: Yeah, but it all depends if you belong there, you're not going to criticize about ...

Stacey: No, but even some people who didn't belong there had no opinion of them, like nothing.

Baba: They had an opinion, but they didn't give it to you.

Stacey: Well ... sometimes there was conflicts in the interviews where you would say something or they would say something and you really disagreed with them and you would say something like, "No, no, I remember it like this."

Baba: I remember, yeah.

Stacey: Do you know what I mean?

Baba: Mm hmm.

Stacey: So I'm trying to understand this thing of a fact because I'm supposed to write this history right, but what's really a fact? There really isn't any.

Baba: There really isn't any because they wouldn't admit what I told them.

Stacey: Well, not only that but you might not be right. You know what I mean? You might have a different perspective on something, like an accident could go on right outside the window and you could say, oh the guy coming down the street hit him or the pedestrian jumped in his way.

Baba: I know, but when it came to the Donovan, I pretty well remember *a lot.*

Stacey: No, you do. I'll give you credit for that.

Baba: You know. And people who said no it was this way, I think that they didn't remember or didn't give you the honest truth.

Stacey: So, do you think that they didn't remember, or do you think they didn't want to talk about it?

Baba: Or didn't want to talk about it. One of the two.[2]

I remember being extremely frustrated during this session, a fact that the recording confirms, as my voice grows increasingly louder and my tone becomes dominant, forceful, and even argumentative. I wanted to have a conceptual conversation with Baba, but she was unwilling or incapable of doing so. I was still too close to the project to realize that she had spent the last year trying to reconstruct her past – her home, her identity, and her community – for me. According to Baba, there was just one truth, her truth. The people she chose as interviewees and her conversations with them, whether I approved or not, were all means to this end. I was also unable to see and understand my own deeply implicated role in the project. Long before I began interviewing, I forged a relationship to the history I was trying to piece together. This undoubtedly shaped both my approach to interviewees and the stories they told us. I had difficulty letting go of the very particular and objective kind of expertise that I thought I was supposed to have as a historian. This retrospective observation is quite different from my thoughts that day: I shut down. Sharing authority could not have been farther from my mind as Baba and I wrestled through this dialogue.

Three years and many telephone conversations later, I returned to Sudbury to revisit Baba's stories and come to terms with the project's methodology. I was finished resisting Baba, recognizing that we both had different kinds of authority that could be shared without compromising my integrity or the quality of my research. Her lived experiences and my academic training did not have to be at odds in the collaborative spaces we created. We could both be ourselves and still effectively and authentically delve into the past. Her truth mattered, telling me a great deal about who she was and how she positioned herself in the Ukrainian community we had worked so hard to understand.

Seeking to engage with the materiality of her past, Baba and I left the comfortable confines of her home and took to the streets of the place that defined her Sudbury: the Donovan.[3] Baba had not lived in this neighbourhood for over fifty years, yet she continued to maintain a powerful imagined connection to it through her stories. In many respects, it was a storehouse for her memories. How would "being there" affect her narrative?[4] Although we had walked down many Sudbury streets together, we had never wandered through the Donovan. This approach would be another way for me to listen to the stories I had heard throughout my life.

A walking interview made a lot of sense, given that nearly all of Baba's memories were rooted in the Donovan, a multicultural neighbourhood that was established around 1907, just northwest of Downtown.[5] Like many men who worked at INCO's nearby Frood Mine, Peter moved his young and growing family there in the early 1920s, settling first in a small rented home on Montague Avenue and then in a boarding house he built on Kathleen Street. The Zymas moved to another home on Frood Road during the Depression, when Peter was unable to pay the mortgage on the Kathleen Street house. Nearly twenty years later, in 1950, the Zymas moved one last time to a home on Baker Street, just steps away from St. Volodymyr's Ukrainian Greek Orthodox Church and the UNF Hall, two organizations that had little bearing on their rigid Catholic lifestyle. Peter and Annie spent their remaining years there, but Baba moved out of the neighbourhood after she married my Gigi in 1951 and, except to visit, never returned. During Baba's childhood, the Donovan was a dynamic part of town, filled with immigrants, boarding houses, shops, and lots of children, thirty-two on her block alone. "It was a really international place," Baba emphasized. This is in stark contrast to what we saw during our 2008 walk: the ethnic makeup had changed, those who once lived in the area had either died or moved away, and the stores and buildings that were vibrant community centres had closed, been vandalized, or torn down. Roaming the Donovan's streets with Baba was therefore "an exciting way of creating more nuanced, embodied, complex, multisensory methods of experiencing and representing [these] surroundings."[6]

The neighbourhood was not simply a series of coordinates on a map. For Baba, it was composed of many "sites of memory" that transcended time, space, and even the place itself. Specifically, the houses, shops, and back alleys that were situated on and near three streets – Kathleen Street, Montague Avenue, and Frood Road – prompted her to tell me a range of stories about herself and her world; these sites were all in close proximity to her childhood homes. Unlike the nationalistic embodiments of memory that Pierre Nora describes as *les lieux de mémoire,* ordinary aspects of the local landscape (Baba's memoryscape) led her recollections to "cohere in complex ways."[7] This is not surprising, given that the "past of a place is," as Doreen Massey insists, "as open to a multiplicity of readings as is the present."[8] As Baba recast, re-envisioned, and reimagined her community through the sites in the Donovan, she alluded to the ways in which it worked and how ethnicity functioned within it.

Baba viewed the Donovan as a unified multicultural neighbourhood, emphasizing that it was a place of socioeconomic equality ("everyone was in the same boat"), cultural homogeneity ("everyone got along"), and solidarity ("everyone helped each other"). Listening and relistening to her tales during our walking interview, however, revealed that there were many problems with these sorts of simple assertions.[9] Baba's community was not limited to the Donovan, and it was quite a bit more complicated than she wanted to admit. Her Ukrainian Catholic identity largely determined who did and did not belong, and these boundaries altered over time as she grew up and her social networks expanded; because she spent most of her spare time at St. Mary's, this is not surprising. Although she seamlessly wove together all kinds of tales, such as ones that focused on her Depression-era experiences, a Croatian man who left the grocery business to start a construction company, and Italian women who wore nothing but black after their husbands died, she confused her expertise with cohesion. Baba prided herself on being an authority when it came to neighbourhood history. Every building, empty lot, and lane had a story. Yet, they told me less about the places and more about Baba and how she envisioned her world. Nostalgia, as Talja Blokland writes, "can

FIGURE 5.1 *(facing page)*   Sudbury skyline from Frood Road, c. 1962 and 2010. Although nearly fifty years separate these photographs, and little seems to have changed, there are subtle differences. In 1972, INCO replaced the small smokestacks, on the right side of the 1962 image, with a superstack, which can be seen just above the stop sign on the right side of the 2010 image, pumping pollution over and beyond the city instead of letting it linger directly above it. Also, INCO's environmental reclamation project, which went hand-in-hand with this initiative, resulted in Sudbury's regreening, explaining the number of trees that appear in the 2010 shot. *Courtesy of Olga and Stacey Zembrzycki*

blur the boundary between community and familiarity."[10] Baba's community, and its social networks, was just one of many that coexisted and conflicted in this place. To this end, "reading community is thus in part an exercise in decoding what this imagined world entailed and how it changed over time."[11]

I spent little time preparing Baba for our walking interview, simply asking her to take me to the places that were important to her and then share her memories about them. I wanted this exchange to be as flexible as possible, allowing Baba to focus on the stories that mattered to her. I hoped that this experiential approach would provide her with a new lens through which to view the past and, in the process, would enable me to access some of the reasons why she told the stories she did. Baba did not see much value in revisiting her tales, telling me that she had nothing new to reveal, but she agreed to humour me anyway.

I arrived at Baba's house just after lunch on 1 November 2008. It was a cold, brisk afternoon but the sun was shining brightly – a typical autumn day in Sudbury. Although three years had passed since our last interview together, little seemed to have changed. Bundled up and waiting in the window between her drawn curtains, Baba waved at me and then disappeared into the background. Moments later she bounded toward the car and fumbled with the door handle. "I don't know what else I can tell you," she said. "Don't worry," I replied, "get in. Where are we going first, Baba?" After pausing for a moment, she declared, "We'll start on Kathleen Street."

The drive from Baba's current residence to the Donovan took a couple of minutes. As soon as I put the car in park, Baba was out on the street, looking at the pink building, which now houses a bakery, in front of her. "This was just an old white house," she enthusiastically declared. I jumped out of the car, recorder and batteries in hand, and asked her to wait a moment. Caught up in her own world, she continued to tell the story of the house, recalling how Mr. McWhitey, a man whom she also held responsible for forcing her family out of their home, had evicted its Depression-era residents: the Pisoskis. McWhitey was a recurring character in her Depression-era narrative, yet she made certain once again to contextualize his relevance in her story. By referring to his machinations, she justified the loss of her family's boarding house and the trying times that followed. Although the Kathleen Street house led Baba to remember this particular Ukrainian family, she revealed little about its members. Rather, she used their eviction to speak about the community to which she belonged. The Donovan was the kind of place where people cared about their neighbours, in this instance feeding and housing the Pisoskis until they recovered. Baba made no distinctions, failing to mention that those who looked after the Pisoskis were Ukrainian Catholics. This tale set the tone of her narrative, hearkening back to a nostalgic time and place that no longer existed.

As we continued east, we stopped at the next set of houses on the street. Baba went into precise details about who had lived there and how they were connected to St. Mary's Ukrainian Catholic Church. Oblivious to the group of children playing in the distance and the constant but light flow of traffic passing by, she was mapping out the particulars of her community, noting those who did and did not belong to it. She focused on her memories of one woman from the church, Mrs. Kuchmar. A long-time resident of the small brick house at 611 Kathleen Street, she lost her husband in a mining accident during the early 1940s and was forced to go on relief to support her four small children. The house was clearly too small to accommodate boarders, one of the few options available to women who lacked a breadwinner in this mining town. Following this, Baba seamlessly transitioned to stories about the building beside Mrs. Kuchmar's home, recalling her childhood excursions to the candy store, which was located on the ground floor, and the dances she attended in the basement, as a teenager. Life went on in this neighbourhood. It was a place where memories of great tragedies and small pleasures coexisted.

In the midst of telling me about Mrs. Okalita, a woman who ran a large boarding house two doors down from Mrs. Kuchmar, Baba went into a shop that sold Ukrainian food. Perplexed but grateful for the opportunity to warm up, I followed her in. She struck up a conversation with the man behind the counter, bickering about the best ways to make perogy dough and telling him about her connection to the Donovan. He could barely get a word in as she explained that her father had once owned the house next door. Incredibly animated, she carried on until it was clear that he had lost interest. Staking a claim to this particular place was very important for her, a place that mattered to her but had nothing to show that she or her family had ever been there.[12]

As we stepped outside, I asked Baba why 587 Kathleen Street, the site of her family's boarding house, was important to her. She stumbled at the outset, telling me that she was unsure whether her father or Mr. McWhitey built it, and then said she had lived there from the age of three to six. She focused on the boarders who had lived with her, emphasizing their good nature. In particular, she remembered that they would give her pennies, which enabled her to buy candy at the store across the street. She explained that this store, Cultrinary's, and another one a block away, Perkovich's, were hubs of activity, where her mother purchased food and other goods for their household. The Zyma home was thereby located in the centre of the neighbourhood. "Was this what your house looked like?" I asked. "Yes, no," she replied and went on to describe the landscape, explaining that her father owned and later sold a number of empty lots around the house. This detail, as well as the fact that Peter owned a second house on Frood Road, which he rented, revealed his importance and status, a crucial element of Baba's narrative. As one story led to another, I tried to get Baba to return to her memories of the Kathleen Street house. She resisted, telling me about another man who lived in the neighbourhood. Although I came prepared to share authority, and to defer to Baba, it continued to be hard work. I bit my tongue and let her ramble on, trying to discern the meanings behind her seemingly disconnected anecdotes. Her tale about the empty lots led to a couple of related stories and finally ended with an account of her work in the general store, Macks', that had been built on one of the vacant lots. She was incredibly proud that she had worked for years before getting married and wanted to convey that to me.

When she had finished, I once again asked her to return to her memories of the house. We walked closer to it, dried leaves crunching under our feet. "What happened to this house and your family?" I asked. Drawing on her well-rehearsed monologue, Baba stated that INCO reduced Peter's and their boarders' shifts during the early 1930s. They could not pay their boarding fees but continued to live with them nonetheless. As the grocery bill accrued at Perkovich's and there was less money, Peter defaulted on his mortgage. "These guys [the boarders] moved up north [to another mine] and they never sent him a nickel, so he was out, you know." Baba added that the Perkovich family eventually took Peter to court and garnisheed his wages until his bill was paid at the store. I had never heard this part of the tale, another villain to add to the men who harmed Baba's family. Baba explained that, because a large French Canadian family that depended on relief, the Lachances, was living in Peter's Frood Road home, he could not simply move his family there at the time. While waiting for the Lachances to relocate, the Zymas moved several times, living in a couple of rented spaces before settling in with friends, who also belonged to St. Mary's. Baba experienced the instability of the 1930s first-hand, even if it was temporary. The Ukrainian Catholic community was, however, instrumental in supporting her and her family when they needed help. "Do you remember your parents talking about losing this house?" I asked. "My father sort of had a nervous breakdown then," she replied. These revelations, which were absent from our past conversations, enabled me to better understand the anxiety that Baba affixed to this period. When I asked her to tell me more about how her parents coped, she shifted to a memory about Christmas, telling me how much it meant to receive a mandarin orange and some candy in her stocking. I kept pushing: "What do you mean that your dad had a bit of a nervous breakdown?" She said, "He was just depressed ... I think his faith carried him through." This was as far as Baba would go, and her reference to Peter's faith supplied a natural transition to a familiar and more straightforward topic, St. Mary's. To restore Peter's character, she once again spoke about his important role in founding the church and the time and energy both her parents gave to sustain it.[13]

"Where to?" I asked when she finished making her point. "There's the Croatian Hall, is that interesting to you?" "'Is it interesting to you?'" she echoed, adding, with a chuckle, "Oh, I danced there like crazy." "Well, let's go then," I said. A welcome diversion, the hall gave her the opportunity to recount good memories about the Donovan, a part of her past she was more willing to explore. That said, her narrative was still quite complicated, referring to the politics of place, her identity as a Ukrainian Catholic, and how her community changed as she grew older. When Baba was a teenager, she surrounded herself with an ethnically diverse group of girls, though it was still dominated by those she befriended at St. Mary's.

FIGURE 5.2   Baba with her brother Mike outside their Kathleen Street home,
c. 1930. *Courtesy of Olga Zembrzycki*

FIGURE 5.3   Baba
outside her former
home on Kathleen
Street, c. 2008. *Photo
by Stacey Zembrzycki*

She was a second-generation Canadian, so her community was not limited to the social network that her parents developed at the church and sustained in their everyday lives. She met a mix of people while playing on the Donovan's multi-ethnic streets, attending an English Catholic school, and eventually working at Macks', a general store that serviced local patrons. Baba and her "gang," as she referred to her girlfriends, spent much of their teens and early twenties dancing their nights away, going to a different ethnic hall nearly every evening. Since St. Mary's did not hold dances on Sundays, they often found themselves at the Croatian Hall, enjoying the music that emanated from the tamborica and learning how to dance the *kolo*, a traditional Croatian folk dance. "So it wasn't a big deal to be at the Croatian Hall?" I asked. "No," because it was an open dance. It was, however, unacceptable to attend a dance at the UNF Hall. "We didn't go [there]," she stressed. The boundaries of Baba's world were constantly being renegotiated, simultaneously including a multi-ethnic group of her neighbours and excluding other Ukrainians. Certainly, Peter and Annie played a big role in determining whom she could befriend. Since they opposed the nationalist and progressive movements, Baba was permitted neither to associate with their members nor attend dances at their halls.

Before I could ask Baba to explain this distinction, she walked off in a new direction, waving at me to follow. In an instant, we had left the years of her adolescence and returned to her childhood, a time when her parents' community was the only one she knew, as she searched for the site of the one-room shack were Mrs. Shustra lived. She and her mother often visited Mrs. Shustra, who was an integral part of Annie's social world. "The shack is gone long time ago," said Baba. "It was almost to the back lane." She was obsessed with showing me its location, so we walked toward the alley behind Kathleen Street. It was important to Baba because this was where she played while living in the boarding house. "Do you remember this lane?" I asked. "Certainly!" she replied. "Let's go to the back of your old house," I said. Baba continued to map the social landscape of her neighbourhood, telling me who had lived in the houses along the lane. In one breath she emphasized its multicultural nature, and in another she referred only to the Ukrainian families that had lived in the area. Again, this was the only kind of community she knew as a young child.

"Now, we're going to the corner, to our famous Harry's Lunch!" she said. "I knew you'd take me there," I replied. A staple in her narrative, Harry's diner was a popular neighbourhood gathering spot, and I had heard about it many times. Now the building housed a photography studio, and I wondered whether seeing it would evoke new memories. "So, Harry's is a big part of your story?" I asked. Instead of speaking about the place itself, Baba focused on its owner: "He's part of our life, to tell you the truth." "Who's Harry?" I asked. She explained that he was a Chinese businessman, with a wife in China, who owned a number of restaurants in the region. She continued, "Harry was a good man, Chinese, but he liked the kids; the kids made him his business." She qualified this by stating that he often loaned money to his young male customers when they were short on cash, and they paid him back when they received their INCO paycheques every second Tuesday at the nearby Toronto Dominion Bank: "He'd open the cash, he wouldn't even ask you to sign anything or take your name, 'Ok, here ... You come back on Tuesday' and you paid him and that's how he operated." Harry made the diner a comfortable and welcoming space: "He was nice and he trusted us," Baba explained. Teens flocked to its booths after dances and stayed into the early hours of the morning, eating french fries and hot chicken sandwiches with gravy and just hanging out. As Baba grew older and her social networks broadened, her community changed. No longer limited to Ukrainians, its boundaries became more porous, including people such as Harry, whom she respected and credited with shaping many of her experiences as a young woman.

This memory was very different from the one that Baba shared with me, about a Chinese launderer, as we walked one block west and turned north onto Montague Avenue. Her stories were both personal and detached, and they easily moved forward and backward through the phases of her life. She continued to weave St. Mary's into them, telling me about more parishioners who had lived in the Donovan and the fundraising ventures they organized together. The church and its members were never far from her mind, defining her experiences in the neighbourhood. Passing houses that were not inhabited by Ukrainians led her to speak of others. "Did people talk to each other even if they were Italian, Jewish, Croatian?" I asked. "Oh yeah!" she said. "'Hello missus.' 'Hello.'" She lived in the same place as they did, but her remarks indicated that they were by no means part of her social network. There were the Irish and Croatian families who lived down the street, the Hungarians who owned the bakery on the corner, the Jew, "the only one in the Donovan," who had a bargain store that sold miners' clothes, and the Italian women "who managed without husbands." These were superficial memories, yet they allowed Baba to demonstrate her knowledge of the neighbourhood. There was also "the Chinaman." I asked Baba to tell me about him and to show me where his laundry was located. Suddenly and seamlessly, our conversation once again jumped back in time, to her early childhood. She said,

> It was directly across from our [Frood Road] house, across from Skakoon hardware, and right across, there's a house in there now, there was an old shack and we'd come at night, when we were playing hide-and-go-seek, there'd be about ten or fifteen of us, eh, we were running from the corner of Frood Road, all around here trying to find somebody 'cause we didn't want to be the stinker. And we'd run past that house and we'd yell, "Chinkie, Chinkie Chinaman, wash my pants, put them in the boiler, and make them dance." And we'd say, "Hey, the Chinaman is coming out with his meat cleaver! Let's go!" So we'd be running all the way up to Bessie Street ... and he'd come out and he'd say, "Go home! Go home!" ... But every night we went to tease him.

This story, which I'd heard before, always made me uncomfortable, and this instance was no exception. Baba thought nothing of uttering these racist remarks, quickly moving on to another memory about her childhood. I do not condone this tale and have no wish to make excuses for Baba, but I do want to understand what it means to her and why it is a part of her narrative. I believe that it speaks to the mutability of her community, highlighting how it worked to include some and exclude others. Unlike Harry's diner, the Frood Road laundry shack was seen as a foreign, racialized space that was off-limits to Baba and her peers. It figured in the experiences of a child, and Baba recalled it in a childlike manner. When she and her friends taunted the "Chinaman," who remained nameless in all her stories, her imagination ran wild, getting the best of her. He was a kind of bogeyman, and she continued to refer to him in a stereotypical manner, othering him and disregarding the important service provided by his business; for men whose boarding house operators did not wash laundry, it was the only place in the Donovan that would do so. At the time, this man was also the only Chinese person in the neighbourhood, and he looked, sounded, and perhaps even behaved in a manner that differed from what Baba saw as normal. When I asked her to tell me more about the meat-cleaver chant, she was brief and to the point, explaining that she was not alone in playing this "game." Many local children played hide-and-seek, and they were "just kids being kids." She added that the cleaver reference stemmed from the fact that most Chinese men who lived in Sudbury owned restaurants and chopped meat with this tool. She said nothing else about this memory. I do not believe that she was trying to be malicious. Rather, fear, curiosity, and childhood ignorance all shaped her understanding of these differences. Whereas as a young adult Baba developed a relationship with Harry, she had no contact with this man. He may have lived right around the corner, but he was a stranger who was outside her community.[14]

Differences also came up when Baba spoke about French Canadians. As we left Montague Avenue and strolled down the lane behind her Frood Road home, she told me a story about the battles that took place there between her brothers and the boys from the Flour Mill. Located about a thirty-minute walk east of the Donovan and also called French Town, the Flour Mill was dominated by French Canadian working-class residents. As a young girl, Baba tagged along with her brothers, and when they either instigated a fight or retaliated against their aggressors, she was often caught in the middle. She remembered running home crying after being hit in the head with the rocks that the two groups threw at each other. Like many boys in their teens, her brothers were constantly getting into trouble, but these sorts of battles had greater implications. They were not simple turf wars between neighbourhood children. For Baba, the telling of this story also spoke to her understanding of her community and the limits she imposed upon it. That she and her brothers had an uneasy relationship with French Canadians can be tied to their elementary school experiences at St. Aloysius, an English Catholic school on MacKenzie Street behind St. Louis de Gonzague, a French Catholic school. Although it stood in a neutral area between the Donovan and the Flour Mill, St. Aloysius was where Baba's communal boundaries took shape and the differences between these places came to a head.

Three generations of my family attended St. Aloysius: Baba, my father, and I. There was nothing extraordinary about the school except its playground: an imaginary boundary wound down the centre. One side was for the exclusive use of French students, and the other was for English students; fraternizing was unacceptable. Teachers supervised the perimeter, and there was absolutely no crossing over. Retrieving a ball that bounced across the line was a complete nightmare. Although the boundary afforded teachers an easy way of controlling their own students, it created needless animosity between the two groups. My experiences were tame compared to Baba's. In particular, she remembered the hostile relations between the students of St. Aloysius and those of St. Louis de Gonzague. The only way to get to St. Aloysius was to pass through the St. Louis de Gonzague schoolyard. According to her, there were always tensions between her friends and a "tough" group of half a dozen French girls. They were bullies who "never let us go by without calling us 'maudit polaque!' We were called polacks when we were young, okay. And we would yell at them 'maudit cochon!' 'Maudit French!' So we were always fighting." Memories like this revealed cracks in Baba's nostalgic narrative. Everyone did not always "get along." Again, "kids will be kids," but this antagonism, and specifically its derogatory exchanges, underscored the complications of growing up ethnic in Sudbury. Baba rarely spoke about French Canadians when she referred to the Donovan, yet like the Lachances, many lived there. Figure 5.4, which shows Baba's multicultural class in 1939, also lacks any French Canadians. Her contact with them was entirely negative, which ultimately shaped her social networks and determined who did and did not belong to her community.

Baba did not make these kinds of connections as we walked through the Donovan. She saw these incidents as unconnected events in her life, isolated snapshots from her youth. Since children often adopt the views of their parents, and certainly Baba's world was shaped by Peter and Annie's networks, I wanted to know how they saw their multicultural neighbours. Did they resent the Chinese launderer? Were they hostile toward the French Canadian families that lived on Frood Road? "No," Baba declared, "they never came into contact with them. They had no

FIGURE 5.4   Baba's grade five class at St. Aloysius on International Day, c. 1939. This photo originally appeared in "Many Nationalities Represented in Sudbury School," *Sudbury Star,* 27 January 1939, 18. Baba is in the back row at the far right. *Courtesy Olga Zembrzycki*

reason to talk to them." Growing up as an ethnic child was therefore a lot more complicated than Baba cared to admit. She negotiated two social realms, living between that of her parents and the one she forged in the Canadian spaces where she played, learned, and later worked. Other Ukrainians who lived in the Donovan had different experiences. Some spoke French, along with Ukrainian and English, learning this third language on the street. Children made choices; they had agency. Baba's stories are therefore representative solely of her experiences.

While I stood in the lane, contemplating communal differences and conflicts, Baba wandered ahead of me, looking for the backyard of her Frood Road home. "Stacey!" she called. "Is this our house?" "I don't know," I replied. "I don't know which one's your house." "Well," she said, "we didn't have [those] outside steps." Throughout the interview, Baba had to come to terms with the transformed landscape around us, demonstrating

FIGURE 5.5

Top: Annie Zyma and her backyard garden on Frood Road, c. 1942. Peter Junior stands beside her. *Courtesy of Olga Zembryzycki*

Left: Baba in the backyard of her former home on Frood Road, c. 2008. *Photo by Stacey Zembrzycki*

the very real tensions between the past and the present that emerge in experiential interviews like this one. So many things had changed, and now she could not even identify the home in which she had lived for nearly twenty years. She used a local landmark, Skakoon's Hardware

Store, to distinguish her house from the others. "Okay, so we're directly across from Skakoon's," she said. "Right here, there's an addition." "So your house looks quite different?" I asked. Baba kept emphasizing the big garden that occupied the backyard. This was difficult to imagine, given that the space was now a parking lot.

She continued to stress the differences between past and present. The original stucco had been covered with grey siding, and an addition replaced the back porch. "So this is really where your memories start?" I asked. "Yeah," she said. "Where we played, where we did everything, where I went to school from, everything." This was also where Baba's community continuously evolved. As we moved to the front of the house, she began to speak about the Burke family, which lived across the street. Irene and Lorraine Burke, who had a Ukrainian father and a Croatian mother, were among her closest friends. Although the Burkes were not members of St. Mary's, they were deeply connected to those who were. The girls played with a doll and a carriage when they were young, skated on the rink that Mr. Burke flooded in a nearby empty lot as they grew older, and frequently enjoyed Mrs. Burke's cooking when they returned home from dances as adolescents. Baba still speaks to Lorraine daily; Irene passed away a number of years ago. "We're still best friends," Baba declared. They spend hours on the telephone, reminiscing about the past, firmly connected to the Donovan through their stories.

Baba and I went to a few other locations during our walking interview, but most were outside the Donovan or on its outskirts: the Polish Hall, her parents' Baker Street house, two other homes where she lived after her marriage, the original site of St. Mary's, and St. Aloysius. Although they were important to her for a variety of reasons, they did not invoke memories of community in quite the same way. Her stories about them were outside the time frame that we chose for the project, and they related to another phase of her life, when she had moved away from the Donovan. We had also spent three intense hours dialoguing about the past and were both tired.

As Baba and I walked through the neighbourhood, she gave me much more than a historical tour of it. Her stories spoke to many of the themes that have emerged throughout this book: home, identity, and most importantly, community. Being there, in the Donovan, did not necessarily lead Baba to tell me new stories, but it did help her better contextualize and expand on old ones. Sometimes you have to hear stories many times before you realize that they are important. For me, these old tales came together in new ways, providing a running commentary on who Baba is and why she sees the world as she does. As she drew on her rehearsed narrative, she shifted the focus from herself and onto others, providing a more nuanced discussion of how ethnicity was lived and the ways it moulded her community. Place gave new meaning to her stories. They also took us inside and outside the neighbourhood and spanned different periods of time. Gender, ethnicity, race, class, age, and region affected her experiences and directed remembering. Who did and did not belong was largely determined by her parents' social world and the friendships she made at St. Mary's. Although her networks broadened over time, her community remained dominated by Ukrainian Catholics. It coexisted and conflicted with others that took root in this multicultural neighbourhood.

ON THIS OCCASION, rather than doing another interview in Baba's home, we took to the streets. We shared authority as we walked, bringing the methodology of this project full circle. I gave Baba the space she needed to recount the stories that mattered to her, asking only those questions that pushed her to go deeper. There was no longer any need to wrestle. She determined the directions in which we went, and I simply tried to understand them. Giving and taking in the interview, and listening, continued to be hard work. It always is. Sometimes I could not connect her tales, but in other instances, they altered how I understood Baba. I still have more questions than answers, but our conversation will, I am sure, continue.

Conclusion

A commitment to sharing authority is a beginning, not a destination.

– Michael Frisch, "Sharing Authority:
Oral History and the Collaborative Process"

WHEN I TELL PEOPLE about my work, what they tend to remember is the description that opens this book, of Baba and I making our way to an interview. Its slapstick humour elicits roaring laughter. "You should make a movie!" many say. Listeners can relate, often because they have been there themselves. Who has not struggled to understand the older people in their lives? Sometimes, however, these conversations turn to the methodological implications of my approach: "What's the point? Why didn't you throw Baba out of the car?" Good questions, I reply. It's always difficult to offer straightforward responses, but I will provide three here.

This book has focused on my attempts to collaborate, as both an oral historian and a granddaughter, with my baba: the process of doing so, the resulting outcomes, and the learning that took place throughout. This is a particular case study about how a theory – sharing authority – works in practice, detailing how I lost authority, wrestled to get it back, and finally came to share it. The interview stories that pepper the preceding pages are purposely honest and, on occasion, raw. They offer a realistic glimpse into the hard work that goes into partnering with communities (in this case my grandmother) when conducting research, noting both the limits and advantages of this methodology.

All oral historians start from a common premise that seeks to redefine and redistribute power, both within and outside the interview, but we chart our own courses through our practice and the people we meet.

Sharing authority is possible, but sometimes there are too many hurdles to overcome. Either way, dialogue is necessary at all junctures, eliciting lessons when the inevitable breakdowns and the glorious breakthroughs occur. These conversations lead us to put structures into place that either work well, fail miserably, or simply continue to evolve. Sharing authority never looks the same twice; there are no formulas. It requires flexibility and a willingness to move forward and roll with the punches. It is about giving up control and seeing a project through to its natural end. This is often frightening and disconcerting; it is hard to let go. The process must, however, dictate the outcome, which, for better or for worse, is rarely what we had in mind at the outset. We often need to distance ourselves from our work to understand how far we have come and where we have ended up. Luckily, there are no rules to break, just new directions in which to forge ahead.[1]

Indeed, if, when I started this project, someone had told me that I would end up writing a history about Sudbury's Ukrainian community through Baba's stories, I would have laughed. I never intended this to be a personal narrative, but circumstances in the field made it my only option; I had to be true to my process. During 2003, between my coursework and exams, I was visiting Baba. This exchange is seared in my memory because it was the first time I spoke to her about the project. She did not understand what a PhD was or why I would want one. After explaining what it entailed, for the umpteenth time, I took a practical approach, simply stating that I wanted to understand what it was like for her, and others of her generation, to grow up in Sudbury's Ukrainian community. As tears welled up in her eyes, the only response she could offer was, "It was great! I wish I could be young again." I knew I had a story but was oblivious to the kind of journey I would have to take, not only to piece it together, but also to appreciate it.

At that point, I had a very particular idea of what the history would look like, privileging written records and supplementing their absences with oral ones. My training had taught me that this was the appropriate approach. Letting go of this notion was difficult, and it certainly explains why there was so much tension between Baba and me. On a practical level, without her, the project would not have existed. That said, it quickly took on a life of its own. We were both heavily invested in it for different reasons that were not necessarily at odds – they were just different. We had to learn how to work together and listen to one another. I sought to reconstruct a history of the community, and Baba wanted to establish and remember her connection to it. This had implications in our exchanges and in those we had with other Ukrainians. As I pieced together an imagined past, I had to keep in mind that Baba had lived it. There was a lot at stake, and I could not simply throw her out of the car. I opted for dialogue instead. Depending on the circumstances, our conversations could be productive or unhelpful. Needless to say, I was always torn. In hindsight, my learning took place when we could not find common ground. Only by wrestling with memories of community did I begin to understand what the project was about and who it was for. It has always been about Baba. It is also about who I am and where I come from. There is a fine line to walk in reflective scholarship; we must be wary of the dangers of narcissism, on the one hand, and the tendency to psychoanalyze, on the other – but writing ourselves out of our narratives is a mistake.[2] Doing oral history and committing to a collaborative approach forces us to pay attention to our own roles in the process. We must own up to the subjectivity we bring to our projects. Whether we care to admit it or not, we undergo important social and self-discoveries throughout the course of our research.[3] Reservations and risks aside, this deserves more attention in our scholarship. If I had given in to the disciplinary insecurity that nearly crippled me as a graduate student, I could not have written this book. Its most important part – the collaboration between Baba and me – would have been silenced. Transparency enables us to hone our craft and push it forward. It is only by interrogating our connections to our work, and the successes and blunders we make along the way, that we can become better listeners, better oral historians.

We cannot all work with family members – nor would we want to – but this approach, of building meaningful relationships with interviewees and engaging in sustained conversations, drives home the potential that sharing authority holds: this is the only way that we can begin to access the meanings implicit in the stories we hear. These projects are time-consuming because they require multiple exchanges. This is good practice although it is important to recognize that it is not always viable or even desirable, in projects with limited budgets or different goals. This book offers a commentary on both the strengths and drawbacks of single and multiple interviews. Baba and I interviewed eighty-two people once, and though these encounters illuminated important patterns across interviews, they limited the meanings I could draw from the narratives themselves. On the other hand, I have spent over thirty years listening to Baba's stories. The more that she and I spoke – over the telephone, in the car, during impromptu visits, at family gatherings – and the closer we became as we spent time together and I forged connections to her social world, the better I was able to understand her stories, why she told them, and how they defined her. Sometimes less is more; there is breadth and then there is depth. I could not have given all our interviewees' stories the same kind of attention that I gave to those told by Baba. Nor could I have created the conditions for sustaining these sorts of conversations. I was not interested in doing so, either. Distance allowed me to recognize the limits of the project and my very particular connection to it. In my case, I dialogued with one person rather than with many. Baba's stories, and the meanings inherent in them, served as an entry point into exploring the history of Sudbury's Ukrainian community. They speak to the agency of the individual in history: how one person's memory can serve as a window into the past.

Although this is a local study that focuses on a particular region, which is largely absent from historiographical discussions, it need not be limited to those who are interested in Sudbury. Its narrative is written by and for, rather than of, the people, speaking to the importance of placing communities, and those who remember them, at the centre of our analyses.[4] I have been incredibly inspired by many of the pathbreaking social histories written about various communities, but I envisioned a new approach to this work by giving a substantial voice to both Baba and those we interviewed.[5] Their stories, as this book makes clear, are significant because they reveal the complicated and often contradictory ways that communities are built, solidified, contested, cultivated, and later remembered. Only by making community a category of analysis and viewing it as an imagined reality, a social interaction, and a process can we begin to make sense of the stories that are told about it.

Like many others, Baba's parents, Peter and Annie Zyma, came to the Sudbury region because it gave them a chance to create a better life for themselves and their children. Upon arriving, they found themselves in a desolate landscape that was dominated by transient men. Life was difficult, and sadly, it did not get much better for them. Informal social networks provided the framework for any initial attempts to build a community, and gender and Old World beliefs determined who did and did not belong. Peter and Annie were firmly rooted in a Catholic network; others established links with progressives. Either way, divisions were always central to this community and its evolution. Power relations between Ukrainians and mining companies also shaped the community and the experiences of its members. Wartime measures and company policies regarding workplace safety, hiring, firing, blacklisting, and even internment had lasting impacts as well.

As more Ukrainians settled in the area, they built public spaces that solidified many informal networks. Peter poured his heart and soul into establishing a Catholic church; others devoted their time to building ULFTA halls, an Orthodox church, and a nationalist hall. In all cases, men, women, and children came together, performing gendered and generational roles, to carve out spaces of their own. The community continued to evolve as its divided members debated and discussed issues that were central to their experiences. The mining companies were never far away, their reach extending into each home and every aspect of life.

As the community grew, it continued to splinter into a number of polarized sub-groups. Confrontations abounded, largely as a response to the circumstances of the Depression. As Ukrainians took to the streets, waging battles from their halls and churches, they negotiated and re-negotiated the boundaries of their highly contested worlds. Identities, and the differences between and among them, played a central role in this process. Baba came to understand these differences as she listened to a group of progressive men swear at her father and vandalize her home; others conceptualized their communities through the places that they themselves were and were not allowed to frequent. These stories, however, were often less important than their meanings, revealing glimpses into who people were and why they viewed their position in either the Catholic, progressive, nationalist, or Orthodox community as they did.

Ironically, the more time that Ukrainians spent defining themselves against each other, the less they were capable of recognizing that all were engaged in a working-class struggle to survive. Baba's family lost a home; others lost their jobs. As they adopted common economic strategies, they had analogous experiences in their homes and in the sub-communities they cultivated.

Of course, living through a period and remembering it are very different processes. When Baba recalled Sudbury Ukrainians, and the particular neighbourhood in which her Catholic sub-group was rooted, she offered a simplified commentary on both, implying that boundaries were firm and straightforward. Our conversations throughout the project, both between ourselves and with others, spoke to another reality. Much like community, memory is complex and ever changing. When Baba and I conducted interviews, for instance, she constantly tried to connect with interviewees. Although I tended to view these random and frequently clear-cut references to the minutiae of everyday life as unwelcome interferences, I now recognize that she was trying to find common ground that would enable her to initiate conversations about community. Had Baba not been in the car, these exchanges would never have occurred. Unity, to be clear, was never our goal, but the intergenerational dialogue that resulted held great potential, sparking important discussions that affected how people imagined, negotiated, and experienced their communities.

Appendix

1. Interviewees

Baba and I interviewed the following men and women. Along with brief biographical details, I note their connections to Baba. They were either family friends or she forged relationships with them at St. Mary's Ukrainian Catholic Church, in the Donovan where she grew up, or in the community at large, usually through everyday activities, such as shopping.

Name	Maiden name/ Name change	Sex	Date of birth	Birthplace	To Sudbury	Neighbourhood	Religion/ Politics	Connection to Baba
Babij, W		M	1926	Coniston, ON	N/A	Polack Town	UCath	Community acquaintance
Babuik, M		M	1916	Swan Plain, SK	1937	Not Given	UOrth	Donovan neighbour
Babuik, V	Havrachysky	F	1925	Ukraine	1935	West End	UOrth	Family friend
Balon, S		M	1926	Timmins, ON	1930	East End	None/ ULFTA	Community acquaintance
Behun, A	Bilowus	F	1931	Coniston, ON	N/A	Polack Town	UCath	Community acquaintance
Behun, P		M	1927	Coniston, ON	N/A	Polack Town	UCath/ UNF	Community acquaintance
Bendick, R	Shyluk	F	1934	North Battle ford, SK	1940	West End	UCath/UNF	Community acquaintance
Bilczuk, V	Bodnarchuk	F	1930	Arbakka, MB	1941	Donovan	UCath	Donovan neighbour
Brydges, M	Ladyk	F	1914	Port Arthur, ON	1922	Donovan	None/ ULFTA	Donovan neighbour
Buchowski, J		M	1929	Coniston, ON	N/A	Polack Town	UCath	Community acquaintance

Name	Maiden name/ Name change	Sex	Date of birth	Birthplace	To Sudbury	Neighbourhood	Religion/ Politics	Connection to Baba
Buchowski, M		F	1944	Sudbury, ON	N/A	West End	N/A	None
Buchowski, S		M	1928	Coniston, ON	N/A	Polack Town	UCath	Community acquaintance
Bzdel, F	Poworoznyk	F	1927	Glen Elder, SK	1952	West End/Lively	UCath	Community acquaintance
Bzdel, J		M	1927	Wishart, SK	1947	West End/Lively	UCath	St. Mary's parishioner
Chitruk, P		M	1924	Sudbury, ON	N/A	East End	UCath/UNF	Family friend
Chmara, W		M	1932	Coniston, ON	N/A	Polack Town	None	Community acquaintance
Chytuk, P	Urchyshyn	F	1919	Regina, SK	1941	East End	None/ULFTA	None
Chyz, P	Demchuk	F	1921	Poland	1940	Downtown/ Coniston	UCath	Family friend
Clouthier, M	Werstiuk	F	1934	Coniston, ON	N/A	Polack Town	UCath	Community acquaintance
Cotnam, H	Cybulka	F	1919	Levack, ON	N/A	French Town	None	Community acquaintance
Crowe, B	Haluschak	F	1930	Fort William, ON	1931	Garson	None/ULFTA	Family friend

Name	Maiden name	Sex	Birth year	Birthplace	Immigration	Location	Religion	Relationship
Dobranski, I	Harmaty	F	1913	Winnipeg, MB	1945	West End	UCath	St. Mary's parishioner
Evanshen, N		M	1924	Sudbury, ON	N/A	East End	UCath/ULFTA	Community acquaintance
Gawalko, R		M	1936	Sudbury, ON	N/A	West End	UCath	Family friend
Giazdoski, H	Daniluk	F	1927	Coniston, ON	N/A	Polack Town	UCath	Community acquaintance
Hayduk, S		M	1931	Falconbridge, ON	N/A	Garson	RC	Community acquaintance
Helash, A	Ciotka	F	1927	Fishing River, MB	1946	Donovan	UCath	Family friend/ Stacey's maternal grandmother
Hickey, M	Danchuk	F	1939	Sudbury, ON	N/A	Donovan/ West End	UCath	St. Mary's parishioner
Holunga, J		M	1925	Coniston, ON	N/A	Polack Town	UCath	Community acquaintance
Jurgilas, L	Burke/ Burkotski	F	1928	Sudbury, ON	N/A	Donovan	UOrth	Donovan neighbour
Kostiw, J	Steczyszyn	F	1921	Poland	1942	Donovan	UCath	St. Mary's parishioner
Kotyluk, L	Kaben	F	1938	Sudbury, ON	N/A	West End	None/ULFTA	Community acquaintance
Kozak, N	Tataryn	F	1922	Espanola, ON	1927	Donovan	UCath	Family friend

Name	Maiden name/ Name change	Sex	Date of birth	Birthplace	To Sudbury	Neighbourhood	Religion/ Politics	Connection to Baba
Kruk, P	Mykoluk	F	1929	Sudbury, ON	N/A	West End	RC	Family friend
Lekun, E	Lyhkun	M	1937	Sudbury, ON	N/A	Creighton	UCath	Donovan friend
Maizuk, E	Kureluik	F	1930	Coniston, ON	N/A	Polack Town	UCath	Community acquaintance
Maizuk, J		M	1922	Coniston, ON	N/A	Polack Town	RC	Community acquaintance
Makarinsky, F		M	1929	Creighton, ON	N/A	Donovan	RC	Donovan neighbour
Martyn, T		M	1944	Sudbury, ON	N/A	Donovan/ West End	UOrth	Community acquaintance
Matschke, A	Kuchmey	F	1923	Sudbury, ON	N/A	West End	UCath	St. Mary's parishioner
Max, B	Maksimovich	M	1931	Sudbury, ON	N/A	East End	UCath	Family friend
Panas, V	Romanchuk	F	1928	Winnipeg, MB	1949	Donovan	UCath/UNF	Community acquaintance
Pihursky, H	Ciotka	F	1926	Colfax, SK	1938	East End	UOrth/UNF	Family friend
Podorozny, A	Ogenchuk	F	1914	Hafford, SK	1937	West End	UCath	St. Mary's parishioner

Name		Sex	Year	Origin	Year	Neighbourhood	Religion	Relationship
Rapsky, C		M	1929	Creighton, ON	1934	West End/Donovan	RC	Family friend
Rohatyn, O	Mysyk	F	1928	Ukraine	1957	Donovan	UCath/UNF	Community acquaintance
Samborski, J	Tyshynski	F	1913	Cudworth, SK	1942	Downtown	UCath	St. Mary's parishioner
Sarmatiuk, D		M	1933	Sudbury, ON	N/A	West End	RC	Family friend
Sawchuk, O		M	1928	Winnipeg, MB	1930	West End	None/ULFTA	Community acquaintance
Semenuk, W		M	1921	Sudbury, ON	N/A	Donovan	UCath	Donovan neighbour
Shelegey, O	Struk	F	1936	Sudbury, ON	N/A	West End	UCath	St. Mary's parishioner
Shelegey, W		M	1925	Ukraine	1939	Polack Town	UCath/UNF	Community acquaintance
Shkrabek, M	Temeriski	F	1913	Fort Frances, ON	1937	Donovan	UOrth	Donovan neighbour
Sitko, M	Wolochatiuk	F	1913	Ethelbert, MB	1938	Donovan	UCath	Donovan neighbour
Smilanich, H	Pasichnyk	F	1926	Levack, ON	N/A	East End	None/ULFTA	Family friend
Solski, E	Kotyluk	F	1929	Chicago, IL	1935	Little Britain	UCath	Donovan neighbour
Solski, N		M	1925	Coniston, ON	N/A	Polack Town	RC	Donovan neighbour

Name	Maiden name/ Name change	Sex	Date of birth	Birthplace	To Sudbury	Neighbourhood	Religion/ Politics	Connection to Baba
Stanyon, M	Kowalchuk	F	1920	MacGregor, MB	1946	Levack	Anglican	Donovan friend
Stefura, J		M	1929	Saskatoon, SK	1929	Donovan	UCath/UNF	Donovan neighbour
Sturby, D	Zaparynuik	F	1929	Sudbury, ON	N/A	Donovan	UOrth	Donovan neighbour
Tarkin, H		M	1932	Winnipeg, MB	1932	Donovan	UCath	Family friend
Timchuk, K	Harach	F	1914	Kroiter, SK	1935	West End	UCath/UNF	Donovan neighbour
Tkach, J		M	1916	Dauphin, MB	1945	West End	UCath	St. Mary's parishioner
Udovicic, S	Kuczma	F	1933	Creighton, ON	N/A	Creighton	UCath	Family friend
Witwicky, S	Makowsky	F	1921	Sundown, MB	1943	Downtown	UCath	Community acquaintance
Yawney, P	Puhach	F	1923	Glen Hope, MB	1943	West End	UCath	St. Mary's parishioner
Zaitz, T	Zayatz	M	1922	Sudbury, ON	N/A	East End	None	Community acquaintance

| Zawierzeniec, M Nykilchyk | F | 1925 | Ukraine | 1938 | West End | UCath/UNF | St. Mary's parishioner |
| Zembrzycki, O Zyma | F | 1927 | Sudbury, ON | N/A | Donovan | UCath | Stacey's paternal grandmother |

RC	Roman Catholic
UCath	Ukrainian Catholic
ULFTA	Ukrainian Labour Farmer Temple Association
UNF	Ukrainian National Federation
UOrth	Ukrainian Orthodox

Thirteen interviewees chose to remain anonymous. To protect their identities, their names, as well as any information about them, do not appear in this table.

2. Interview Questionnaire

First and Second Generation Background Information

What were your parents' names? What was your mother's maiden name?

What year were your parents born in?

Where were your parents born? What country, region, town/village were they born in?

How did your parents meet?

When did your parents get married? Where did they get married?

Did your parents attend school? Up to what grade? Could they read or write?

Did they work in their native country?

How old were your parents when they came to Canada?

Did their entire family or members of their community come to Canada with them? Did they all settle in Sudbury or elsewhere?

What was their voyage route to Canada? Do you remember any specifics about their immigration process/experience? Where was the first place they settled when they came to Canada?

Did your parents become Canadian citizens? When?

When did your parents come to Sudbury?

Why did they come to Sudbury?

Where did they work in Sudbury?

When were you born?

Where were you born? What were the circumstances of your birth?

Do you have any siblings? What was their birth order?

Were you or any of your siblings named after someone or something?

Were you and your siblings baptized? Where? How long after birth?

Neighbourhood and Childhood/Adolescent Associations

Can you describe where you lived in Sudbury? What was the neighbourhood called?

What was your family's position in this neighbourhood/community?

Was this neighbourhood ethnically diverse?

Did you have free time to play with other children in the neighbourhood? How was your free time spent? What kinds of games did you play? Who did you play them with? What were the rules? Did you have any equipment or toys?

Did you have friends from other ethnicities? How did these friends influence you?

Did your parents have friends from other ethnicities?

Whom did you associate with as a teenager? Were your friends from different ethnicities? Were you permitted to date? Were those you dated Ukrainian? Did they practice the same religion as you? What kinds of activities did you participate in?

The Ukrainian Home

Can you describe your family dwelling? What was the floor plan of your house? Did any of your siblings share bedrooms?

Were there boarders in the house? Who were they? How many were there? Who tended to their needs? Did these boarders work? Where did they work? How did they end up staying at your house?

What were your mother's household responsibilities? What kinds of decisions did she make? What were your father's responsibilities? What kinds of decisions did he make? What role did children play in the household?

How did your family spend time together? Were there family holidays or reunions?

Do you have any special memories about any births, weddings, or funerals you attended or heard about? What kinds of traditions surrounded these events?

What was the role of Ukrainian heritage in your family? Did you speak Ukrainian at home or English? Why do you think you spoke this language? What language did your parents converse in? Did you celebrate Ukrainian holidays? Which ones? What kinds of traditions did you follow?

Gender Relations within the Family

What kinds of responsibilities did you have in your parents' home and in the family? Were there differences between boys' and girls' responsibilities?

Who disciplined the children? How were you disciplined?

What were your father's attitudes toward women? What were your mother's thoughts on women and their roles?

What were your father's attitudes toward men? What were your mother's thoughts on men and their roles?

Did you have any major disputes with your parents? How were they resolved?

Consumption

Which meals did your family eat together? What was the pattern of seating at the table? What kinds of issues were discussed during meals? Did your father's schedule include shift-work? How did this affect mealtime? Did it impact the time at which you ate? What you ate?

What was your favourite food as a child?

How important has Ukrainian food been to you and your family? Do you cook Ukrainian food? What is your specialty? Who taught you how to make it? How old were you when you learned how to make it?

What sounds, smells, and/or tastes do you associate with your family's home? With the community?

Education

Where did you go to school? Do you remember any one teacher having a particular influence on you? What level of education did you receive? What kinds of things did you learn in school? What was your favourite part about school? What kinds of school activities did you participate in?

What were your parents' attitudes toward education? Did they feel it was important for you and your siblings to learn Ukrainian? How important? Did your parents have different expectations for male and female children?

What other forms of schooling did you participate in? Did you enrol in night school, Ukrainian language school, union classes, or religious classes? Did you participate in any organizations through school, like Girl Guides, Red Cross, and sports or music groups?

Did you have any special training or preparation for a job/career? What kinds of opportunities were available to you (choices)? For women: Was it assumed that you would stay at home? For men: Was it assumed that your brothers/male friends would work at the mine?

Religion and Politics

Were your parents involved in the Ukrainian community?

Were your parents religious? What church did they belong to? Did they participate in any church organizations?

What were your parents' political beliefs?

Are you a member of any particular church in Sudbury? Have you been involved in the Ukrainian church in any way? What was your role in this organization? Was this an important part of your life? How important was the ethnic church? What role did it play in the community? Do you remember if there were any Communist attacks upon the church?

Negotiating a Place in the Host Society

Did your parents speak English? If yes, how did they learn this language?

Do you know of any occasions in which your parents were discriminated against for being Ukrainian? For example, were they interned, did they have run-ins with the police?

What do you remember about the Depression? Do you have any family stories about the Depression? How was your family affected by the Depression? Were there any economic impacts? Did anyone lose jobs, boarders, houses? Did you always have enough food to eat? Do you remember anything about the growth of Bolshevism in the region?

Do you remember the Royal Visit of 1939?

Do you have any family stories about World War I? World War II? Did anyone in your family participate in the First or Second World War effort, either on the home or war front? (Factory work, charity work, local opportunities – i.e. more work) What was your family's reaction/particular views toward the first war? To the second war? How did your family react to these wars? How was your family affected by these wars? What was the economic impact? Were you recruited during this period? Did you relocate to another region? If you helped with the war effort, was the Ukrainian church involved?

How did the war impact attitudes about Ukrainians? Did your family change after the war? Was your family treated differently after the war?

Did your family have connections with other family members in Ukraine before either war? Did the war affect this connection?

How were Ukrainians treated and regarded by other races? Were Ukrainian men and women treated differently by the ethnic community? By the larger community?

Have you or anyone you know ever been racially profiled by the local police? Do you remember hearing of many Ukrainian men/women who committed crimes? Do you remember any hangings that took place in Sudbury?

Material Culture and Consumerism

Can you give a general description of any reading materials you had? Did your family subscribe to any newspapers, local or ethnic? Did you subscribe to any of this material?

What kinds of clothing did you wear? Who made this clothing? Did you wear any kinds of Ukrainian clothing?

What kinds of hairstyles did you have in your adolescence?

Did you have any heroes/idols?

Adulthood

What was your first job? How was it obtained? Can you trace your work career in terms of place, positions, conditions, wages, and numbers of men/women? Were there any differentials in wages and conditions among ethnicities or among men and women? Were you involved in any union activities?

Where did you live when you were working?

Did you control your earnings? How did you spend your money?

Marriage

Have you ever been married? Have you remained single?

What is your spouse's name? When was he/she born? Where was he/she born? How did you meet him/her? Was he/she Ukrainian? Did he/she have the same religious background as you? Did your parents approve of him/her? Describe your wedding and any special customs, traditions, and beliefs that occurred on that day.

For women: Did you continue to work outside the home? What was your role inside the home? What was your husband's role?

What was your spouse's background? Was he/she educated? Where did he/she work?

Did he/she work shift work? Did you have to adapt to that lifestyle? How?

Did you have children? How many?

Who raised the children? Who made decisions about the children? How did you spend time with your children? Did you follow any child-rearing guides or advice? Who gave you advice?

Did you or your spouse speak Ukrainian to the children? Did you celebrate any Ukrainian traditions? Did you send the children to Ukrainian school? Did you raise them in the Ukrainian church? Which one? Were they members of any Ukrainian organizations?

What kind of social life did you have as a parent? What kinds of activities did you partake in outside the home? With whom? Were you a member of any organizations/clubs? Any Ukrainian organizations? Did you interact with other ethnicities or other ethnic-specific organizations? Were members strictly Ukrainian? What other social outlets were available to you?

Did being a member of a specific organization divide your family, your friends, your neighbourhood, your community?

Were you involved in any union movements? Did you participate in any strikes? How? Why?

Have you volunteered or participated in any other organization not discussed?

Do you have any feelings about Ukraine? Have you supported nationalist campaigns? Have you done any charity work for Ukraine?

Unmarried, Divorced, Separated

If separated, divorced, widowed, explore reasons. How did you support your family? Discuss any difficulties with being a single parent. How did your life change without a spouse?

If single, where did you work? What kinds of social relationships did you have? What are your attitudes toward marriage? Did you experience any pressure to marry? What kinds of living arrangements did you have? What kinds of things did you do in your spare time?

Did you experience any economic pressures?

Closing Remarks

Do you have any reflections on any changes that have occurred in the Ukrainian community or in Sudbury in general?

How important was it for you to be a Canadian? Did you ever feel any tensions between being Ukrainian and being Canadian? Was being a Ukrainian more important than being a Canadian or vice versa?

Did you ever feel isolated from the larger community or discriminated against because your family was "foreign"? Were you ever discriminated against for being Ukrainian or for belonging to a Ukrainian organization?

Do you know of any stereotypes/perceptions used to describe Ukrainians?

How important was/is the Ukrainian community to you?

What does being Ukrainian mean to you?

Is there anything else you wish to share?

Do you have any photos or memorabilia you wish to share?

Do you have any friends or relatives who may be interested in participating in this study?

Notes

Introduction

1 Between October 2004 and June 2005, Baba and I conducted seventy-two life story, oral history interviews with Ukrainians who were either born or raised in the Sudbury region or came to it prior to 1945; I conducted ten other interviews on my own. Of the interviewees, fifty were women and thirty-two were men. The group was politically, religiously, and ideologically diverse: nine identified as progressives, six were members of the Orthodox community, fourteen did not identify with any Ukrainian community, and fifty-three were Ukrainian Catholics; fourteen Ukrainian Catholics also belonged to the Ukrainian National Federation (UNF). We stopped interviewing when we reached eighty-two people because this was more than enough to discern patterns across the collection. On the other hand, Baba and I could have done more, and certainly wanted to, because we were both committed to preserving a collective narrative about this community. Time and financial constraints, however, made this unfeasible. For more information about our interviewees and Baba's connection to them, see the Appendix. Thirteen interviewees chose to remain anonymous. To protect their identities, their names and any information that may be used to identify them do not appear in the text of this book.

2 See Stacey Zembrzycki, "Memory, Identity, and the Challenge of Community among Ukrainians in the Sudbury Region, 1901-1939" (PhD diss., Carleton University, 2007).

3 Linda Shopes also reminds us of the common disconnect between oral historians and their interviewees in "Sharing Authority," *Oral History Review* 30, 1 (January 2003): 105.

4 Michael Frisch, *A Shared Authority: Essays on the Craft and Meaning of Oral and Public History* (Albany: State University of New York Press, 1990).

5 Michael Frisch, "Sharing Authority: Oral History and the Collaborative Process," *Oral History Review* 30, 1 (January 2003): 113. Although their language differed from that of Frisch, feminist oral historians also focused on process and on how the unique dynamics of the interview space affected the stories told and the narratives that were written as a result. See Sherna Berger Gluck and Daphne Patai, eds., *Women's Words: The Feminist Practice of Oral History* (New York: Routledge, 1991).

6 Frisch, "Sharing Authority," 113.

7 Katharine C. Corbett and Howard S. Miller, "A Shared Inquiry into Shared Inquiry," *Public Historian* 28, 1 (Winter 2006): 20.

8 For the reference to "mantra," see Shopes, "Sharing Authority," 103.

9 Shopes makes a similar point in ibid., 104.

10 "Shared Authority," special feature in *Oral History Review* 30, 1 (January 2003): 23-113; Corbett and Miller, "A Shared Inquiry," 15-38; Steven High, Lisa Ndejuru, and Kristen O'Hare, eds., "Special Issue of Sharing Authority: Community-University Collaboration in Oral History, Digital Storytelling, and Engaged Scholarship," *Journal of Canadian Studies* 43, 1 (Winter 2009).

11 I have just co-edited a collection that takes this point as its premise: Anna Sheftel and Stacey Zembrzycki, eds., *Oral History off the Record: Toward an Ethnography of Practice* (New York: Palgrave Macmillan, 2013).

12 Public archives are complicated and highly political sites of knowledge and power that ultimately determine the national narratives we can and cannot write. See, for instance, Jacques Derrida, *Archive Fever: A Freudian Impression*, trans. Eric Prenowitz (Chicago: University of Chicago Press, 1996); Antoinette Burton, *Dwelling in the Archive: Women Writing House, Home, and History in Late Colonial India* (Oxford: Oxford University Press, 2003); Marlene Manoff, "Theories of the Archive from across the Disciplines," *Libraries and the Academy* 4, 1 (January 2004): 9-25; and Antoinette Burton, ed., *Archive Stories: Facts, Fictions, and the Writing of History* (Durham: Duke University Press, 2005).

13 For similar reflections on putting theory into practice, see, for instance, Donald Ritchie, *Doing Oral History: A Practical Guide* (New York: Oxford University Press, 2003); Lynn Abrams, *Oral History Theory* (London: Routledge, 2010); Donald Ritchie, ed., *The Oxford Handbook of Oral History* (New York: Oxford University Press, 2010).

14 Martha Norkunas, *Monuments and Memory: History and Representation in Lowell, Massachusetts* (Washington, DC: Smithsonian Institution Press, 2002), 25.

15 My thinking here is inspired by Carolyn Steedman, *Landscape for a Good Woman: A Story of Two Lives* (New Brunswick, NJ: Rutgers University Press, 1986), 8-12; Penny Summerfield, *Reconstructing Women's Wartime Lives: Discourse and Subjectivity in Oral Histories of the Second World War* (Manchester: Manchester University Press, 1998), x; Franca Iacovetta, "Post-Modern Ethnography, Historical Materialism, and Decentring the (Male) Authorial Voice: A Feminist Conversation," *Histoire sociale/Social History* 32, 64 (November 1999): 275-93; and Pamela Sugiman, "'These Feelings That Fill My Heart': Japanese Canadian Women's Memories of Internment," *Oral History* 34, 2 (Autumn 2006): 69-84. Although other scholars have used the memories of family members to construct their histories, they have spent very little time critically exploring their subjective links to the resulting narratives.

16 Frances Swyripa, *Wedded to the Cause: Ukrainian-Canadian Women and Ethnic Identity, 1891-1991* (Toronto: University of Toronto Press, 1993), 216-17.

17 Olga Zembrzycki (née Zyma), interview by author, Sudbury, 6 October 2004.

18 It must be noted that I returned to the original oral records to write this book, using Stories Matter – free open-source database-building software developed at the Centre for Oral History and Digital Storytelling – to relisten to the interviews that Baba and I conducted. For more on Stories Matter, see http://storytelling.concordia.ca/ storiesmatter/.

19 Alicia Rouverol, "Collaborative Oral History in a Correctional Setting: Promise and Pitfalls," *Oral History Review* 30, 1 (January 2003): 83.

20 Henry Greenspan, *On Listening to Holocaust Survivors: Recounting and Life History* (Westport: Praeger Press, 1998), xvii.

21 Names enclosed in quotation marks are pseudonyms.

22 Anonymous interview. Any information that can be used to identify interviewees, including the dates and locations of interviews, does not appear in the notes.

23 Swyripa, *Wedded to the Cause*, 241-43; Karen Dubinsky, "'Who Do You Think Did the Cooking?': Baba in the Classroom," in *Changing Lives: Women and Northern Ontario*, ed. Margaret Kechnie and Marge Reitsma-Street (Toronto: Dundurn Press, 1996), 193-97.

24 Luisa Passerini's work is best known for doing this: see Luisa Passerini, *Fascism in Popular Memory: The Cultural Experience of the Turin Working Class*, trans. Robert Lumley and Jude Bloomfield (Cambridge: Cambridge University Press, 1987); and Luisa Passerini, ed., *Memory and Totalitarianism* (Oxford: Oxford University Press, 1992). Also see the chapters written by Alexander Freund, Luis van Isschot, and Anna Sheftel in Sheftel and Zembrzycki, *Oral History off the Record*.

25 Since all our interviews were in English, I believe that this response was related to familiarity rather than language.

26 Barbara Myerhoff, *Number Our Days* (New York: Simon and Schuster, 1978). For similar discussions on interviewing the elderly, see Mark Klempner, "Navigating Life Review Interviews with Survivors of Trauma," in *The Oral History Reader*, 2nd ed., ed. Robert Perks and Alistair Thomson (New York: Routledge, 2006), 198-210; and Katrina Srigley, "Stories of Strife? Remembering the Great Depression," in "Special Issue: Remembering Family, Analyzing Home: Oral History and the Family," ed. Katrina Srigley and Stacey Zembrzycki, *Oral History Forum d'histoire orale* 29 (2009): http://www.oralhistoryforum.ca/.

27 For related reflections, see Lorraine Sitzia, "A Shared Authority: An Impossible Goal?" *Oral History Review* 30, 1 (January 2003): 87-101. Although the purpose of her project was very different from mine, Katherine Borland also speaks about the challenges of working with her grandmother in "'That's Not What I Said': Interpretive Conflict in Oral Narrative Research," in Gluck and Patai, *Women's Words*, 63-75.

28 See, for instance, Ruth Behar, *Translated Woman: Crossing the Border with Esperanza's Story* (Boston: Beacon Press, 1993); and Ruth Behar, *The Vulnerable Observer: Anthropology That Breaks Your Heart* (Boston: Beacon Press, 1996).

29 In *On Listening to Holocaust Survivors,* Henry Greenspan pioneered this way of thinking about the dynamics of interviews. See also Henry Greenspan and Sidney Bolkosky, "When Is an Interview an Interview? Notes from Listening to Holocaust Survivors," *Poetics Today* 27, 2 (2006): 431-49.

30 Ritchie, *Doing Oral History,* 87.

31 Childhood is a separate and socially constructed stage of existence that complicates the creation of a memory text; all our interviewees were under thirteen years old prior to 1939. See Neil Sutherland, "When You Listen to the Winds of Childhood, How Much Can You Believe?" in *Histories of Canadian Children and Youth,* ed. Nancy Janovicek and Joy Parr (Oxford: Oxford University Press, 2003), 19-34.

32 Gluck and Patai, *Women's Words*; Caroline B. Brettell, *When They Read What We Write: The Politics of Ethnography* (Westport, CT: Bergin and Garvey, 1993); Joan Sangster, "Telling Our Stories: Feminist Debates and the Use of Oral History," *Women's History Review* 3, 1 (March 1994): 5-28.

33 Greenspan and Bolkosky, "When Is an Interview an Interview?," 432.

34 Talja Blokland, "Bricks, Mortar, Memories: Neighbourhood and Networks in Collective Acts of Remembering," *International Journal of Urban and Regional Research* 25, 2 (June 2001): 279.

35 Alessandro Portelli, *The Death of Luigi Trastulli and Other Stories: Form and Meaning in Oral History* (Albany: State University of New York Press, 1991), viii-ix. As Pamela Sugiman points out, whereas written sources present a raw version of the past, that of their oral counterparts often changes over time. Sugiman, "'These Feelings,'" 81.

36 Portelli, *The Death of Luigi Trastulli,* 99.

37 Shopes, "Sharing Authority," 106.

38 Annette Kuhn, *Family Secrets: Acts of Memory and Imagination* (London: Verso, 1995). Also see Norkunas, *Monuments and Memory*; Mary Patrice Erdmans, *The Grasinski Girls: The Choices They Had and the Choices They Made* (Athens: Ohio University Press, 2004); and Katrina Srigley and Stacey Zembrzycki, "Introduction," in Srigley and Zembrzycki, "Special Issue: Remembering Family."

39 For a related discussion, see Anna Sheftel and Stacey Zembrzycki, "Only Human: A Reflection on the Ethical and Methodological Challenges of Working with 'Difficult' Stories," *Oral History Review* 37, 2 (Summer-Fall 2010): 191-241.

40 Lara Campbell writes that Canadian historiography that focuses on the Depression is "surprisingly fragmented and incomplete," usually subsumed into studies that address the interwar years or other thematic issues. Lara Campbell, *Respectable Citizens: Gender, Family, and Unemployment in Ontario's Great Depression* (Toronto: University of Toronto Press, 2009), 7. Although Campbell's work and the studies by Denyse Baillargeon and Katrina Srigley begin to address this shortcoming, more work is needed on the social history of this period as well as the first two decades of the twentieth century. Denyse Baillargeon, *Making Do: Women, Family, and Home in Montreal during the Great Depression,* trans. Yvonne Klein (Waterloo: Wilfrid

Laurier University Press, 1999); Katrina Srigley, *Breadwinning Daughters: Young Working Women in a Depression-Era City, 1929-1939* (Toronto: University of Toronto Press, 2010).

41 See, for instance, Vera Lysenko, *Men in Sheepskin Coats* (Toronto: Ryerson Press, 1947); Vladimir Kaye, *Early Ukrainian Settlements in Western Canada, 1895-1900* (Toronto: University of Toronto Press, 1964); Manoly Lupul, ed., *A Heritage in Transition: Essays in the History of Ukrainians in Canada* (Toronto: McClelland and Stewart, 1982); Michael H. Marunchak, *The Ukrainian Canadians: A History* (Winnipeg: Ukrainian Academy of Arts and Sciences in Canada, 1982); O.W. Gerus and J.E. Rea, *The Ukrainians in Canada* (Ottawa: Canadian Historical Association, 1985); Jaroslav Petryshyn, *Peasants in the Promised Land: Canada and the Ukrainians, 1891-1914* (Toronto: Lorimer, 1985); and Lubomyr Luciuk and Stella Hryniuk, eds., *Canada's Ukrainians: Negotiating an Identity* (Toronto: University of Toronto Press, 1991). Exceptions to this trend include Swyripa, *Wedded to the Cause;* Rhonda Hinther, "'Sincerest Revolutionary Greetings': Progressive Ukrainians in the Twentieth Century" (PhD diss., McMaster University, 2005); and Rhonda Hinther and Jim Mochoruk, eds., *Re-Imagining Ukrainian-Canadians: History, Politics, and Identity* (Toronto: University of Toronto Press, 2011). Orest Martynowych's rich study lacks a political agenda, but "it is essentially a history of public events and institutions, punctuated by dramatic episodes caused by prominent (male) personalities." See Orest Martynowych, *Ukrainians in Canada: The Formative Period, 1891-1924* (Edmonton: Canadian Institute of Ukrainian Studies Press, 1991), xxv.

42 John C. Walsh and Steven High, "Rethinking the Concept of Community," *Histoire sociale/Social History* 32, 64 (November 1999): 255-57. Also see Anthony P. Cohen, *The Symbolic Construction of Community* (London: Routledge, 1985); Ewa Morawska, *For Bread with Butter: The Life-Worlds of East Central Europeans in Johnstown Pennsylvania, 1890-1940* (Cambridge: Cambridge University Press, 1985); Franca Iacovetta, *Such Hardworking People: Italian Immigrants in Postwar Toronto* (Montreal and Kingston: McGill-Queen's University Press, 1992); Royden Loewen, *Family, Church, and Market: A Mennonite Community in the Old and New Worlds, 1850-1930* (Toronto: University of Toronto Press, 1993); Henry Glassie, *Passing the Time in Ballymenone: Culture and History of an Ulster Community* (Bloomington: Indiana University Press, 1995); Dolores Hayden, *The Power of Place: Urban Landscapes as Public History* (Cambridge, MA: MIT Press, 1995); Doreen Massey, "Places and Their Pasts," *History Workshop Journal* 39, 1 (1995): 182-92; Miranda Joseph, *Against the Romance of Community* (Minneapolis: University of Minnesota Press, 2002); Kerry Abel, *Changing Places: History, Community, and Identity in Northeastern Ontario* (Montreal and Kingston: McGill-Queen's University Press, 2006); Jordan Stanger-Ross, *Staying Italian: Urban Change and Ethnic Life in Postwar Toronto and Philadelphia* (Chicago: University of Chicago Press, 2009); and James Opp and John C. Walsh, eds., *Placing Memory and Remembering Place in Canada* (Vancouver: UBC Press, 2010).

43 Lynne Marks, *Revivals and Roller Rinks: Religion, Leisure, and Identity in Late-Nineteenth-Century Small-Town Ontario* (Toronto: University of Toronto Press, 1996).

44 For the most part, those who have written about northern Ontario have focused almost exclusively on resource development, labour radicalism, urban settlement patterns, and industrial development in single-industry communities. For a discussion of this historiographical problem, see Kerry Abel, "History and the Provincial Norths: An Ontario Example," in *Northern Visions: New Perspectives on the North in Canadian History*, ed. Kerry Abel and Ken Coates (Peterborough: Broadview Press, 2001), 127-40; and Nancy Forestell, "Women, Gender and the Provincial North," in Abel and Coates, *Northern Visions*, 107-16. Notable exceptions include Ian Radforth, *Bushworkers and Bosses: Logging in Northern Ontario, 1900-1980* (Toronto: University of Toronto Press, 1987); Thomas Dunk, *It's a Working Man's Town: Male Working-Class Culture in Northwestern Ontario* (Montreal and Kingston: McGill-Queen's University Press, 1991); Karen Dubinsky, *Improper Advances: Rape and Heterosexual Conflict in Ontario, 1880-1929* (Chicago: Chicago University Press, 1993); Nancy Forestell, "All That Glitters Is Not Gold: The Gender Dimensions of Work, Family, and Community Life in the Northern Ontario Gold Mining Town of Timmins, 1901-1950" (PhD diss., University of Toronto, 1993); Nancy Forestell, "Bachelors, Boarding Houses, and Blind Pigs: Gender Construction in a Multi-Ethnic Mining Camp, 1909-1920," in *A Nation of Immigrants: Women, Workers, and Communities in Canadian History, 1840s-1960s*, ed. Franca Iacovetta, Paula Draper, and Robert Ventresca (Toronto: University of Toronto Press, 1998), 251-90; Nancy Forestell, "The Miner's Wife: Working-Class Femininity in a Masculine Context, 1920-1950," in *Gendered Pasts: Historical Essays in Femininity and Masculinity in Canada*, ed. Kathryn McPherson, Cecilia Morgan, and Nancy Forestell (Oxford: Oxford University Press, 1999), 139-57; Oiva W. Saarinen, *Between a Rock and a Hard Place: A Historical Geography of the Finns in the Sudbury Area* (Waterloo: Wilfrid Laurier University Press, 1999); and Françoise Noël, *Family and Community Life in Northeastern Ontario: The Interwar Years* (Montreal and Kingston: McGill-Queen's University Press, 2009).

45 Walsh and High, "Rethinking the Concept of Community," 262, 267.

46 To learn more about the creation of this website, see Stacey Zembrzycki, "Bringing Stories to Life: Using New Media to Disseminate and Critically Engage with Oral History Interviews," *Oral History* 41, 1 (Spring 2013): 98-107.

47 Michael Frisch, "Oral History and the Digital Revolution: Toward a Post-Documentary Sensibility," in Perks and Thomson, *The Oral History Reader*, 2nd ed., 32-42; Alistair Thomson, "Four Paradigm Transformations in Oral History," *Oral History Review* 34, 1 (2007): 68-70; Michael Frisch, "Three Dimensions and More: Oral History beyond the Paradoxes of Method," in *Handbook of Emergent Methods*, ed. S. Nagy Hess-Biber and P. Leavy (New York: Guilford Press, 2008), 221-38; Steven High and David Sworn, "After the Interview: The Interpretive Challenges of Oral History Video Indexing," *Digital Studies/Le champ numérique* 1, 2 (2009): http://www.digitalstudies.

org/; Steven High, "Telling Stories: A Reflection on Oral History and New Media," *Oral History* 38, 1 (Spring 2010): 101-12; Erin Jessee, Stacey Zembrzycki, and Steven High, "*Stories Matter*: Conceptual Challenges in the Development of Oral History Database Building Software," *Forum Qualitative Sozialforschung/Forum: Qualitative Social Research* 12, 1 (January 2011): http://www.qualitative-research.net/; Steven High, Jessica J. Mills, and Stacey Zembrzycki, "Telling Our Stories/Animating Our Past: A Status Report on Oral History and Digital Media," *Canadian Journal of Communication* 37, 3 (September 2012): 1-22.

Chapter 1: Building

1   Although a Ukrainian nationalist movement worked to transmit a sense of Ukrainian identity among citizens in Austria-Hungary, most, and especially peasant migrants like Peter, tended to identify with their own regions or villages rather than with a broader nationality. See Stella Hryniuk, *Peasants with Promise: Ukrainians in Southeastern Galicia, 1880-1900* (Edmonton: Canadian Institute of Ukrainian Studies Press, 1991). For a related discussion about the multi-layered nature of Italian identity in Toronto prior to the Second World War, see John Zucchi, *Italians in Toronto: Development of a National Identity, 1875-1935* (Montreal and Kingston: McGill-Queen's University Press, 1988).

2   This story is pieced together from three formal audio-recorded interviews that I conducted with Baba and many informal conversations I had with her before and throughout this project: Olga Zembrzycki (née Zyma), interviews by author, Sudbury, 6 October 2004, 18 June 2005, 1 November 2008. Where possible, maiden names have been included in this work. Since many women married men who descended from other ethnicities, and thus assumed non-Ukrainian surnames, this inclusion is meant to denote their Ukrainian heritage.

3   On family narratives and mythmaking, see, for instance, Raphael Samuel and Paul Thompson, eds., *The Myths We Live By* (New York: Routledge, 1990); Katherine Borland, "'That's Not What I Said': Interpretive Conflict in Oral Narrative Research," in *Women's Words: The Feminist Practice of Oral History,* ed. Sherna Berger Gluck and Daphne Patai (New York: Routledge, 1991), 63-75; Daniel Bertaux and Paul Thompson, eds., *Between Generations: Family Models, Myths, and Memories* (London: Transaction, 1993); Alexander Freund and Laura Quilici, "Exploring Myths in Women's Narratives: Italian and German Immigrant Women in Vancouver, 1947-1961," *BC Studies* 105-6 (Spring-Summer 1995): 159-82; Annette Kuhn, *Family Secrets: Acts of Memory and Imagination* (London: Verso, 1995); Pamela Sugiman, "'These Feelings That Fill My Heart': Japanese Canadian Women's Memories of Internment," *Oral History* 34, 2 (Autumn 2006): 69-84; Alexander Freund, "A Canadian Family Talks about Oma's Life in Nazi Germany: Three-Generational Interviews and Communicative Memory," in "Special Issue: Remembering Family, Analyzing Home: Oral History and the Family," ed. Katrina Srigley and Stacey Zembrzycki,

Oral History Forum d'histoire orale 29 (2009): http://www.oralhistoryforum.ca/; and Katrina Srigley, "Stories of Strife? Remembering the Great Depression," in Srigley and Zembrzycki, "Special Issue: Remembering Family, Analyzing Home."

4 Personal truths affect how individuals speak about their lives. They are revealed through the collective threads of an interview. On self-representation and truth, see, for instance, Luisa Passerini, *Fascism in Popular Memory: The Cultural Experience of the Turin Working Class,* trans. Robert Lumley and Jude Bloomfield (Cambridge: Cambridge University Press, 1987); Alessandro Portelli, *The Death of Luigi Trastulli and Other Stories: Form and Meaning in Oral History* (Albany: State University of New York Press, 1991); Joan Sangster, "Telling Our Stories: Feminist Debates and the Use of Oral History," Women's History Review 3, 1 (March 1994): 5-28; Alessandro Portelli, *Battle of Valle Giulia: Oral History and the Art of Dialogue* (Madison: University of Wisconsin Press, 1997); Marlene Epp, *Women without Men: Mennonite Refugees of the Second World War* (Toronto: University of Toronto Press, 1999); Alessandro Portelli, *The Order Has Been Carried Out: History, Memory, and Meaning of a Nazi Massacre in Rome* (New York: Palgrave Macmillan, 2003); Michael Riordon, *An Unauthorized Biography of the World* (Toronto: Between the Lines, 2004); Pamela Sugiman, "Passing Time, Moving Memories: Interpreting Wartime Narratives of Japanese Canadian Women," *Histoire sociale/Social History* 37, 73 (May 2004): 51-79; and Alessandro Portelli, *They Say in Harlan County: An Oral History* (Oxford: Oxford University Press, 2011).

5 C.M. Wallace, "The 1880s," in *Sudbury: Rail Town to Regional Capital,* ed. C.M. Wallace and Ashley Thomson (Toronto: Dundurn Press, 1993), 21-27.

6 Eileen Goltz, "A Corporate View of Housing and Community in a Company Town: Copper Cliff, 1886-1920," *Ontario History* 82, 1 (March 1990): 38.

7 Ibid., 39-40.

8 Ashley Thomson, "The 1890s," in Wallace and Thomson, *Sudbury,* 52.

9 Mike Solski, *The Coniston Story* (Sudbury: Journal Printing, 1983), 10.

10 Kerry Abel problematizes the debates surrounding company towns, questioning whether their "welfare capitalism" benefited residents or acted as a mechanism for social control. See Kerry Abel, *Changing Places: History, Community, and Identity in Northeastern Ontario* (Montreal and Kingston: McGill-Queen's University Press, 2006), 248.

11 Hryniuk, *Peasants with Promise,* 205; Orest Martynowych, *Ukrainians in Canada: The Formative Period, 1891-1924* (Edmonton: Canadian Institute of Ukrainian Studies Press, 1991), 3.

12 Martynowych, *Ukrainians in Canada,* 109-28; Alexander Biega and Myroslaw Diakowsky, eds., *The Ukrainian Experience in Quebec* (Toronto: Basilian Press, 1994). For a detailed analysis of the 1901 aggregate and manuscript census data, see Stacey Zembrzycki, "Memory, Identity, and the Challenge of Community among Ukrainians in the Sudbury Region, 1901-1939" (PhD diss., Carleton University, 2007), 39-45.

See also Canada, Bureau of the Census, *Population,* Vol. 1 (Ottawa: S.E. Dawson, 1902); Canada, Census of Canada, 1901, Sudbury, McKim, Snider and Waters, and Dryden, Neelon, and Garson sub-districts, Library and Archives Canada (LAC), http://www.collectionscanada.ca/; and Eric W. Sager and Peter Baskerville, eds., *Household Counts: Canadian Households and Families in 1901* (Toronto: University of Toronto Press, 2007).

13 For an in-depth discussion and deconstruction of the 1911 aggregate and manuscript census, see Zembrzycki, "Memory, Identity, and the Challenge," 45-67. Also see Canada, Bureau of the Census, *Population,* Vol. 1 (Ottawa: C.H. Parmelee, 1913); Canada, Bureau of the Census, *Religions, Origins, Birthplace, Citizenship, Literacy and Infirmities,* Vol. 2 (Ottawa: C.H. Parmelee, 1913); Census of Canada, 1911, Sudbury, Copper Cliff, Creighton, Snider and Waters, and Garson and Neelon sub-districts, LAC, http://www.collectionscanada.ca/.

14 See Nancy Forestell, "All That Glitters Is Not Gold: The Gender Dimensions of Work, Family, and Community Life in the Northern Ontario Gold Mining Town of Timmins, 1901-1950" (PhD diss., University of Toronto, 1993); Nancy Forestell, "Bachelors, Boarding Houses, and Blind Pigs," in *A Nation of Immigrants: Women, Workers, and Communities in Canadian History, 1840s-1960s,* ed. Franca Iacovetta, Paula Draper, and Robert Ventresca (Toronto: University of Toronto Press, 1998), 251-90; Abel, *Changing Places,* 93, 103-35, 227.

15 Guy Gaudreau's study about French Canadian miners highlights similar patterns: Guy Gaudreau, *L'histoire des mineurs du nord ontarien et québécois* (Sillery, QC: Septentrion, 2003).

16 Zembrzycki interview, 1 November 2008.

17 Archives of Ontario, Toronto (AO), Multicultural History Society of Ontario Fonds, F 1405, Series 56-27, Ukrainian Canadian Papers, Mary Hansen Papers, typed article for the *Sudbury Star,* dated 1952.

18 Multicultural History Society of Ontario, Toronto (MHSO), Oral History Collection, no. 437-0979-ZAR, Maria Zarichny (née Vasiliuk), interview by Mary Stefura, Kirkland Lake, Ontario, 14 June 1977.

19 The demographics of Garson are outlined in Zembrzycki, "Memory, Identity, and the Challenge," 46, 61-62.

20 Maria's story about loneliness, isolation, and domestic abuse builds upon the work in Frances Swyripa, *Wedded to the Cause: Ukrainian-Canadian Women and Ethnic Identity, 1891-1991* (Toronto: University of Toronto Press, 1993), 28-42; and Frances Swyripa, "Negotiating Sex and Gender in the Ukrainian Bloc Settlement: East Central Alberta between the Wars," *Prairie Forum* 20, 2 (Fall 1995): 149-74. For a more general discussion about domestic violence, see, for instance, Karen Dubinsky, *Improper Advances: Rape and Heterosexual Conflict in Ontario, 1880-1929* (Chicago: Chicago University Press, 1993); and Franca Iacovetta, *Gatekeepers: Reshaping Immigrant Lives in Cold War Canada* (Toronto: Between the Lines, 2006), 222-31.

21 Between 1913 and 1939, there were seven capital murder trials in the Sudbury region; five involved Ukrainian working-class immigrants. See Stacey Zembrzycki, "'I'll Fix You!': Domestic Violence and Murder in a Ukrainian Working-Class Immigrant Community in Northern Ontario," in *Re-Imagining Ukrainian-Canadians: History, Politics, and Identity,* ed. Rhonda Hinther and Jim Mochoruk (Toronto: University of Toronto Press, 2011), 436-64.

22 "Twin Children Were Destroyed," *Sudbury Star,* 25 July 1914, 1; "Guilty, but Clemency Asked for 18-Year-Old Murderess," *Sudbury Star,* 24 October 1914, 1; LAC, Record Group (RG) 13, Volume (vol.) 1479, file CC 30, Catherine Hawryluk, Memorandum dated 14 February 1918.

23 Dubinsky, *Improper Advances,* 15.

24 Hryniuk, *Peasants with Promise,* 86-114.

25 Ian Radforth, *Bushworkers and Bosses: Logging in Northern Ontario, 1900-1980* (Toronto: University of Toronto Press, 1987), 107-110, makes a similar statement about Finnish men who worked in northern Ontario lumber camps, declaring that the vitality of radicalism was also rooted in the tough working conditions that they experienced.

26 "Fatal Stabbing at Garson Mine," *Sudbury Star,* 20 June 1914, 1. John Weaver's claim, that immigrants often killed, assaulted, or stole from other immigrants in the same ethnic group, highlights a pattern that could be applied to boarding houses. See John Weaver, *Crimes, Constables, and Courts: Order and Transgression in a Canadian City, 1816-1970* (Montreal and Kingston: McGill-Queen's University Press, 1995), 219.

27 On boarding house culture, see, for instance, Robert Harney, "Boarding and Belonging: Thoughts on Sojourner Institutions," *Urban History Review* 2 (1978): 8-37; Robert Harney, "Men without Women: Italian Immigrants in Canada," *Canadian Ethnic Studies* 11, 1 (1979): 22-44; and Forestell, "All That Glitters," 111-26.

28 Zembrzycki interview, 6 October 2004.

29 Pauline Kruk (née Mykoluk), interview by Olga and Stacey Zembrzycki, Sudbury, 20 January 2005. Unless otherwise indicated, Baba and I conducted all interviews.

30 Ivan Rohozhynsky, "Copper Cliff," *Robochyi narod,* 26 March 1913, 5. Unless otherwise stated, Larissa Stavroff translated all Ukrainian-language newspaper articles. In 1909 and 1910, Ukrainian socialists formed the FUSD to unite all socialist organizations under one centrally coordinated leadership; it was aligned with the Canadian Social Democratic Party. The organization's early years were, however, complicated by infighting, poor leadership, and the fact that its central executive was located in Montreal, whereas its newspaper, *Robochyi narod,* was in Winnipeg. See Peter Krawchuk, *Our History: The Ukrainian Labour-Farmer Movement in Canada, 1907-1991,* trans. Mary Skrypnyk (Toronto: Lugus, 1996), 7-17.

31 Solski, *The Coniston Story.*

32 Steve Buchowski, interview, Coniston, 16 May 2005.

33   John Herd Thompson, *Ethnic Minorities during Two World Wars* (Ottawa: Canadian Historical Association, 1991), 5-7.

34   Martynowych, *Ukrainians in Canada,* 420.

35   Although proponents of the recent Ukrainian redress campaign view internment as a "war against ethnicity," others argue that this depiction constitutes "simple history." See all the essays in Franca Iacovetta, Roberto Perin, and Angelo Principe, eds., *Enemies Within: Italian and Other Internees in Canada and Abroad* (Toronto: University of Toronto Press, 2000); and Lubomyr Luciuk, *In Fear of the Barbed Wire Fence: Canada's First National Internment Operations and the Ukrainian Canadians, 1914-1920* (Kingston: Kashten Press, 2001).

36   John Higham defines nativism as including "every type and level of antipathy toward aliens, their institutions, and their ideas." John Higham, *Strangers in the Land: Patterns of American Nativism* (New York: Atheneum, 1963), 3. Also see Edmund Bradwin, *The Bunkhouse Man: A Study of Work and Pay in the Camps of Canada, 1903-1914* (Toronto: University of Toronto Press, 1929), 92, 105-6; Thompson, *Ethnic Minorities,* 3-4; and Abel, *Changing Places,* 407.

37   Thompson, *Ethnic Minorities,* 7.

38   Martynowych, *Ukrainians in Canada,* 419, 427-36. Also see Ian McKay, *Reasoning Otherwise: Leftists and the People's Enlightenment in Canada, 1890-1920* (Toronto: Between the Lines, 2008).

39   Matt Bray, "1910-1920," in Wallace and Thomson, *Sudbury,* 91-93.

40   Ibid.

41   The Canadian government banned the USDP in September 1918 for its condemnation of the war. See Krawchuk, *Our History,* 18.

42   "Sudbury," *Robochyi narod,* 29 May 1918, 3.

43   See Mary Stefura, "Aspects of Culture in the Ukrainian Community of the Sudbury Area," *Polyphony* 5, 2 (Fall-Winter 1983): 29-32.

44   "From the Life of the Workers in Creighton Mine," *Robochyi narod,* 21 September 1918, 4.

45   For a discussion about restrictions on the foreign-language press and foreign literature, see Martynowych, *Ukrainians in Canada,* 436-37.

46   LAC, RG 13, vol. 226, Series A-2, file 1918-1974, "Seditious Literature Found on One Mechnavech at Sudbury (August 20, 21, 1918)"; "Who Needs War," 4, 6; LAC, RG 13, vol. 228, Series A-2, file 1918-2295, "Seditious Literature Is Seized"; "Co. Police Make Nine Arrests," *Sudbury Star,* 24 August 1918, 4; "From the Life of the Workers," 4; INCO or Canadian Copper Employment Records, 1912-39, Ukrainians in Sudbury Collection, in author's possession.

47   This argument supports those made by Frances Swyripa in "The Politics of Redress: The Contemporary Ukrainian-Canadian Campaign," in Iacovetta, Perin, and Principe, *Enemies Within,* 362.

48 In the early 1950s, archivists at the Public Archives of Canada were faced with storage problems. As a result, they selected which First World War files were to be preserved and, in the process, destroyed the individual files of Canadian soldiers as well as those pertaining to Ukrainian internees. This step seemed logical at the time, given that Canadian historians were not doing social or ethnic history. In recent years, however, some historians, especially those involved in the Ukrainian redress campaign, have interpreted it as a deliberate attempt to cover up a "dark" chapter of Canadian history. These individuals, it must be noted, have said little about the connection between internees and socialism, and whether it led them to commit crimes. See, for instance, Luciuk, *In Fear of the Barbed Wire Fence;* Bohdan Kordan, *Enemy Aliens, Prisoners of War: Internment in Canada during the Great War* (Montreal and Kingston: McGill-Queen's University Press, 2002); and Ukrainian Canadian Civil Liberties Association, "Project Roll Call," InfoUkes: An Information Resource about Ukraine and Ukrainians, http://www.infoukes.com/. I am grateful to Myron Momryk for explaining LAC's lack of files pertaining to Ukrainian internees and the subsequent debates that have ensued in the community.

49 "More about Arrests in the Sudbury Area," *Robochyi narod,* 21 September 1918, 4.

50 Despite a number of attempts, I was unable to gain access to the INCO archive. That said, fragmented sources indicate there is a complex and interesting story about the company's use of the wartime measures, and internment in particular, which remains to be written.

51 "Please Help Mikhnievych," *Robochyi narod,* 21 September 1918, 4.

52 Although Mary Anne and Steve Buchowski are distant cousins, they do not know each other personally. Neither one could discuss the connection/disconnection between their families, though they both knew that Steve's father, John, worked at the Buchowski General Store at some point.

53 "Comrade W.N. Buchowski Has Died," obituary in Mary Anne Buchowski's personal collection.

54 Mary Anne Buchowski, interview by author, Ottawa, 13 March 2006.

55 "Buchowski General Store Burning," 19 November 1917, from Mary Anne Buchowski's personal collection.

56 "Letter from Wasyl Buchowski regarding the General Store's Burning," 6 May 1920, from Mary Anne Buchowski's personal collection.

57 Mary Anne Buchowski interview.

58 Donald Avery, *Reluctant Host: Canada's Response to Immigrant Workers, 1896-1994* (Toronto: McClelland and Stewart, 1995), 76.

59 Canada, Royal Commission on Industrial Relations, *Report of Commission Appointed under Order-in-Council P.C. 670 to Enquire into Industrial Relations in Canada Together with a Minority Report* (Ottawa: King's Printer, 1919), 1902.

60 Ibid., 1934.

61 Ibid., 1949.
62 Ibid., 1953.

Chapter 2: Solidifying

1 St. Mary's Ukrainian Catholic Church Centenary Committee, *Centenary of the Ukrainian Catholic Church in Greater Sudbury* (Sudbury: St. Mary's Ukrainian Catholic Church, 2009).

2 Informal conversations between Baba and author; Olga Zembrzycki (née Zyma), interviews by author, Sudbury, 6 October 2004, 18 June 2005, 1 November 2008.

3 Up to 1918, I refer to those who belonged to the Ukrainian left as "socialists," and after 1918, I call them "progressives." Ottawa outlawed the Ukrainian Social Democratic Party in 1918, and after the Russian Revolution, the Ukrainian left rejected all socialist parties and movements that opposed Bolshevism, which meant that the socialist label no longer applied to these individuals. I also employ "progressive" because interviewees referred to themselves in this way. For more on these terms, see Orest Martynowych, *Ukrainians in Canada: The Formative Period, 1891-1924* (Edmonton: Canadian Institute of Ukrainian Studies Press, 1991), xxix; and John Boyd, "Editor Preface," in Peter Krawchuk, *Our History: The Ukrainian Labour-Farmer Movement in Canada, 1907-1991,* trans. Mary Skrypnyk (Toronto: Lugus, 1996), v-vii.

4 Margaret Bertulli and Rae Swan, eds., *A Bit of the Cliff: A Brief History of the Town of Copper Cliff, Ontario: 1901-1972* (Copper Cliff: Copper Cliff Museum, 1982), 39; Michael Marunchak, *The Ukrainian Canadians: A History* (Winnipeg: Ukrainian Academy of Arts and Sciences in Canada, 1982), 215; St. Mary's Ukrainian Catholic Church, *Centenary of the Ukrainian Catholic Church;* and Theodore Pryjma, "St. Mary's Ukrainian Catholic Parish: A History" (unpublished paper, n.d.), 2.

5 See Royden Loewen, *Family, Church, and Market: A Mennonite Community in the Old and New Worlds, 1850-1930* (Toronto: University of Toronto Press, 1993); Lynne Marks, *Revivals and Roller Rinks: Religion, Leisure, and Identity in Late-Nineteenth-Century Small-Town Ontario* (Toronto: University of Toronto Press, 1996), 22-51; and Kerry Abel, *Changing Places: History, Community, and Identity in Northeastern Ontario* (Montreal and Kingston: McGill-Queen's University Press, 2006), 227-31.

6 Mary Stefura, "Sudbury Ukrainian Time Line," *Polyphony* 10 (1988): 66-67.

7 Sudbury's population more than doubled between 1911 and 1921, and the population in Coniston and Levack quadrupled during this period. See Canada, Bureau of the Census, *Population,* vol. 1 (Ottawa: F.A. Acland, 1924).

8 A.D. Gilbert, "The 1920s," in *Sudbury: Rail Town to Regional Capital,* ed. C.M. Wallace and Ashley Thomson (Toronto: Dundurn Press, 1993), 113-23; Matt Bray and A.D. Gilbert, "The Mond-International Nickel Merger of 1929: A Case Study in Entrepreneurial Failure," *Canadian Historical Review* 76, 1 (March 1995): 19-42.

9 Gilbert, "The 1920s," 114.

10 For the reasons behind these name changes, see Krawchuk, *Our History,* 28-38.

11 "Letter from V.S. – Sudbury," *Ukrainski robitnychi visti,* 27 April 1921, 4.

12 "Letter from Sudbury – A Worker," *Ukrainski robitnychi visti,* 19 October 1921, 4.

13 "Letter Submitted by I. Pereima, Coniston," *Ukrainski robitnychi visti,* 12 April 1924, 4.

14 Mond Nickel Company Employment Records, 1912-30, Ukrainians in Sudbury Collection, in author's possession; Sudbury Regional Police Museum, Sudbury, Constable Boucher's Daily Journal, 1922; Sudbury Regional Police Museum, Constable Boucher's Daily Journal, 1923; Sudbury Regional Police Museum, Constable Brennan's Report Book, Coniston, 1927.

15 Mike Solski, *The Coniston Story* (Sudbury: Journal Printing, 1983), 40.

16 "History of the ULFTA Branch in Coniston," in *Almanac, 1918-1929,* trans. Larissa Stavroff (Winnipeg: Ukrainian Labour Farmer Temple Association, 1930), 133. Also see Solski, *The Coniston Story,* 82-86.

17 "Sudbury – A Worker," *Ukrainski robitnychi visti,* 26 June 1924, 3; "Coniston, from a Member of the Proletariat," *Ukrainski robitnychi visti,* 10 July 1924, 3; "Sudbury – Ivan Soroka," *Ukrainski robitnychi visti,* 15 November 1924, 3.

18 Progressives were merely following the directives of the national executive, which voted to organize youth sections in 1924. See "Coniston, from a Member of the Proletariat," 3.

19 This name was adopted at the ULTA's fifth national convention to appeal to farmers in Western Canada.

20 Rhonda Hinther, "'Sincerest Revolutionary Greetings': Progressive Ukrainians in the Twentieth Century" (PhD diss., McMaster University, 2005), 15.

21 "The ULFTA Branch, Sudbury, Ontario," in *Almanac, 1918-1929,* 132.

22 Library and Archives Canada, Ottawa (LAC), Peter Krawchuk Fonds, Manuscript Group (MG) 30, vol. 21, Series D403, file 5, *ULFTA Sudbury Minute Book, 1926-1931,* trans. Larissa Stavroff. Ukrainians and Finns formed similar alliances in Timmins, Ontario. See Abel, *Changing Places,* 120-21.

23 Hinther, "'Sincerest Revolutionary Greetings,'" 17.

24 Frances Swyripa, *Wedded to the Cause: Ukrainian-Canadian Women and Ethnic Identity, 1891-1991* (Toronto: University of Toronto Press, 1993), 151.

25 Hinther, "'Sincerest Revolutionary Greetings,'" 117-18. For a related discussion about women's roles in other socialist and left-wing organizations, as well as in religious and right-wing groups, see Wendy Mitchinson, "The WCTU: 'For God, Home and Native Land': A Study of Nineteenth Century Feminism," in *A Not Unreasonable Claim: Women and Reform in Canada, 1880s-1920s,* ed. Linda Kealey (Toronto: Women's Press, 1979), 151-67; Joan Sangster, *Dreams of Equality: Women on the Canadian Left, 1920-1950* (Toronto: McClelland and Stewart, 1989); Mariana Valverde, *The Age of Light, Soap, and Water: Moral Reform in English Canada, 1885-1925* (Toronto: McClelland and Stewart, 1991), 58-61; Varpu Lindström, *Defiant Sisters:*

A Social History of Finnish Immigrant Women in Canada (Toronto: Multicultural History Society of Ontario, 1992); Janice Newton, *The Feminist Challenge to the Canadian Left, 1900-1918* (Montreal and Kingston: McGill-Queen's University Press, 1995); Marks, *Revivals and Roller Rinks*, 95-101; Linda Kealey, *Enlisting Women for the Cause: Women, Labour, and the Left in Canada, 1890-1920* (Toronto: University of Toronto Press, 1998); and Craig Heron, *Booze: A Distilled History* (Toronto: Between the Lines, 2003), 153-57.

26 Swyripa, *Wedded to the Cause*, 144.

27 Hinther, "'Sincerest Revolutionary Greetings,'" 129-30.

28 LAC, Peter Krawchuk Fonds, MG 30, vol. 21, Series D403, file 7, *Coniston Minute Book, 1924-1926*, trans. Larissa Stavroff, 70.

29 See the regional letters published in *Ukrainski robitnychi visti* and *Robitnytsia* (Working woman), a national progressive semi-monthly newspaper published by men for women between April 1924 and August 1937; Hinther, "'Sincerest Revolutionary Greetings,'" 145; and Joan Sangster, "*Robitnytsia*, Ukrainian Communists, and the 'Porcupinism' Debate: Reassessing Ethnicity, Gender, and Class in Early Canadian Communism, 1922-1930," *Labour/Le Travail* 56 (Fall 2005): 51-89. On illiteracy rates, see Swyripa, *Wedded to the Cause*, 24.

30 "Coniston," *Ukrainski robitnychi visti*, 13 October 1925, 4.

31 *Coniston Minute Book, 1924-1926*, 86, 89.

32 Ibid., 101, 108.

33 "Sudbury – Letter from Elena Bezkrovna and M. Matvitchuk," *Robitnytsia*, 15 February 1925, 21.

34 *ULFTA Sudbury Minute Book, 1926-1931*.

35 Hinther, "'Sincerest Revolutionary Greetings,'" 120-21, 135.

36 *ULFTA Sudbury Minute Book, 1926-1931*, 113.

37 Swyripa, *Wedded to the Cause*, 155-66; Hinther, "'Sincerest Revolutionary Greetings,'" 132-34.

38 Hinther, "'Sincerest Revolutionary Greetings,'" 208-9.

39 Until recently, Canadian children lacked a history that focused on their agency. Notable exceptions include David Nasaw, *Children of the City: At Work and at Play* (Garden City: Anchor Press, 1985); Bettina Bradbury, "Gender at Work at Home: Family Decisions, the Labour Market, and Girls' Contributions to the Family Economy," in *Canadian Family History*, ed. Bettina Bradbury (Toronto: Copp Clark Pitman, 1992), 177-98; John Bullen, "Hidden Workers: Child Labour and the Family Economy in Late Nineteenth Century Urban Ontario," in Bradbury, *Canadian Family History*, 199-219; Enrico T. Carlson Cumbo, "'As the Twig Is Bent, the Tree's Inclined': Growing Up Italian in Toronto, 1905-1940" (PhD diss., University of Toronto, 1996); Neil Sutherland, *Growing Up: Childhood in English Canada from the Great War to the Age of Television* (Toronto: University of Toronto Press, 1997); Robert McIntosh,

Boys in the Pits: Child Labour in Coal Mines (Montreal and Kingston: McGill-Queen's University Press, 2000); and Hinther, "'Sincerest Revolutionary Greetings.'"

40 This statement is taken from Mercedes Steedman's Personal Oral History Collection, Sudbury, Anne Macks (née Ladyk), interview by Mercedes Steedman, Sudbury, 3 May 1993. Although I met Anne and asked her for an interview, she declined my request. She passed away shortly thereafter.

41 Mary Brydges (née Ladyk), interview, Sudbury, 28 October 2004.

42 "Coniston – Letter from Nastusia Pereima," *Robitnytsia*, 1 September 1924, 16; "Sudbury – Maria Bezkrovna," *Robitnytsia*, 15 March 1926, 26.

43 "For the Youth Section," *Robitnytsia*, 15 May 1926, 27; "Sudbury – From One of the Amateur Players," *Robitnytsia*, 15 November 1926, 22.

44 "Sudbury," *Svit molodi*, April 1929, 14; LAC, Record Group (RG) 146, Record of the Canadian Security Intelligence Service (CSIS), Part 1, Request Number (No.) AH 2003 00297, "News 183 Ukrainian Labour News 23-1-26, Sudbury," 146.

45 Hinther, "'Sincerest Revolutionary Greetings,'" 226.

46 Ibid., 207-83.

47 Anonymous interview.

48 On working-class leisure, see Marks, *Revivals and Roller Rinks*; and Abel, *Changing Places*.

49 Father Kolsun's letter was instrumental in getting George Boluk rehired as a converter labourer at INCO's Copper Cliff Smelter.

50 For more on these relationships, see "Pastor Relates Methods Used by Communists," *Sudbury Star*, 15 December 1928, 1; "*Vapaus* Editor Is Arrested on Sedition Charge," *Sudbury Star*, 15 December 1928, 1; and Mercedes Steedman, "Godless Communists and Faithful Wives, Gender Relations and the Cold War: Mine Mill and the 1958 Strike against the International Nickel Company," in *Mining Women: Gender in the Development of a Global Industry, 1670-2005*, ed. Jaclyn G. Gier and Laurie Mercier (New York: Palgrave Macmillan, 2006), 236.

51 Informal conversation between Baba and author. Also see "Creighton – Letter from Kliuvychenko," *Ukrainski robitnychi visti*, 15 December 1928, 3.

52 "New Ukrainian Parish Serves Flock of 10,000," *Sudbury Star*, 13 October 1928, 13; "New Ukrainian Church Bound to Christianity," *Sudbury Star*, 19 December 1928, 13; "Ukrainians Avow Loyalty; Bar Communism," *Sudbury Star*, 23 February 1929, 13.

53 Father Mykola Shumsky, a priest in the region from 1921 to 1925, was responsible for bringing in the CSO, founding branches in Coniston and Creighton in 1925. LAC, RG 146-3, Royal Canadian Mounted Police (RCMP), Request No. 94-A-00180, vol. 38, file 1, Ukrainian United Hetman Organization, 1928-1942, report dated 18 February 1925; "Creighton," *Ukrainski robitnychi visti*, 25 April 1925, 4.

54 Orest Martynowych, "The Hetmanite Movement and the Ukrainian Catholic Church in Canada, 1924-1940: Allies or Adversaries?" (Paper presented at the annual

conference of the Canadian Association of Slavists, Winnipeg, 1 June 2004), 1-2. The CSO was affiliated with and largely modelled after the Canadian General Council of the Boy Scouts Association until 1935, when the Boy Scouts came under heavy RCMP scrutiny and severed its ties with the organization, declaring that the CSO did not "do enough scouting to influence them [boy scouts] along the right lines." See LAC, RG 146-3, RCMP, Request No. 94-A-00180, vol. 38, file 1, Ukrainian United Hetman Organization, 1928-1942, Canadian General Council of the Boy Scouts Association to the RCMP, 25 November 1935; S.T. Wood to Mr. Blair, 12 December 1936. Similarly, the church's alliance with the CSO was strained by the late 1930s.

55 Swyripa, *Wedded to the Cause,* 148.

56 Pryjma, "St. Mary's Ukrainian Catholic Parish," 5.

57 Swyripa, *Wedded to the Cause,* 164. For a related discussion of cultural exchanges between Anglican women and Aboriginals in northern British Columbia, the Yukon, and the Canadian Arctic, see Myra Rutherdale, *Women and the White Man's God: Gender and Race in the Canadian Mission Field* (Vancouver: UBC Press, 2002).

58 Archives of Ontario, Toronto (AO), Multicultural History Society of Ontario Fonds, Reverend Theodore Pryjma, Microfilm MFN 115, St. Mary's Ukrainian Catholic Church, *Minute Book of the Ukrainian Junior Catholic Women's League of Sudbury.*

59 Ibid.

60 Eugenia Maizuk (née Kureluik), interview, Sudbury, 19 January 2005.

61 Marks, *Revivals and Roller Rinks,* 53-69.

62 Ibid.

63 For a related discussion about class inequalities among female parishioners, see ibid., 72.

64 A handful of interviewees, including Baba, used the term "fina panis" to refer to women who refused to do menial tasks, believing that these jobs were beneath them. See Helen Pihursky (née Ciotka), interview, Sudbury, 13 January 2005; and Anne Matschke (née Kuchmey), interview, Sudbury, 7 May 2005. Also see "Coniston," *Robitnytsia,* 15 August 1927, 16.

65 Unfortunately, "gossip" is a gendered word that tends to have negative connotations. That said, it is time that we, as oral historians, take gossip seriously and regard it as another way of knowing and learning about the past. If we dismiss this important form of communication, we risk missing a crucial aspect of interviewees' daily lives and the ways they understand them. This book demonstrates what we can learn when we sit back, listen, and sometimes even gossip ourselves. For a related discussion, see Franca Iacovetta, "Gossip, Contest, and Power in the Making of Suburban Bad Girls: Toronto, 1945-1960," *Canadian Historical Review* 80, 4 (December 1999): 585-623; Lynne Marks, "Railing, Tattling, and General Rumour: Gossip, Gender, and Church Regulation in Upper Canada," *Canadian Historical Review* 81, 3 (September 2000): 380-402; and Luise White, *Speaking with Vampires: Rumor and History in Colonial Africa* (Berkeley: University of California Press, 2000).

66 Anonymous interview. Identifying information, such as Elena's community affiliations, has been left out of this description, so as to protect her identity.

67 For an insightful study that problematizes adolescence, see Cynthia Comacchio, *The Dominion of Youth: Adolescence and the Making of Modern Canada, 1920 to 1950* (Waterloo: Wilfrid Laurier University Press, 2006).

68 "Fr. N.J. Bartman Is Optimistic," *Sudbury Star,* 22 May 1929, 16.

Chapter 3: Contesting

1 For a discussion of the challenges that historians face when adult interviewees recall their childhoods, see Neil Sutherland, "When You Listen to the Winds of Childhood, How Much Can You Believe?" in *Histories of Canadian Children and Youth*, ed. Nancy Janovicek and Joy Parr (Oxford: Oxford University Press, 2003), 23.

2 Annette Kuhn writes that families are sites of safety, closeness, intimacy, and identity making. They also rarely lack secrets, which almost always inhabit the borderlands of memory. See Annette Kuhn, *Family Secrets: Acts of Memory and Imagination* (London: Verso, 1995), 1-2.

3 Informal conversations between Baba and author; Olga Zembrzycki (née Zyma), interviews by author, Sudbury, 6 October 2004, 18 June 2005, 1 November 2008.

4 For related discussions about the public airing of differences, see Mary Ryan, *Civic Wars: Democracy and Public Life in the American City during the Nineteenth-Century* (Berkeley: University of California Press, 1997); Michael Cottrell, "St. Patrick's Day Parades in Nineteenth-Century Toronto: A Study of Immigrant Adjustment and Elite Control," in *A Nation of Immigrants: Women, Workers, and Communities in Canadian History, 1840s-1960s*, ed. Franca Iacovetta, Paula Draper, and Robert Ventresca (Toronto: University of Toronto Press, 1998), 35-54; and Scott W. See, "The Orange Order and Social Violence in Mid-Nineteenth Century Saint John," in Iacovetta, Draper, and Ventresca, *A Nation of Immigrants*, 5-34. On notions of respectable citizenship during the Depression, see Lara Campbell, *Respectable Citizens: Gender, Family, and Unemployment in Ontario's Great Depression* (Toronto: University of Toronto Press, 2009).

5 Canada, Bureau of the Census, *Population by Areas*, vol. 2 (Ottawa: J.O. Patenaude, 1933).

6 Ibid.; C.M. Wallace, "The 1930s," in *Sudbury: Rail Town to Regional Capital*, ed. C.M. Wallace and Ashley Thomson (Toronto: Dundurn Press, 1993), 139.

7 See, for instance, Michiel Horn, *The Dirty Thirties: Canadians in the Great Depression* (Toronto: Copp Clark, 1972); Blair Neatby, *The Politics of Chaos: Canada in the Thirties* (Toronto: Macmillan of Canada, 1972); Barry Broadfoot, *Ten Lost Years, 1929-1939: Memories of Canadians Who Survived the Depression* (Toronto: Doubleday Canada, 1973); Allen Seager and John Thompson, *Canada, 1922-1939: Decades of Discord* (Toronto: McClelland and Stewart, 1985); Michiel Horn, *The Depression in Canada: Responses to Economic Crisis* (Toronto: Copp Clark, 1988); Pierre Berton,

The Great Depression, 1929-1939 (Toronto: McClelland and Stewart, 1990); Robert Collins, *You Had to Be There: An Intimate Portrait of the Generation That Survived the Depression, Won the War, and Re-invented Canada* (Toronto: McClelland and Stewart, 1997); Denyse Baillargeon, *Making Do: Women, Family, and Home in Montreal during the Great Depression*, trans. Yvonne Klein (Waterloo: Wilfrid Laurier University Press, 1999); Barbara Ann Lambert, *Rusty Nails and Ration Books: Memories of the Great Depression and WWII, 1929-1945* (Victoria: Trafford, 2002); Campbell, *Respectable Citizens*; and Katrina Srigley, *Breadwinning Daughters: Young Working Women in a Depression-Era City, 1929-1939* (Toronto: University of Toronto Press, 2010).

8 "Sudbury Mecca for Hundreds Seeking Work," *Sudbury Star*, 19 April 1930, 22.

9 This arrangement is outlined in Ukrainian Catholic Archeparchy of Winnipeg Archive, Winnipeg (UCAWA), Nicholas Bartman File, NB 65, Bishop Ladyka to Nicholas Bartman, 4 April 1931, trans. Orest Martynowych; and UCAWA, Nicholas Bartman File, NB 42-44, Vasyl Iavorsky to Bishop Ladyka, 2 January 1931, trans. Orest Martynowych.

10 "Coniston – Letter from Maksym," *Ukrainski robitnychi visti*, 20 February 1930, 4; "Sudbury's Unemployed Demand Work or Bread, But the Police Beat Them with Clubs," *Ukrainski robitnychi visti*, 13 November 1930, 4.

11 The preferred workers' celebration for socialists and communists, May Day was a time of defiance and protest that explicitly threatened the social order of the nation. See Cottrell, "St. Patrick's Day Parades," 37-38; and Craig Heron and Steve Penfold, *The Workers' Festival: A History of Labour Day in Canada* (Toronto: University of Toronto Press, 2005), 187.

12 "Line Broken Up by Police Squad; 18 Are Arrested," *Sudbury Star*, 3 May 1930, 1; "Report from a Member of the CPC," *Ukrainski robitnychi visti*, 8 May 1930, 4; "'Reds' in Court Are Sentenced for Disturbing," *Sudbury Star*, 17 May 1930, 1; "First of May Celebration," *Robitnytsia*, 1 June 1930, 28.

13 "Ukrainians Combat 'Red' Propaganda," *Sudbury Star*, 19 March 1930, 12; "Parochial Work of Ukrainians Fast Expanding," *Sudbury Star*, 2 August 1930, 21.

14 "Ukrainians Combat 'Red' Propaganda," 12.

15 This organization was also called the Ukrainian Rifleman's Association (URA). See *Ukrainian National Federation of Canada, Sudbury Branch, Anniversary Book, Twenty-Five Years of the Branch*, trans. Larissa Stavroff (Sudbury: Ukrainian National Federation, 1957), 19.

16 Ibid., 20. Headed by Colonel Evhen Konovalets, the OUN was a mass revolutionary organization "dedicated to an uncompromising armed and political struggle against the Soviet, Polish, Romanian, and Czechoslovak regimes occupying various regions of Ukraine." Oleh Gerus, "Consolidating the Community: The Ukrainian Self-Reliance League," in *Canada's Ukrainians: Negotiating an Identity*, ed. Lubomyr Luciuk and Stella Hryniuk (Toronto: University of Toronto Press, 1991), 166.

17 "The Face of the Rifleman's Community Is Thoroughly Fascist," *Ukrainski robitnychi visti*, 22 November 1930, 6.

18 Although both the CSO and the UWVA lobbied for the creation of an independent Ukrainian state in Europe, the CSO believed that it should be a monarchy ruled by Hetman Pavlo Skoropadsky and his descendants, whereas the UWVA argued for a republic, initially ruled by a revolutionary nationalist elite and then by a democratic-ally elected government. The CSO, which claimed to stand for order and authority, and rejected any tactics that led to chaos and anarchy, also took strong exception to the UWVA's acceptance of sabotage, armed expropriations, and political assassina-tions, all of which characterized OUN actions in what is now western Ukraine. I am grateful to Orest Martynowych for clarifying these differences.

19 *Ukrainian Rifleman's Community in Canada, 1928-1938*, trans. Myron Momryk (Saskatoon: *Novyi shliakh*, 1938), 69; "Military Drill Being Sought by Ukrainians," *Sudbury Star*, 24 December 1930, 1.

20 Wallace, "The 1930s," 143; "As a Soldier, I Fought for This Country and Now I'm Starving," *Ukrainski robitnychi visti*, 24 February 1931, 4; A. Kostiuchek, "I Wandered into Sudbury in Search of Work," *Ukrainski robitnychi visti*, 4 July 1931, 4.

21 "There's Misery in the World Because People Don't Want to Pray Says Sudbury Priest," *Ukrainski robitnychi visti*, 8 January 1931, 4. Also see "They Put Their Last Pennies in the Collection Plate at the ULT," *Ukrainski robitnychi visti*, 6 February 1932, 4.

22 Nellie Kozak (née Tataryn), interview, Sudbury, 6 June 2005.

23 Meetings were often held immediately after meals so as to attract new unemployed members to the ULFTA. Myron Kostaniuk, "Recollections from the Life of a Ukrain-ian Pioneer," *Ukrainian Canadian*, October 1990, 36; "Winter Approaching, Neces-sary to Prepare for Sharper Class Struggles," *Ukrainski robitnychi visti*, 1 October 1931, 4.

24 "Even Though I Was Severely Ill, I Rallied and Went to the February 25th Demon-stration," *Ukrainski robitnychi visti*, 10 March 1931, 5.

25 "Sudbury Unemployed in Brave Struggle with Police; Blood in the Streets," *Ukrainski robitnychi visti*, 5 March 1931, 4. Also see "Participant in the Demonstration," *Robitnytsia*, 1 April 1931, 25.

26 "Reds Remanded on Appearance in Police Court," *Sudbury Star*, 28 February 1931, 1.

27 "Bench Scores Seven Accused for Defying Law," *Sudbury Star*, 7 March 1931, 1.

28 "The Sudbury Workers Condemn Police Terror and Pogroms of February 25th," *Ukrainski robitnychi visti*, 12 March 1931, 5.

29 "On Streets of Sudbury, Workers in Heated Battle with Police Legion and Firemen," *Ukrainski robitnychi visti*, 23 April 1931, 4; "Four Are Fined for Part Taken in Disturbance," *Sudbury Star*, 2 May 1931, 1.

30 "Lack of Funds Forces Church to Close Doors," *Sudbury Star*, 29 April 1931, 23.

31 "Parish Control Is Transferred," *Sudbury Star*, 2 May 1931, 1.

32 Anne Matschke (née Kuchmey), interview, Sudbury, 7 May 2005.

33 Iavorsky to Ladyka, 2 January 1931; UCAWA, Nicholas Bartman File, NB 47-48, N. Melnyk to Bishop Ladyka, 3 March 1931, trans. Orest Martynowych.

34 UCAWA, Nicholas Bartman File, NB 61, Bishop Ladyka to Nicholas Bartman, 23 March 1931, trans. Orest Martynowych; Ladyka to Bartman, 4 April 1931.

35 UCAWA, Nicholas Bartman File, NB 69, Nicholas Bartman to Bishop Ladyka, 18 April 1931, trans. Orest Martynowych; UCAWA, Nicholas Bartman File, NB 72-73, J.W. Arsenych (lawyer) to Ruthenian Greek Catholic Episcopal Corporation, 12 May 1931, trans. Orest Martynowych.

36 See, for instance, UCAWA, Nicholas Bartman File, NB 137, Bishop James Morrison (Antigonish) to Bishop Ladyka, 3 January 1933, trans. Orest Martynowych.

37 Matschke interview.

38 "We're Working in the Mines to the Point of Exhaustion," *Ukrainski robitnychi visti*, 4 August 1931, 4; "Miner Being Kept from Working," *Ukrainski robitnychi visti*, 27 October 1931, 4; D. Barabash, "INCO Preparing to Cut Miners' Salaries," *Ukrainski robitnychi visti*, 29 October 1931, 4.

39 "18 Arrested in Battle over Flag as Communists Attempt May Day Parade," *Sudbury Star*, 4 May 1932, 5. Also see Kelly Saxberg, dir., *Letters from Karelia* (Montreal: National Film Board of Canada, 2004), for a fascinating depiction of this confrontation.

40 "Police and Hirelings Attacked the Workers," *Ukrainski robitnychi visti*, 12 May 1932, 4.

41 "Special Telegram," *Ukrainski robitnychi visti*, 3 May 1932, 1; "One, Two, Three, We Don't Fear the Bourgeoisie," *Ukrainskyi holos*, 4 May 1932, 1. It must be noted that police did not raid the Coniston ULFTA Hall, because it was no longer in operation, closing some time between late 1931 and early 1932.

42 "18 Arrested in Battle," 4; "No More Meetings Will Be Tolerated; Parade Prevented," *Sudbury Star*, 7 May 1932, 1.

43 "May It Be the Last Parade," *Sudbury Star*, 4 May 1932, 4.

44 Heron and Penfold, *The Workers' Festival*, 10-11.

45 Kostaniuk was later interned in Canadian facilities during the Second World War. See "May Day Disturber Denies Ever Seeing Red Flag in Parade," *Sudbury Star*, 25 May 1932, 1; "May Day Rioter Receives Term 6 to 18 Months," *Sudbury Star*, 28 May 1932, 2; and Kostaniuk, "Recollections from the Life," 37.

46 Mary Kardash, "Untitled," in *Reminiscences of Courage and Hope: Stories of Ukrainian Canadian Women Pioneers*, ed. Peter Krawchuk, trans. Michael Ukas (Toronto: Kobzar, 1991), 297-98.

47 Nick Evanshen, interview, Sudbury, 14 May 2005.

48 Wallace, "The 1930s," 144; "Coniston, Creighton and Garson Closing for Three Months," *Sudbury Star*, 27 July 1932, 1.

49 Zynovy Knysh, ed., *Toward National Unity: Fifty Years of Service by the Ukrainian National Federation, 1932-1982*, trans. Larissa Stavroff (Toronto: Ukrainian National

Federation of Canada, 1982), 483; Irene Knysh, ed., *In Service of Our Homeland: The Ukrainian Women's Organization of Canada, Twenty-Fifth Anniversary,* trans. Larissa Stavroff (Winnipeg: Ukrainian Women's Organization of Canada, 1956), 335.

50 UCAWA, John Kolsun File, JKO 84, John Kolsun to Bishop Ladyka, 15 March 1932, trans. Orest Martynowych.

51 See UCAWA, John Kolsun File, JKO 100-104, John Kolsun to Bishop Ladyka, 14 September 1932, trans. Orest Martynowych.

52 Orest Martynowych, *Ukrainians in Canada: The Formative Period, 1891-1924* (Edmonton: Canadian Institute of Ukrainian Studies Press, 1991), 247.

53 Knysh, *In Service of Our Homeland,* 338-39; Knysh, *Toward National Unity,* 485. According to Swyripa, the UNF prepared Ukrainian nationalist women to be loyal Canadian citizens as well as good mothers and homemakers. See Frances Swyripa, *Wedded to the Cause: Ukrainian-Canadian Women and Ethnic Identity, 1891-1991* (Toronto: University of Toronto Press, 1993), 157.

54 UCAWA, Peter Kamenetsky File, PK 125-29, Peter Kamenetsky to Bishop Ladyka, 27 December 1933, trans. Orest Martynowych.

55 UCAWA, Peter Kamenetsky File, PK 170-72, N. Stuss to Bishop Ladyka, 5 February 1935, trans. Orest Martynowych.

56 See UCAWA, Peter Kamenetsky File, PK 134-35, Peter Kamenetsky to Bishop Ladyka, 19 January 1934, trans. Orest Martynowych.

57 By defeating the "parish aristocracy," which was composed of CSO members, and drawing nationalists back to the church, Kamenetsky increased its membership base to well over two hundred members by March 1935, and by December 1935 he had paid off the church mortgage. See UCAWA, Peter Kamenetsky File, PK 179-81, Peter Kamenetsky to Bishop Ladyka, 2 March 1935, trans. Orest Martynowych; UCAWA, Peter Kamenetsky File, PK 202, Bishop Ladyka to Peter Kamenetsky, 2 December 1935, trans. Orest Martynowych; UCAWA, Peter Kamenetsky File, PK 223-24, Bishop Ladyka to Peter Kamenetsky, 4 September 1937, trans. Orest Martynowych.

58 "Greek Orthodox Members Form Sudbury Church," *Sudbury Star,* 20 February 1935, 10; Archives of the Ukrainian Greek Orthodox Church of Canada, Winnipeg, Father Andrii Sarmatiuk File, Andrii Sarmatiuk to Bishop [name unknown], 23 September 1940, trans. by Orest Martynowych.

59 Gerus, "Consolidating the Community," 161.

60 Ibid., 162.

61 Martynowych, *Ukrainians in Canada,* 493.

62 Swyripa, *Wedded to the Cause,* 8.

63 Martynowych, *Ukrainians in Canada,* 496.

64 See, for instance, UCAWA, Michael Irkha File, MI 111-112, Michael Irkha to Bishop Ladyka, 26 August 1940, trans. Orest Martynowych.

65 Osyp Hryhorovych, "Sudbury," *Ukrainski robitnychi visti,* 10 February 1934, 5.

66 Wallace, "The 1930s," 144.

67 N. Siry, "Nickel Industry in Sudbury Working for the Impending War," *Ukrainski robitnychi visti,* 8 December 1934, 4. Also see "Hitlerite Agents in Sudbury Won't Be Allowed to Smash Labour Unity," *Ukrainski robitnychi visti,* 18 July 1935, 3.

68 "*Novyi shliakh*'s Fascist Liars Eating Away at the ULN," *Ukrainski robitnychi visti,* 5 February 1935, 4; "All Mines, Smelters and Refineries in INCO's Hands (In Sudbury Area)," *Ukrainski robitnychi visti,* 8 July 1935, 3; "Minister of Ontario Mines P. Ledok Refuses to Speak to Miner's Grievances," *Ukrainski robitnychi visti,* 13 July 1935, 2.

69 My requests for RCMP documents through Library and Archives Canada's Access to Information and Privacy (ATIP) program turned up few documents. Moreover, Sudbury is rarely mentioned in the RCMP Bulletins in Gregory Kealey and Reg Whitaker, eds., *R.C.M.P. Security Bulletins: The Depression Years,* 5 vols. (St. John's: Canadian Committee on Labour History, 1993, 1995, 1996, 1997). Scholars whose requests focused on other locales were swamped with documents. See, for instance, Kerry Abel, *Changing Places: History, Community, and Identity in Northeastern Ontario* (Montreal and Kingston: McGill-Queen's University Press, 2006).

70 · N. Stus, "Mass Anti-Communist Rally in Sudbury," *Novyi shliakh,* 1 December 1936, 7.

71 See, for instance, "Dance Ukrainian Folk Rounds in Colorful Costumes," *Sudbury Star,* 16 October 1936, 3.

72 As explained above, UHO members pushed for the establishment of a Ukrainian monarchy that was modelled on the British imperial system of government; they believed that Pavlo Skoropadsky, Danylo's father, was Ukraine's only legitimate and hereditary ruler because he was a direct descendant of Hetman Ivan Skoropadsky, who had ruled Ukraine two centuries before.

73 "Sees Ukraine Established on British Lines," *Sudbury Star,* 6 December 1937, 6. Also see John Esaiw, *For Ukraine: Danylo Skoropadsky's Tour of the USA and Canada, Fall 1937-Spring 1938,* trans. Larissa Stavroff (Chicago: United Hetman Organization, 1938), 178-88.

74 Orest Martynowych, "The Hetmanite Movement and the Ukrainian Catholic Church in Canada, 1924-1940: Allies or Adversaries?" (Paper presented at the annual conference of the Canadian Association of Slavists, Winnipeg, 1 June 2004), 13-14.

75 Ibid., 8.

76 Ibid., 14.

77 Note that the USRL was formed in December 1927 by the same intelligentsia that had established the Ukrainian Greek Orthodox Church of Canada.

78 "Glory to Ukraine," *Ukrainskyi holos,* 6 April 1938, 4; "The Appearance of a New Ukrainian Disease," *Ukrainskyi holos,* 20 April 1938, 5; A Nationalist, "Isn't This Banditry?" *Ukrainskyi holos,* 20 April 1938, 6; P.I. Lazarovych and I. Kyriak, "Our Position," *Ukrainskyi holos,* 4 May 1938, 4.

79 "Sudbury," *Narodna hazeta,* 14 May 1938, 2.

80 "Sudbury," *Novyi shliakh,* 7 June 1938, 3; "Use Rocks and Chairs during Racial Battle," *Sudbury Star,* 13 June 1938, 1. Also see Library and Archives Canada (LAC), RG 146-3, RCMP, Request No. AH-2003-00299, vol. 4121, file 38-06-14/57-11-19, Ukrainian National Federation of Canada, Sudbury, Ontario, "The Riot at Sudbury," 14 June 1938.

81 "Despicable Deeds on the Part of Ukrainian Fascists in Canada," *Narodna hazeta,* 21 June 1938, 3; "UNF Is the Enemy of the Ukrainians in Canada," *Narodna hazeta,* 21 June 1938, 3; "We Condemn the Actions of Ukrainian Fascists in Sudbury," *Narodna hazeta,* 21 June 1938, 3; "They Persuaded the Bolsheviks with Rocks and Chairs," *Ukrainskyi holos,* 22 June 1938, 5; Mike Szander, "The Kingdom of INCO and Its UNF Ruffians," *Narodna hazeta,* 27 June 1938, 3.

82 Gerus, "Consolidating the Community," 171.

83 It must be noted that few interviewees saw their organizational affiliations as Oryst did, as having inhibited them or limited their opportunities. The ways that children negotiated community divisions were not always as simple and straightforward as he suggested. As the previous chapter made clear, some children were less devoted than their parents to political and religious institutions. Also, they decided where and with whom they would spend their time, even if this meant breaking their parents' rules. Baba, for instance, never passed up a chance to attend a dance, even at a ULFTA Hall. Others had friends who belonged to opposing organizations, and they either hid these relationships from their parents or their parents turned a blind eye to them.

84 Oryst Sawchuk, interview by author, Sudbury, 26 January 2005.

85 John Stefura, interview by author, Sudbury, 24 January 2005.

86 Sawchuk interview.

87 Ibid.

88 "Ukrainian Fascists – Enemies of the People," *Narodna hazeta,* 17 December 1938, 5. For a sampling of the activities in which nationalists participated during the first year of the war, see "Ukrainians Boost Finnish War Chest Funds," *Sudbury Star,* 25 January 1940, 1; "To Assist at Canadian Legion Concert," *Sudbury Star,* 12 February 1940, 16; "Native Groups Make Concert Big Success," *Sudbury Star,* 19 February 1940, 6; "Folk Dances to Feature Red Cross Concert," *Sudbury Star,* 5 April 1940, 6; and "Many Nations Represented at Concert for Red Cross," *Sudbury Star,* 7 October 1940, 6.

89 Thomas Prymak, *Maple Leaf and Trident: The Ukrainian Canadians during the Second World War* (Toronto: Multicultural History Society of Ontario, 1988), 138-43.

90 Anonymous interview.

91 Peter Krawchuk, *Our History: The Ukrainian Labour-Farmer Movement in Canada, 1907-1991,* trans. Mary Skrypnyk (Toronto: Lugus, 1996), 45. Also see "Two Halls, Paper May Feel Weight of New Regulations," *Sudbury Star,* 6 June 1940, 1; "Police Making Full Check on Outlaw Groups," *Sudbury Star,* 7 June 1940, 1; "Aliens Swear Their Loyalty to Dominion," *Sudbury Star,* 15 June 1940, 8; "Aliens in City Make Rush to Obey the Law," *Sudbury Star,* 24 June 1940, 8.

92 "Seized Halls to Be Returned," *Sudbury Star,* 15 October 1943, 1. Also see "Editorial – Keep Them Closed," *Sudbury Star,* 7 April 1943, 4; and "Backs *Sudbury Star* Stand on Ukrainian Hall Issue," *Sudbury Star,* 12 April 1943, 12.

Chapter 4: Cultivating

1 For related discussions about masculinity during the Depression, see Margaret Jane Hillyard Little, *'No Car, No Radio, No Liquor Permit': The Moral Regulation of Single Mothers in Ontario, 1920-1997* (Oxford: Oxford University Press, 1998); Lara Campbell, *Respectable Citizens: Gender, Family, and Unemployment in Ontario's Great Depression* (Toronto: University of Toronto Press, 2009), 57-83; and Katrina Srigley, "Stories of Strife? Remembering the Great Depression," in "Special Issue: Remembering Family, Analyzing Home: Oral History and the Family," ed. Katrina Srigley and Stacey Zembrzycki, *Oral History Forum d'histoire orale* 29 (2009): http://www.oralhistoryforum.ca/.

2 Michael Riordon, *An Unauthorized Biography of the World* (Toronto: Between the Lines, 2004), 230 (emphasis in original).

3 It is important to broach the term "like family" critically, recognizing that the boundaries of Ukrainian families were quite fluid and largely emanated from relationships of co-residence and authority. See Naomi Tadmor, "The Concept of the Household-Family in Eighteenth-Century England," *Past and Present* 151 (1996): 113, 120-25.

4 Informal conversations between Baba and author; Olga Zembrzycki (née Zyma), interviews by author, 6 October 2004, 18 June 2005, 1 November 2008.

5 Denyse Baillargeon makes a similar point about working-class housewives in Montreal, noting that they were already used to unemployment, low wages, and frugal living before the Depression crippled the economy. See Denyse Baillargeon, *Making Do: Women, Family, and Home in Montreal during the Great Depression,* trans. Yvonne Klein (Waterloo: Wilfrid Laurier University Press, 1999), 107.

6 For discussions relating to nostalgia and collective memory making, see Talja Blokland, "Bricks, Mortar, Memories: Neighbourhood and Networks in Collective Acts of Remembering," *International Journal of Urban and Regional Research* 25, 2 (June 2001): 268-83; and Srigley, "Stories of Strife?"

7 Zembrzycki interview, 6 October 2004. The labour force in Canada's coal mines was also family-based. See Robert McIntosh, *Boys in the Pits: Child Labour in Coal Mines* (Montreal and Kingston: McGill-Queen's University Press, 2000), 42.

8 Nick Evanshen, interview by author, Sudbury, 14 May 2005.

9 See Nancy Forestell, "All That Glitters Is Not Gold: The Gender Dimensions of Work, Family, and Community Life in the Northern Ontario Gold Mining Town of Timmins, 1901-1950" (PhD diss., University of Toronto, 1993), 167-256; and Nancy Forestell, "The Miner's Wife: Working-Class Femininity in a Masculine Context, 1920-1950," in *Gendered Pasts: Historical Essays in Femininity and Masculinity in*

Canada, ed. Kathryn McPherson, Cecilia Morgan, and Nancy Forestell (Oxford: Oxford University Press, 1999), 145-56.

10 Nellie Kozak (née Tataryn), interview, Sudbury, 6 June 2005.

11 Steve Balon, interview, Sudbury, 20 April 2005.

12 See Forestell, "All That Glitters"; Nancy Forestell, "Bachelors, Boarding Houses, and Blind Pigs: Gender Construction in a Multi-Ethnic Mining Camp, 1909-1920," in *A Nation of Immigrants: Women, Workers, and Communities in Canadian History, 1840s-1960s,* ed. Franca Iacovetta, Paula Draper, and Robert Ventresca (Toronto: University of Toronto Press, 1998), 251-90; Forestell, "The Miner's Wife"; and Kerry Abel, *Changing Places: History, Community, and Identity in Northeastern Ontario* (Montreal and Kingston: McGill-Queen's University Press, 2006), 70-97. Joy Parr's study does not focus on a mining community, but it does discuss the gendering of work in the industrial towns of Paris and Hanover, Ontario. See Joy Parr, *The Gender of Breadwinners: Women, Men and Change in Two Industrial Towns, 1880-1950* (Toronto: University of Toronto Press, 1990).

13 For an important discussion about women's employment in Canada and shifting familial gender roles, see Campbell, *Respectable Citizens;* and Katrina Srigley, *Breadwinning Daughters: Young Working Women in a Depression-Era City, 1929-1939* (Toronto: University of Toronto Press, 2010).

14 North American historians who discuss boarding house culture have focused on the experiences of male boarders or female boarding house operators. Although some have used oral history interviews to analyze the gendering of boarding house roles, memories have not constituted a central source. As a result, we know very little about the family dynamics of these types of households and even less about children's experiences in them. See Robert Harney, "The Commerce of Migration," *Canadian Ethnic Studies* 9 (1977): 42-53; Robert Harney, "Boarding and Belonging: Thoughts on Sojourner Institutions," *Urban History Review* 2 (1978): 8-37; Robert Harney, "Men without Women: Italian Immigrants in Canada," *Canadian Ethnic Studies* 11, 1 (1979): 22-44; Virginia Yans-McLaughlin, *Family and Community: Italian Immigrants in Buffalo, 1880-1930* (Ithaca, NY: Cornell University Press, 1982), 68, 173-74; Bettina Bradbury, "Pigs, Cows, and Boarders: Non-Wage Forms of Survival among Montreal Families, 1861-91," *Labour/Le travail* 14 (Fall 1984): 9-46; Joanne Meyerowitz, *Women Adrift: Independent Wage Earners in Chicago, 1880-1930* (Chicago: University of Chicago Press, 1988); Forestell, "All That Glitters"; Forestell, "Bachelors, Boarding Houses"; and Diane Vecchio, *Merchants, Midwives and Labouring Women: Italian Migrants in Urban America* (Chicago: University of Illinois Press, 2006).

15 Vecchio, *Merchants, Midwives and Labouring Women,* 67; Bradbury, "Pigs, Cows, and Boarders," 32; Varpu Lindström, *Defiant Sisters: A Social History of Finnish Immigrant Women in Canada* (Toronto: Multicultural History Society of Ontario, 1992); Bettina Bradbury, *Working Families: Age, Gender, and Daily Survival in Industrializing Montreal* (Toronto: McClelland and Stewart, 1993), 175, 178.

16 How much men paid for boarding arrangements is unclear since our interviewees, as children, were not involved in the financial end of these businesses. Taking in boarders, it must be noted, was not always an option for working-class families in other parts of the country. See, for instance, Baillargeon, *Making Do*, 97.

17 See Harney, "Boarding and Belonging"; Harney, "Men without Women"; John Zucchi, *Italians in Toronto: Development of a National Identity, 1875-1935* (Montreal and Kingston: McGill-Queen's University Press, 1988).

18 For a discussion of Depression-era budgeting, see Baillargeon, *Making Do*, 91-111.

19 Harney, "Boarding and Belonging," 27.

20 Food is central to understanding the narratives of immigrants, especially immigrant women. See, for example, Marlene Epp, "The Semiotics of Zwieback: Feast and Famine in the Narratives of Mennonite Refugee Women," in *Sisters or Strangers? Immigrant, Ethnic, and Racialized Women in Canadian History*, ed. Marlene Epp, Franca Iacovetta, and Frances Swyripa (Toronto: University of Toronto Press, 2004), 314-40; Franca Iacovetta and Valerie J. Korinek, "Jell-O Salads, One-Stop Shopping, and Maria the Homemaker: The Gender Politics of Food," in Epp, Iacovetta, and Swyripa, *Sisters or Strangers?* 190-230; Franca Iacovetta, *Gatekeepers: Reshaping Immigrant Lives in Cold War Canada* (Toronto: Between the Lines, 2006), 137-69; and Franca Iacovetta, Valerie J. Korinek, and Marlene Epp, eds., *Edible Histories, Cultural Politics: Towards a Canadian Food History* (Toronto: University of Toronto Press, 2012).

21 Frances Swyripa, *Wedded to the Cause: Ukrainian-Canadian Women and Ethnic Identity, 1891-1991* (Toronto: University of Toronto Press, 1993), 26. Also see Rhonda Hinther, "'Sincerest Revolutionary Greetings,' Progressive Ukrainians in the Twentieth Century" (PhD diss., McMaster University, 2005), 128-29.

22 Baillargeon, *Making Do*, 42.

23 Although male interviewees openly admitted that their parents treated them better than their sisters, they were defensive when it came to this omission, always pointing out that they themselves had contributed to the family economy nevertheless.

24 Michael Frisch, "Working-Class Public History in the Context of Deindustrialization: Dilemmas of Authority and the Possibilities of Dialogue," *Labour/Le travail* 51 (Spring 2003): 153-64.

25 Paul Behun, interview, Coniston, 12 May 2005; Angela Behun, interview, Coniston, 12 May 2005. For a discussion of mothers' allowances and the moral regulation of women, see Little, *'No Car, No Radio'*; Margaret Jane Hillyard Little, "'A Fit and Proper Person': The Moral Regulation of Single Mothers in Ontario, 1920-1940," in McPherson, Morgan, and Forestell, *Gendered Pasts*, 123-38; and Campbell, *Respectable Citizens*.

26 For more on the connections that are both made and not made in interviews, see Anna Sheftel and Stacey Zembrzycki, "Only Human: A Reflection on the Ethical and Methodological Challenges of Working with 'Difficult' Stories," *Oral History Review* 37, 2 (Summer-Fall 2010): 191-241.

27 William Semenuk, interview, Sudbury, 10 November 2004.

28 In his interviews with Holocaust survivors, Henry Greenspan speaks about their "usual spiel" and the deep and meaningful stories that are told when a trusting, collaborative, and engaging interviewing style is employed. These kinds of difficult stories take time to rear their ugly heads, if in fact they ever do. See Henry Greenspan, *On Listening to Holocaust Survivors: Recounting and Life History* (Westport: Praeger Press, 1998). Srigley also speaks about how generational divisions can silence interviewees, in Srigley, *Breadwinning Daughters*, 10.

29 For thoughtful explorations on the intersection of morality, immigrants, and social spaces, see James Opp, "Re-imaging the Moral Order of Urban Space: Religion and Photography in Winnipeg, 1900-1914," *Journal of the Canadian Historical Association* 13 (2002): 86; and Maddalena Tirabassi, "Bourgeois Men, Peasant Women: Rethinking Domestic Work and Morality in Italy," in *Women, Gender, and Transnational Lives: Italian Workers of the World,* ed. Donna Gabaccia and Franca Iacovetta (Toronto: University of Toronto Press, 2002), 106-29.

30 For a related discussion about the informal communal regulation of marital affairs, see Frances Swyripa, "Negotiating Sex and Gender in the Ukrainian Bloc Settlement: East Central Alberta between the Wars," *Prairie Forum* 20, 2 (Fall 1995): 149-74.

31 Donna Gabaccia and Franca Iacovetta, "Introduction," in Gabaccia and Iacovetta, *Women, Gender, and Transnational Lives,* 3-41; Donna Gabaccia, Franca Iacovetta, and Fraser Ottanelli, "Laboring across National Borders: Class, Gender, and Militancy in the Proletarian Mass Migrations," *International Labor and Working-Class History* 66 (Fall 2004): 69.

32 For more on bootlegging, see Lindström, *Defiant Sisters*, 102-10; Judith Bennett, *Ale, Beer, and Brewsters in England: Women's Work in a Changing World, 1300-1600* (Oxford: Oxford University Press, 1996); John Hallwas, *The Bootlegger: A Story of Small-Town America* (Urbana: University of Illinois Press, 1998); Antonio Nicaso, *Rocco Perri: The Story of Canada's Most Notorious Bootlegger* (Toronto: John Wiley and Sons, 2004); and Vecchio, *Merchants, Midwives and Labouring Women,* 70-71.

33 Drinking was "a display of manhood equivalent to the display of strength and courage underground ... something of a vehicle of empowerment for men who were relatively powerless at the bottom of a workplace hierarchy." Abel, *Changing Places,* 201. Also see Forestell, "All That Glitters," 267-74; Lynne Marks, *Revivals and Roller Rinks: Religion, Leisure, and Identity in Late-Nineteenth-Century Small-Town Ontario* (Toronto: University of Toronto Press, 1996), 81-106; and Forestell, "Bachelors, Boarding Houses," 251-90.

34 When Prohibition ended in Ontario in 1927, the government opened its first liquor stores, giving men a legitimate place to purchase spirits. Craig Heron, *Booze: A Distilled History* (Toronto: Between the Lines, 2003), 276.

35 Peter Chitruk, interview, Sudbury, 10 January 2005.

36 William Babij, interview, Sudbury, 16 December 2004.

37 Chitruk interview.

38 In the late nineteenth century, the municipal governments of Sudbury and Copper Cliff enacted bylaws that prohibited small animals from being kept close to houses, but Coniston did not do so until 1934. See Mike Solski, *The Coniston Story* (Sudbury: Journal Printing, 1983), 13-17; and Ashley Thomson, "The 1890s," in *Sudbury: Rail Town to Regional Capital*, ed. C.M. Wallace and Ashley Thomson (Toronto: Dundurn Press, 1993), 33-57. For a related discussion that is situated in Montreal, see Bradbury, "Pigs, Cows, and Boarders," 9-46; and Bradbury, *Working Families*, 163-68.

39 Bodies, as Joy Parr writes, are archives. Our "tacit knowledge," what "we know but cannot tell," is rooted in local culture and enables us to hold on to what has passed out of our minds. Put simply, smells, tastes, sounds, sights, and textures are a way of knowing. See Joy Parr, *Sensing Change: Technologies, Environments, and the Everyday, 1953-2003* (Vancouver: UBC Press, 2010), 1-21.

40 Charlie Rapsky, interview by author, Sudbury, 6 June 2005.

41 Little, 'No Car, No Radio,' 76-89; Campbell, *Respectable Citizens*.

42 Campbell, *Respectable Citizens*, 57.

43 Nick Solski, interview, Sudbury, 7 December 2004.

Chapter 5: Remembering

1 For a discussion on another kind of post-interview experience, see Wendy Rickard, "Oral History – 'More Dangerous Than Therapy'?: Interviewees' Reflections on Recording Traumatic or Taboo Issues," *Oral History* 26, 2 (Autumn 1998): 34-48.

2 Olga Zembrzycki (née Zyma), interview by author, 18 June 2005. To listen to this exchange, go to Stacey Zembrzycki, "According to Baba: A Collaborative Oral History of Sudbury's Ukrainian Community," http://www.sudburyukrainians.ca/project.html. It can be found in the second link to the audio clips; it is the fourth clip.

3 Although some oral historians, especially those who are engaged in community, arts, and new media projects that examine place, identity, and urban change, have begun to embrace walking interviews, this approach, along with wandering, driving, cycling, and "bumbling," is more common among geographers. On these mobile approaches, see Jon Anderson, "Talking Whilst Walking: A Geographical Archaeology of Knowledge," *Area* 36, 3 (2004): 254-61; Mimi Sheller and John Urry, "The New Mobilities Paradigm," *Environment and Planning* A 38 (2006): 207-26; Mark Riley and David Harvey, "Talking Geography: On Oral History and the Practice of Geography," *Social and Cultural Geography* 8, 3 (June 2007): 1-4; Jane Ricketts Hein, James Evans, and Phil Jones, "Mobile Methodologies: Theory, Technology and Practice," *Geography Compass* 2, 5 (September 2008): 1266-85; Lyndsay Brown and Kevin Durrheim, "Different Kinds of Knowing: Generating Qualitative Data through Mobile Interviewing," *Qualitative Inquiry* 15, 5 (June 2009): 911-30; and Richard M. Carpiano,

"Come Take a Walk with Me: The 'Go-Along' Interview as a Novel Method for Studying the Implications of Place for Health and Well-Being," *Health and Place* 15 (2009): 263-72. Note that the walking interview I conducted with Baba was not a soundwalk. These, and the soundscapes that result, focus on the sounds of place and how they trigger meanings, feelings, and associations. See Tom Hall, Brett Lashua, and Amanda Coffey, "Sound and the Everyday in Qualitative Research," *Qualititative Inquiry* 14, 6 (2008): 1019-40; Lisa Gasior, "Griffintown Soundscape," http://www.griffinsound.ca/.

4 I thank Steven High for pushing me to examine the impact of place on Baba's storytelling.

5 This exchange took place on 1 November 2008. Readers who are interested in getting a sense of the stories that Baba told on this occasion can listen to edited clips at Zembrzycki, "According to Baba," http://www.sudburyukrainians.ca/memoryscape.html. Although listening to the clips and viewing the accompanying images online is nothing like experiencing the place itself – the power of place and the inherent tensions between past and present that undergird the sites recalled cannot be harnessed on a website – I hope that it will allow visitors to explore the multi-layered and plural memories of place.

6 Toby Butler, "Memoryscape: How Audio Walks Can Deepen Our Sense of Place by Integrating Art, Oral History, and Cultural Geography," *Geography Compass* 1, 3 (2007): 369; also see Toby Butler and G. Miller, "Linked: A Landmark in Sound, a Public Walk of Art," *Cultural Geographies* 12, 1 (2005): 77-88. For a thorough discussion about the state of oral history and new media and a synopsis of inspiring projects that take mobile methodologies seriously, see Steven High, Jessica J. Mills, and Stacey Zembrzycki, "Telling Our Stories/Animating Our Past: A Status Report on Oral History and Digital Media," *Canadian Journal of Communication* 37, 3 (September 2012): 1-22.

7 Dolores Hayden, *The Power of Place: Urban Landscapes as Public History* (Cambridge, MA: MIT Press, 1995), 43. For lieux de mémoire, see Pierre Nora, "Between Memory and History: *Les Lieux de Mémoire*," *Representations* 26 (Spring 1989): 7-24. For more on the importance of the locality of place, see Henry Glassie, *Passing the Time in Ballymenone: Culture and History of an Ulster Community* (Bloomington: Indiana University Press, 1995); Keith H. Basso, *Wisdom Sits in Places: Landscape and Language among the Western Apache* (Albuquerque: University of New Mexico Press, 1996); Julie Cruikshank, *Do Glaciers Listen? Local Knowledge, Colonial Encounters, and Social Imagination* (Vancouver: UBC Press, 2005); and James Opp and John c. Walsh, eds., *Placing Memory and Remembering Place in Canada* (Vancouver: UBC Press, 2010).

8 Doreen Massey, "Places and Their Pasts," *History Workshop Journal* 39, 1 (1995): 184-85.

9   For a related discussion about making sense of contradictions in the interview space, see Pamela Sugiman, "'Life Is Sweet': Vulnerability and Composure in the Wartime Narratives of Japanese Canadians," *Journal of Canadian Studies* 43, 1 (Winter 2009): 186-218.

10 Talja Blokland, "Bricks, Mortar, Memories: Neighbourhood and Networks in Collective Acts of Remembering," *International Journal of Urban and Regional Research* 25, 2 (June 2001): 272.

11 John C. Walsh and Steven High, "Rethinking the Concept of Community," *Histoire sociale/Social History* 32, 64 (November 1999): 269.

12 The work of Martha Norkunas is instructive here. Norkunas tried to recover her family's connection to Lowell, Massachusetts, and to link these memories to the landscape. See Martha Norkunas, *Monuments and Memory: History and Representation in Lowell, Massachusetts*, (Washington, DC: Smithsonian Institution Press, 2002).

13 Lenore Layman views reticence as a means through which interviewees may assert power, thus balancing the academic and interpretive authority of the interviewer; according to her, the refusal to address topics is an important way to assert power in the interview relationship, and thus it is worthy of serious study. See Lenore Layman, "Reticence in Oral History Interviews," *Oral History Review* 36, 2 (Summer-Fall 2009): 207-30.

14 For a discussion of how racism can be used to interpret deeper meanings in a narrative, see Anna Sheftel and Stacey Zembrzycki, "Only Human: A Reflection on the Ethical and Methodological Challenges of Working with 'Difficult' Stories," *Oral History Review* 37, 2 (Summer-Fall 2010): 191-241.

Conclusion

1   For a similar reflection, see Alicia Rouverol, "Collaborative Oral History in a Correctional Setting: Promise and Pitfalls," *Oral History Review* 30, 1 (January 2003): 82.

2   To this end, Franca Iacovetta adds that "the personal and emotional can be legitimate forms of scholarly writing." Franca Iacovetta, "Post-Modern Ethnography, Historical Materialism, and Decentring the (Male) Authorial Voice: A Feminist Conversation," *Histoire sociale/Social History* 32, 64 (November 1999): 283.

3   Michael Frisch makes this point in "Sharing Authority: Oral History and the Collaborative Process," *Oral History Review* 30, 1 (January 2003): 112.

4   For a similar type of narrative, see Alessandro Portelli, *They Say in Harlan County: An Oral History* (Oxford: Oxford University Press, 2011).

5   I am referring, for instance, to Franca Iacovetta, *Such Hardworking People: Italian Immigrants in Postwar Toronto* (Montreal and Kingston: McGill-Queen's University Press, 1992); Royden Loewen, *Family, Church, and Market: A Mennonite Community*

in the Old and New Worlds, 1850-1930 (Toronto: University of Toronto Press, 1993); Lynne Marks, *Revivals and Roller Rinks: Religion, Leisure, and Identity in Late-Nineteenth-Century Small-Town Ontario* (Toronto: University of Toronto Press, 1996); and Kerry Abel, *Changing Places: History, Community, and Identity in Northeastern Ontario* (Montreal and Kingston: McGill-Queen's University Press, 2006).

Bibliography

Archival Sources

Archives of Ontario, Toronto (AO)
Department of Justice
Multicultural History Society of Ontario Fonds
Ukrainian National Federation of Canada Fonds

Archives of the Ukrainian Greek Orthodox Church of Canada, Winnipeg
Father Andrii Sarmatiuk File

Greater Sudbury Public Library, Sudbury
Regional Collection
Vernon's Sudbury Directory

Laurentian University Archives, Sudbury
George Prusila Papers
Sudbury and District Historical Society Fonds
Sudbury and District Ministerial Association Fonds

Library and Archives Canada, Ottawa (LAC)
Association of United Ukrainian Canadians Fonds
Canadian Security Intelligence Service (CSIS)
Communist Party of Canada Fonds
Department of Citizenship and Immigration
Department of External Affairs
Department of Justice
Department of Labour
Department of Mines and Resources
Department of the Secretary of State of Canada
Finnish Organization of Canada Fonds
Frontier College Fonds

Frontier College Oral History Collection
Manuscript Census of Canada, 1901, 1911
Michael Horoshko Fonds
Peter Krawchuk Fonds
Records of the Immigration Branch
Royal Canadian Mounted Police (RCMP)
Ukrainian National Youth Federation of Canada Fonds

Multicultural History Society of Ontario, Toronto (MHSO)
Ethnic Newspaper Collection
Finnish Canadian Historical Society Collection
Oral History Collection
Sudbury Collection

St. Mary's Ukrainian Catholic Church, Sudbury
Marriage Register, 1933-37
Parish Register, 1928 on
Records of Baptisms, Confirmations, Marriages, and Burials, 1927-28
Records of Baptisms, 1929-34, 1939 on

Stacey Zembrzycki's Personal Archive
Ukrainians in Sudbury Collection

Sudbury Regional Police Museum, Sudbury
Constable Boucher's Daily Journal, 1922 (Coniston, Garson)
Constable Boucher's Daily Journal, 1923
Constable Brennan's Report Book, Coniston, 1927
Criminal Register, 1930-39
Prisoners Records Book: Neelon, Garson, Coniston, May 1921-July 1925

Ukrainian Catholic Archeparchy of Winnipeg Archive, Winnipeg (UCAWA)
John Kolsun File
Michael Irkha File
Nicholas Bartman File
Peter Kamenetsky File

Printed Government Sources
Canada. Census of Canada, 1901-31.
Canada. *Report of Commission Appointed under Order-in-Council P.C. 670 to Enquire into Industrial Relations in Canada Together with a Minority Report.* Ottawa: King's Printer, 1919.

Ontario. *Annual Report on Common Gaols, Prisons and Reformatories,* 1930-39.
Ontario. *Annual Report on the Mining Accidents in Ontario,* 1900-39.

Newspapers and Magazines

English-Language Newspapers
Sudbury Journal (1891-1918)
Sudbury Star (1910-39)

Ukrainian-Language Newspapers
Boiova molod (1930-32)
Holos robitnytsi (1923-24)
Narodna hazeta (1937-41)
Novyi shliakh (1932-39)
Robitnytsia (1924-37)
Robochyi narod (1909-18)
Svit molodi (1927-30)
Ukrainski robitnychi visti (1919-37)
Ukrainskyi holos (1910-39)
Ukrainskyi robitnyk (1934-39)

Interviews

Conducted by Olga and Stacey Zembrzycki
William Babij, Sudbury, Ontario, 16 December 2004.
Michael Babuik, Sudbury, Ontario, 24 November 2004.
Vera Babuik (Havrachysky), Sudbury, Ontario, 24 November 2004.
Steve Balon, Sudbury, Ontario, 20 April 2005.
Angela Behun (Bilowus), Coniston, Ontario, 12 May 2005.
Paul Behun, Coniston, Ontario, 12 May 2005.
Victoria Bilczuk (Bodnarchuk), Sudbury, Ontario, 10 November 2004.
Mary Brydges (Ladyk), Sudbury, Ontario, 28 October 2004.
John Buchowski, Sudbury, Ontario, 18 May 2005.
Steve Buchowski, Coniston, Ontario, 16 May 2005.
Frances Bzdel (Poworoznyk), Val Caron, Ontario, 10 January 2005.
Jacob Bzdel, Val Caron, Ontario, 10 January 2005.
Peter Chitruk, Sudbury, Ontario, 10 January 2005.
Walter Chmara, Sudbury, Ontario, 15 December 2004.
Pearl Chyz (Demchuk), Garson, Ontario, 28 January 2005.
Mary Clouthier (Werstiuk), Coniston, Ontario, 16 May 2005.
Helen Cotnam (Cybulka), Sudbury, Ontario, 2 May 2005.
Bernice Crowe (Haluschak), Sudbury, Ontario, 17 May 2005.
Isobel Dobranski (Harmaty), Sudbury, Ontario, 1 November 2004.

Robert Gawalko, Sudbury, Ontario, 23 November 2004.

Helen Gniazdoski (Daniluk), Sudbury, Ontario, 13 May 2005.

Stanley Hayduk, Garson, Ontario, 19 May 2005.

Mary Hickey (Danchuk), Sudbury, Ontario, 2 December 2004.

John Holunga, Coniston, Ontario, 16 May 2005.

Lorraine Jurgilas (Burke/Burkotski), Sudbury, Ontario, 8 November 2004.

Jeanette (Yevania) Kostiw (Steczyszyn), Hanmer, Ontario, 14 January 2005.

Lovey Kotyluk, Copper Cliff, Ontario, 10 May 2005.

Nellie Kozak (Tataryn), Sudbury, Ontario, 6 June 2005.

Pauline Kruk (McCollick/Mykoluk), Sudbury, Ontario, 20 January 2005.

Ernie Lekun (Lyhkun), Sudbury, Ontario, 9 May 2005.

Eugenia Poland Maizuk (Kureluik), Sudbury, Ontario, 19 January 2005.

Joseph Maizuk, Sudbury, Ontario, 25 January 2005.

Frank Makarinsky, Sudbury, Ontario, 4 May 2005.

Terry (Taras) Martyn, Sudbury, Ontario, 17 December 2004.

Anne Matschke (Kuchmey), Sudbury, Ontario, 7 May 2005.

Boris Max (Maksimovich), Sudbury, Ontario, 11 May 2005.

Victoria Panas (Romanchuk), Sudbury, Ontario, 14 December 2004.

Helen Pihursky (Ciotka), Sudbury, Ontario, 13 January 2005.

Anne Podorozny (Ogenchuk), Sudbury, Ontario, 9 November 2004.

Olga Rohatyn (Mysyk), Sudbury, Ontario, 27 January 2005.

Jean Samborski (Tyshynski), Sudbury, Ontario, 5 November 2004.

Don Sarmatiuk, Sudbury, Ontario, 3 May 2005.

William Semenuk, Sudbury, Ontario, 10 November 2004.

Olga Shelegey (Struk), Coniston, Ontario, 12 May 2005.

Walter Shelegey, Coniston, Ontario, 12 May 2005.

Mary Shkrabek (Temeriski), Sudbury, Ontario, 5 November 2004.

Mary Sitko (Wolochatiuk), Sudbury, Ontario, 3 November 2004.

Helen Smilanich (Pasichnyk), Sudbury, Ontario, 20 April 2005.

Elsie Solski (Kotyluk), Sudbury, Ontario, 7 December 2004.

Nick Solski, Sudbury, Ontario, 7 December 2004.

Mary Ducisk Stanyon (Kowalchuk), Sudbury, Ontario, 25 January 2005.

Doris Sturby (Zaparynuik), Sudbury, Ontario, 13 December 2004.

Henry Tarkin (Terkovich), Sudbury, Ontario, 1 December 2004.

Katherine Timchuk (Harach), Sudbury, Ontario, 2 November 2004.

John Tkach, Sudbury, Ontario, 12 January 2005.

Sophie Udovicic (Kuczma), Sudbury, Ontario, 24 January 2005.

Stella Witwicky (Makowsky), Sudbury, Ontario, 29 November 2004.

Pauline Yawney (Puhach), Sudbury, Ontario, 11 January 2005.

Tom Zaitz (Zayatz), Sudbury, Ontario, 25 November 2004.

Mary Zawierzeniec (Nykilchyk), Sudbury, Ontario, 3 December 2004.

Conducted by Stacey Zembrzycki
Ramona Bendick (Shyluk), Sudbury, Ontario, 15 November 2004.
Mary Anne Buchowski, Ottawa, Ontario, 13 March 2006.
Patricia Chytuk (Urchyshyn), Sudbury, Ontario, 18 January 2005.
Nick Evanshen, Sudbury, Ontario, 14 May 2005.
Alice Helash (Ciotka), Sudbury, Ontario, 17 January 2005.
Charlie Rapsky, Sudbury, Ontario, 6 June 2005.
Oryst Sawchuk, Sudbury, Ontario, 26 January 2005.
John Stefura, Sudbury, Ontario, 24 January 2005.
Olga Zembrzycki (Zyma), Sudbury, Ontario, 6 October 2004, 18 June 2005, 1 November 2008.

All interviews conducted for this project are accessible at the City of Greater Sudbury Archives and the Centre for Oral History and Digital Storytelling at Concordia University.

Frontier College Oral History Collection, Library and Archives Canada, Ottawa (LAC)
Howard Rockeby-Thomas, interview by Marjorie Robinson, Toronto, Ontario, 21 May 1976.
O.E. Walli, interview by Marjorie Robinson, Toronto, Ontario, 3 June 1975.
Dr. J. Wendell McLeod, interview by Marjorie Robinson, Toronto, Ontario, 4 July 1975.
Jack Willard, interview by Marjorie Robinson, Toronto, Ontario, 21 May 1976.

Memories and Music: Oral History Interviews with International Nickel Company Pensioners, Greater Sudbury Public Library, Sudbury
Jack Halco, interview by Don MacMillan, Sudbury, Ontario, n.d.
Bill Jarrett, interview by Don MacMillan, Sudbury, Ontario, n.d.
Ted Kucharuk, interview by Don MacMillan, Sudbury, Ontario, n.d.
Harry Navasneck, interview by Don MacMillan, Sudbury, Ontario, n.d.
Eli Shpaiuk, interview by Don MacMillan, Sudbury, Ontario, n.d.
Harry Tarkin, interview by Don MacMillan, Sudbury, Ontario, n.d.

Mercedes Steedman's Personal Oral History Collection, Sudbury
Anne Macks, interview by Mercedes Steedman, Sudbury, Ontario, 3 May 1993.

Oral History Collection, Multicultural History Society of Ontario, Toronto (MHSO)
Fred Anaka, interview by Ihor Dawydiak, location unknown, 1 June 1978.
Mary Hansen, interview by Mary Stefura, Sudbury, Ontario, n.d.
Steve Hrycyshyn, interview by Mary Stefura, Kirkland Lake, Ontario, 9 June 1975.
William Krystia, interview by Mary Stefura, Sudbury, Ontario, 30 November 1981.
John Shelestynsky, interview by Mary Stefura, Kirkland Lake, Ontario, 7 June 1978.

Other Sources

Abel, Kerry. *Changing Places: History, Community, and Identity in Northeastern Ontario.* Montreal and Kingston: McGill-Queen's University Press, 2006.

–. "History and the Provincial Norths: An Ontario Example." In Abel and Coates, *Northern Visions: New Perspectives on the North in Canadian History,* 127-40.

Abel, Kerry, and Ken Coates, eds. *Northern Visions: New Perspectives on the North in Canadian History.* Peterborough: Broadview Press, 2001.

Abrams, Lynn. *Oral History Theory.* London: Routledge, 2010.

Anderson, Benedict. *Imagined Communities: Reflections on the Origin and Spread of Nationalism.* London: Verso, 1991.

Anderson, J.T.M. *The Education of the New-Canadian: A Treatise on Canada's Greatest Educational Problem.* Toronto: J.M. Dent and Sons, 1918.

Anderson, Jon. "Talking Whilst Walking: A Geographical Archaeology of Knowledge." *Area* 36, 3 (2004): 254-61.

Avery, Donald. *"Dangerous Foreigners": European Immigrant Workers and Labour Radicalism in Canada, 1896-1932.* Toronto: McClelland and Stewart, 1979.

–. *Reluctant Host: Canada's Response to Immigrant Workers, 1896-1994.* Toronto: McClelland and Stewart, 1995.

Backhouse, Constance. *Petticoats and Prejudice: Women and Law in Nineteenth-Century Canada.* Toronto: Women's Press, 1991.

Baillargeon, Denyse. *Making Do: Women, Family, and Home in Montreal during the Great Depression.* Trans. Yvonne Klein. Waterloo: Wilfrid Laurier University Press, 1999.

Baldwin, Doug. "A Study in Social Control: The Life of the Silver Miner in Northern Ontario." *Labour/Le travail* 2 (1977): 79-106.

Basso, Keith H. *Wisdom Sits in Places: Landscape and Language among the Western Apache.* Albuquerque: University of New Mexico Press, 1996.

Beach, Noel. "Nickel Capital: Sudbury and the Nickel Industry, 1905-1925." *Laurentian University Review* 16, 3 (1974): 55-74.

Beavis, Mary Ann, ed. *Municipal Development in Northeastern Ontario: Copper Cliff and Sudbury.* Winnipeg: Institute of Urban Studies, 1991.

Behar, Ruth. *Translated Woman: Crossing the Border with Esperanza's Story.* Boston: Beacon Press, 1993.

–. *The Vulnerable Observer: Anthropology That Breaks Your Heart.* Boston: Beacon Press, 1996.

Bennett, Judith. *Ale, Beer, and Brewsters in England: Women's Work in a Changing World, 1300-1600.* Oxford: Oxford University Press, 1996.

Bertaux, Daniel, and Paul Thompson, eds. *Between Generations: Family Models, Myths, and Memories.* London: Transaction, 1993.

Berton, Pierre. *The Great Depression, 1929-1939.* Toronto: McClelland and Stewart, 1990.

Bertulli, Margaret, and Rae Swan, eds. *A Bit of the Cliff: A Brief History of the Town of Copper Cliff, Ontario: 1901-1972.* Copper Cliff: Copper Cliff Museum, 1982.

Biega, Alexander, and Myroslaw Diakowsky, eds. *The Ukrainian Experience in Quebec.* Toronto: Basilian Press, 1994.

Blokland, Talja. "Bricks, Mortar, Memories: Neighbourhood and Networks in Collective Acts of Remembering." *International Journal of Urban and Regional Research* 25, 2 (June 2001): 268-83.

Bodnar, John. *The Transplanted: A History of Immigrants in Urban America.* Bloomington: Indiana University Press, 1985.

Borland, Katherine. "'That's Not What I Said': Interpretive Conflict in Oral Narrative Research." In Gluck and Patai, *Women's Words: The Feminist Practice of Oral History,* 63-75.

Boyd, John. "Editor Preface." In Krawchuk, *Our History: The Ukrainian Labour-Farmer Movement in Canada, 1907-1991,* v-vii.

Bradbury, Bettina. "Gender at Work at Home: Family Decisions, the Labour Market, and Girls' Contributions to the Family Economy." In *Canadian Family History,* ed. Bettina Bradbury, 177-98. Toronto: Copp Clark Pitman, 1992.

–. "Pigs, Cows, and Boarders: Non-Wage Forms of Survival among Montreal Families, 1861-91." *Labour/Le travail* 14 (Fall 1984): 9-46.

–. *Working Families: Age, Gender, and Daily Survival in Industrializing Montreal.* Toronto: McClelland and Stewart, 1993.

Bradley, Harriet. "The Seductions of the Archive: Voices Lost and Found." *History of the Human Sciences* 12, 2 (May 1999): 107-22.

Bradwin, Edmund. The *Bunkhouse Man: A Study of Work and Pay in the Camps of Canada, 1903-1914.* Toronto: University of Toronto Press, 1929.

Bray, Matt. "1910-1920." In Wallace and Thomson, *Sudbury: Rail Town to Regional Capital,* 86-112.

Bray, Matt, and Ernie Epp, eds. *A Vast and Magnificent Land: An Illustrated History of Northern Ontario.* Toronto: Ontario Ministry of Northern Affairs, 1984.

Bray, Matt, and A.D. Gilbert. "The Mond-International Nickel Merger of 1929: A Case Study in Entrepreneurial Failure." *Canadian Historical Review* 76, 1 (March 1995): 19-42.

Bray, Matt, and Ashley Thomson, eds. *At the End of the Shift: Mines and Single-Industry Towns in Northern Ontario.* Toronto: Dundurn Press, 1992.

Brettell, Caroline B. *When They Read What We Write: The Politics of Ethnography.* Westport, CT: Bergin and Garvey, 1993.

Broadfoot, Barry. *Ten Lost Years, 1929-1939: Memories of Canadians Who Survived the Depression.* Toronto: Doubleday Canada, 1973.

Brown, Lyndsay, and Kevin Durrheim. "Different Kinds of Knowing: Generating Qualitative Data through Mobile Interviewing." *Qualitative Inquiry* 15, 5 (June 2009): 911-30.

Bullen, John. "Hidden Workers: Child Labour and the Family Economy in Late Nineteenth Century Urban Ontario." In *Canadian Family History,* ed. Bettina Bradbury, 199-219. Toronto: Copp Clark Pitman, 1992.

Burton, Antoinette, ed. *Archive Stories: Facts, Fictions, and the Writing of History.* Durham: Duke University Press, 2005.

–. *Dwelling in the Archive: Women Writing House, Home, and History in Late Colonial India.* Oxford: Oxford University Press, 2003.

Butler, Toby. "Memoryscape: How Audio Walks Can Deepen Our Sense of Place by Integrating Art, Oral History, and Cultural Geography." *Geography Compass* 1, 3 (2007): 360-72.

Butler, Toby, and G. Miller. "Linked: A Landmark in Sound, a Public Walk of Art." *Cultural Geographies* 12, 1 (2005): 77-88.

Campbell, Lara. *Respectable Citizens: Gender, Family, and Unemployment in Ontario's Great Depression.* Toronto: University of Toronto Press, 2009.

Campbell, Peter J. "The Cult of Spontaneity: Finnish-Canadian Bushworkers and the Industrial Workers of the World in Northern Ontario, 1919-1934." *Labour/Le travail* 41 (Spring 1988): 117-46.

Careless, J.M.S. "'Limited Identities' in Canada." *Canadian Historical Review* 50, 1 (March 1969): 1-10.

Carpiano, Richard M. "Come Take a Walk with Me: The 'Go-Along' Interview as a Novel Method for Studying the Implications of Place for Health and Well-Being." *Health and Place* 15 (2009): 263-72.

Cohen, Anthony P. *The Symbolic Construction of Community.* London: Routledge, 1985.

Collins, Robert. *You Had to Be There: An Intimate Portrait of the Generation That Survived the Depression, Won the War, and Re-invented Canada.* Toronto: McClelland and Stewart, 1997.

Comacchio, Cynthia. *The Dominion of Youth: Adolescence and the Making of Modern Canada, 1920 to 1950.* Waterloo: Wilfrid Laurier University Press, 2006.

Conner, Ralph. *The Foreigner: A Tale of Saskatchewan.* Toronto: Westminster, 1909.

Corbett, Katharine C., and Howard S. Miller. "A Shared Inquiry into Shared Inquiry." *Public Historian* 28, 1 (Winter 2006): 15-38.

Cottrell, Michael. "St. Patrick's Day Parades in Nineteenth-Century Toronto: A Study of Immigrant Adjustment and Elite Control." In Iacovetta, Draper, and Ventresca, *A Nation of Immigrants: Women, Workers, and Communities in Canadian History, 1840s-1960s,* 35-54.

Cruikshank, Julie. *Do Glaciers Listen? Local Knowledge, Colonial Encounters, and Social Imagination.* Vancouver: UBC Press, 2005.

Cruikshank, Julie, Angela Sidney, Kitty Smith, and Annie Ned. *Life Lived Like A Story: Life Stories of Three Yukon Aboriginal Elders.* Lincoln: University of Nebraska Press, 1990.

Cumbo, Enrico T. Carlson. "'As the Twig Is Bent, the Tree's Inclined': Growing Up Italian in Toronto, 1905-1940." PhD diss., University of Toronto, 1996.

Cuthbert-Brandt, Gail. "The Development of French-Canadian Social Institutions in Sudbury, Ontario, 1883-1920." *Laurentian University Review* 11, 2 (February 1979): 5-22.

Czumer, William. *Recollections about the Life of the First Ukrainian Settlers in Canada.* Edmonton: Canadian Institute of Ukrainian Studies Press, 1981.

Darcovich, William, ed. *A Statistical Compendium on the Ukrainians in Canada, 1891-1976.* Ottawa: University of Ottawa Press, 1980.

Dennie, Donald. "Sudbury 1883-1946: A Social Historical Study of Property and Class." PhD diss., Carleton University, 1989.

Derrida, Jacques. *Archive Fever: A Freudian Impression.* Trans. Eric Prenowitz. Chicago: University of Chicago Press, 1996.

Dorian, Charles. *The First 75 Years; A Headline History of Sudbury, Canada.* Ilfracombe, UK: A.H. Stockwell, 1959.

Dubinsky, Karen. *Improper Advances: Rape and Heterosexual Conflict in Ontario, 1880-1929.* Chicago: Chicago University Press, 1993.

–. "'Who Do You Think Did the Cooking?': Baba in the Classroom." In Kechnie and Reitsma-Street, *Changing Lives: Women and Northern Ontario,* 193-97.

Dubinsky, Karen, and Franca Iacovetta. "Murder, Womanly Virtue, and Motherhood: The Case of Angelina Napolitano, 1911-1922." *Canadian Historical Review* 77, 4 (December 1991): 505-31.

Dunk, Thomas. *It's a Working Man's Town: Male Working-Class Culture in Northwestern Ontario.* Montreal and Kingston: McGill-Queen's University Press, 1991.

Epp, Marlene. "The Memory of Violence: Soviet and East European Mennonite Refugees and Rape in the Second World War." *Journal of Women's History* 9, 1 (Spring 1997): 58-87.

–. "The Semiotics of Zwieback: Feast and Famine in the Narratives of Mennonite Refugee Women." In Epp, Iacovetta, and Swyripa, *Sisters or Strangers? Immigrant, Ethnic, and Racialized Women in Canadian History,* 314-40.

–. *Women without Men: Mennonite Refugees of the Second World War.* Toronto: University of Toronto Press, 1999.

Epp, Marlene, Franca Iacovetta, and Frances Swyripa, eds. *Sisters or Strangers? Immigrant, Ethnic, and Racialized Women in Canadian History.* Toronto: University of Toronto Press, 2004.

Erdmans, Mary Patrice. *The Grasinski Girls: The Choices They Had and the Choices They Made.* Athens: Ohio University Press, 2004.

Esaiw, John. *For Ukraine: Danylo Skoropadsky's Tour of the USA and Canada, Fall 1937-Spring 1938.* Trans by. Larissa Stavroff. Chicago: United Hetman Organization, 1938.

Fitzpatrick, Alfred. *The University in Overalls: A Plea for Part-Time Study*. Toronto: Frontier College Press, 1923.

Forestell, Nancy. "All That Glitters Is Not Gold: The Gender Dimensions of Work, Family, and Community Life in the Northern Ontario Gold Mining Town of Timmins, 1901-1950." PhD diss., University of Toronto, 1993.

–. "Bachelors, Boarding Houses, and Blind Pigs: Gender Construction in a Multi-Ethnic Mining Camp, 1909-1920." In Iacovetta, Draper, and Ventresca, *A Nation of Immigrants: Women, Workers, and Communities in Canadian History, 1840s-1960s*, 251-90.

–. "The Miner's Wife: Working-Class Femininity in a Masculine Context, 1920-1950." In McPherson, Morgan, and Forestell, *Gendered Pasts: Historical Essays in Femininity and Masculinity in Canada*, 139-57.

–. "Women, Gender and the Provincial North." In Abel and Coates, *Northern Visions: New Perspectives on the North in Canadian History*, 107-16.

Frager, Ruth. *Sweatshop Strife: Class, Ethnicity, and Gender in the Jewish Labour Movement of Toronto, 1900-1939*. Toronto: University of Toronto Press, 1992.

Freund, Alexander. "A Canadian Family Talks about Oma's Life in Nazi Germany: Three-Generational Interviews and Communicative Memory." In "Special Issue: Remembering Family, Analyzing Home: Oral History and the Family," ed. Katrina Srigley and Stacey Zembrzycki. *Oral History Forum d'histoire orale* 29 (2009): http://www.oralhistoryforum.ca/.

Freund, Alexander, and Laura Quilici. "Exploring Myths in Women's Narratives: Italian and German Immigrant Women in Vancouver, 1947-1961." *BC Studies* 105-6 (Spring-Summer 1995): 159-82.

Frisch, Michael. "Oral History and the Digital Revolution: Toward a Post-Documentary Sensibility." In Perks and Thomson, *The Oral History Reader*, 2nd ed., 32-42.

–. *A Shared Authority: Essays on the Craft and Meaning of Oral and Public History*. Albany: State University of New York Press, 1990.

–. "Sharing Authority: Oral History and the Collaborative Process." *Oral History Review* 30, 1 (January 2003): 111-13.

–. "Three Dimensions and More: Oral History beyond the Paradoxes of Method." In *Handbook of Emergent Methods*, ed. S. Nagy Hess-Biber and P. Leavy, 221-38. New York: Guilford Press, 2008.

–. "Working-Class Public History in the Context of Deindustrialization: Dilemmas of Authority and the Possibilities of Dialogue." *Labour/Le travail* 51 (Spring 2003): 153-64.

Gabaccia, Donna, and Franca Iacovetta. "Introduction." In Gabaccia and Iacovetta, *Women, Gender, and Transnational Lives: Italian Workers of the World*, 3-41.

–, eds. *Women, Gender, and Transnational Lives: Italian Workers of the World*. Toronto: University of Toronto, 2002.

Gabaccia, Donna, Franca Iacovetta, and Fraser Ottanelli. "Laboring across National Borders: Class, Gender, and Militancy in the Proletarian Mass Migrations." *International Labor and Working-Class History* 66 (Fall 2004): 57-77.

Gasior, Lisa. "Griffintown Soundscape." http://www.griffinsound.ca/.

Gaudreau, Guy. *L'histoire des mineurs du nord ontarien et québécois*. Sillery, QC: Septentrion, 2003.

Gerus, O.W., and J.E. Rea. *The Ukrainians in Canada*. Ottawa: Canadian Historical Association, 1985.

Gerus, Oleh. "Consolidating the Community: The Ukrainian Self-Reliance League." In Luciuk and Hryniuk, *Canada's Ukrainians: Negotiating an Identity*, 157-86.

Gilbert, A.D. "The 1920s." In Wallace and Thomson, *Sudbury: Rail Town to Regional Capital*, 113-37.

Glassie, Henry. *Passing the Time in Ballymenone: Culture and History of an Ulster Community*. Bloomington: Indiana University Press, 1995.

Gluck, Sherna Berger, and Daphne Patai, eds. *Women's Words: The Feminist Practice of Oral History*. New York: Routledge, 1991.

Goltz, Eileen. "A Corporate View of Housing and Community in a Company Town: Copper Cliff, 1886-1920." *Ontario History* 82, 1 (March 1990): 29-52.

–. "The Exercise of Power in a Company Town: Copper Cliff, 1886-1980." PhD diss., University of Guelph, 1988.

Gordon, Linda. *Heroes of Their Own Lives: The Politics and History of Family Violence, Boston 1880-1960*. New York: Penguin Books, 1988.

Greenspan, Henry. *On Listening to Holocaust Survivors: Recounting and Life History*. Westport: Praeger Press, 1998.

Greenspan, Henry, and Sidney Bolkosky. "When Is an Interview an Interview? Notes from Listening to Holocaust Survivors." *Poetics Today* 27, 2 (2006): 431-49.

Hall, Tom, Brett Lashua, and Amanda Coffey. "Sound and the Everyday in Qualitative Research." *Qualitative Inquiry* 14, 6 (2008): 1019-40.

Hallwas, John. *The Bootlegger: A Story of Small-Town America*. Urbana: University of Illinois Press, 1998.

Handlin, Oscar. *The Uprooted*. Boston: Little Brown, 1973.

Harney, Robert. "Boarding and Belonging: Thoughts on Sojourner Institutions." *Urban History Review* 2 (1978): 8-37.

–. "The Commerce of Migration." *Canadian Ethnic Studies* 9 (1977): 42-53.

–, ed. *Gathering Place: Peoples and Neighbourhoods of Toronto, 1834-1945*. Toronto: Multicultural History Society of Ontario, 1985.

–. "Men without Women: Italian Immigrants in Canada." *Canadian Ethnic Studies* 11, 1 (1979): 22-44.

Hayden, Dolores. *The Power of Place: Urban Landscapes as Public History*. Cambridge, MA: MIT Press, 1995.

Hein, Jane Ricketts, James Evans, and Phil Jones. "Mobile Methodologies: Theory, Technology and Practice." *Geography Compass* 2, 5 (September 2008): 1266-85.

Heron, Craig. *Booze: A Distilled History.* Toronto: Between the Lines, 2003.

Heron, Craig, and Steve Penfold. *The Workers' Festival: A History of Labour Day in Canada.* Toronto: University of Toronto Press, 2005.

Higgins, E.G. *Twelve O'Clock and All's Well: A Pictorial History of Law Enforcement in the Sudbury District: 1883-1978.* Sudbury: Journal Printing, 1978.

High, Steven. *Industrial Sunset: The Making of North America's Rust Belt, 1969-1984.* Toronto: University of Toronto Press, 2003.

–. "Telling Stories: A Reflection on Oral History and New Media." *Oral History* 38, 1 (Spring 2010): 101-12.

High, Steven, Jessica J. Mills, and Stacey Zembrzycki. "Telling Our Stories/Animating Our Past: A Status Report on Oral History and Digital Media." *Canadian Journal of Communication* 37, 3 (September 2012): 1-22.

High, Steven, Lisa Ndejuru, and Kristen O'Hare, eds. "Special Issue of Sharing Authority: Community-University Collaboration in Oral History, Digital Storytelling, and Engaged Scholarship." *Journal of Canadian Studies* 43, 1 (Winter 2009).

High, Steven, and David Sworn. "After the Interview: The Interpretive Challenges of Oral History Video Indexing." *Digital Studies/Le champ numérique* 1, 2 (2009): http://www.digitalstudies.org/.

Higham, John. *Strangers in the Land: Patterns of American Nativism.* New York: Atheneum, 1963.

Hillmer, Norman, Bohdan Kordan, and Lubomyr Luciuk, eds. *On Guard for Thee: War, Ethnicity, and the Canadian State, 1939-45.* Ottawa: Canadian Committee for the History of the Second World War, 1988.

Hinther, Rhonda. "'Sincerest Revolutionary Greetings': Progressive Ukrainians in the Twentieth Century." PhD diss., McMaster University, 2005.

Hinther, Rhonda, and Jim Mochoruk, eds. *Re-Imagining Ukrainian-Canadians: History, Politics, and Identity.* Toronto: University of Toronto Press, 2011.

"History of the ULFTA Branch in Coniston." In *Almanac, 1918-1929,* trans. Larissa Stavroff, 133-35. Winnipeg: Ukrainian Labour Farmer Temple Association, 1930.

Horn, Michiel. *The Depression in Canada: Responses to Economic Crisis.* Toronto: Copp Clark, 1988.

–. *The Dirty Thirties: Canadians in the Great Depression.* Toronto: Copp Clark, 1972.

Hryniuk, Stella. *Peasants with Promise: Ukrainians in Southeastern Galicia, 1880-1900.* Edmonton: Canadian Institute of Ukrainian Studies Press, 1991.

Hunchuck, Suzanne Holyck. "A House Like No Other: An Architectural and Social History of the Ukrainian Labour Temple, 523 Arlington Avenue, Ottawa, 1923-1967." Master's thesis, Carleton University, 2001.

Iacovetta, Franca. *Gatekeepers: Reshaping Immigrant Lives in Cold War Canada.* Toronto: Between the Lines, 2006.

–. "Gossip, Contest, and Power in the Making of Suburban Bad Girls: Toronto, 1945-1960." *Canadian Historical Review* 80, 4 (December 1999): 585-623.

–. "Manly Militants, Cohesive Communities, and Defiant Domestics: Writing about Immigrants in Canadian Historical Scholarship." *Labour/Le travail* 36 (Fall 1995): 217-52.

–. "Post-Modern Ethnography, Historical Materialism, and Decentring the (Male) Authorial Voice: A Feminist Conversation." *Histoire sociale/Social History* 32, 64 (November 1999): 275-93.

–. *Such Hardworking People: Italian Immigrants in Postwar Toronto.* Montreal and Kingston: McGill-Queen's University Press, 1992.

–. *The Writing of English Canadian Immigrant History.* Ottawa: Canadian Historical Association, 1997.

Iacovetta, Franca, Paula Draper, and Robert Ventresca, eds. *A Nation of Immigrants: Women, Workers, and Communities in Canadian History, 1840s-1960s.* Toronto: University of Toronto Press, 1998.

Iacovetta, Franca, and Valerie J. Korinek. "Jell-O Salads, One-Stop Shopping, and Maria the Homemaker: The Gender Politics of Food." In Epp, Iacovetta, and Swyripa, *Sisters or Strangers? Immigrant, Ethnic, and Racialized Women in Canadian History,* 190-230.

Iacovetta, Franca, Valerie J. Korinek, and Marlene Epp, eds. *Edible Histories, Cultural Politics: Towards a Canadian Food History.* Toronto: University of Toronto Press, 2012.

Iacovetta, Franca, and Wendy Mitchinson, eds. *On the Case: Explorations in Social History.* Toronto: University of Toronto Press, 1998.

Iacovetta, Franca, Roberto Perin, and Angelo Principe, eds. *Enemies Within: Italian and Other Internees in Canada and Abroad.* Toronto: University of Toronto Press, 2000.

Iacovetta, Franca, and Mariana Valverde, eds. *Gender Conflicts: New Essays in Women's History.* Toronto: University of Toronto Press, 1992.

Jacobson, Matthew Frye. *Whiteness of a Different Color: European Immigrants and the Alchemy of Race.* Cambridge, MA: Harvard University Press, 1998.

James, Daniel. *Doña María's Story: Life, History, Memory, and Political Identity.* Durham: Duke University Press, 2000.

Jessee, Erin, Stacey Zembrzycki, and Steven High. "*Stories Matter*: Conceptual Challenges in the Development of Oral History Database Building Software." *Forum Qualitative Sozialforschung/Forum: Qualitative Social Research* 12, 1 (January 2011): http://www.qualitativeresearch.net/.

Joseph, Miranda. *Against the Romance of Community.* Minneapolis: University of Minnesota Press, 2002.

Kardash, Mary. "Untitled." In Krawchuk, *Reminiscences of Courage and Hope: Stories of Ukrainian Canadian Women Pioneers*, 297-98.

Kaye, Vladimir. *Early Ukrainian Settlements in Western Canada, 1895-1900*. Toronto: University of Toronto Press, 1964.

Kealey, Gregory, and Reg Whitaker, eds. *R.C.M.P. Security Bulletins: The Depression Years*. 5 vols. St. John's: Canadian Committee on Labour History, 1993, 1995, 1996, 1997.

–. *R.C.M.P. Security Bulletins: The Early Years, 1919-1929*. St. John's: Canadian Committee on Labour History, 1994.

Kealey, Linda. *Enlisting Women for the Cause: Women, Labour, and the Left in Canada, 1890-1920*. Toronto: University of Toronto Press, 1998.

Kean, Hilda. *London Stories: Personal Lives, Public Histories*. London: Rivers Oram Press, 2004.

Kechnie, Margaret, and Marge Reitsma-Street, eds. *Changing Lives: Women and Northern Ontario*. Toronto: Dundurn Press, 1996.

Kelley, Ninette, and Michael Trebilcock. *The Making of the Mosaic: A History of Canadian Immigration Policy*. Toronto: University of Toronto Press, 1998.

Kinsman, Gary, Dieter Buse, and Mercedes Steedman, eds. *Whose National Security? Canadian State Surveillance and the Creation of Enemies*. Toronto: Between the Lines, 2000.

Klempner, Mark. "Navigating Life Review Interviews with Survivors of Trauma." In Perks and Thomson, *The Oral History Reader*, 2nd ed., 198-210.

Knysh, Irene, ed. *In Service of Our Homeland: The Ukrainian Women's Organization of Canada, Twenty-Fifth Anniversary*. Trans. Larissa Stavroff. Winnipeg: Ukrainian Women's Organization of Canada, 1956.

Knysh, Zynovy, ed. *Toward National Unity: Fifty Years of Service by the Ukrainian National Federation, 1932-1982*. Trans. Larissa Stavroff. Toronto: Ukrainian National Federation of Canada, 1982.

Kordan, Bohdan. *Canada and the Ukrainian Question, 1939-1945: A Study in Statecraft*. Montreal and Kingston: McGill-Queen's University Press, 2001.

–. *Enemy Aliens, Prisoners of War: Internment in Canada during the Great War*. Montreal and Kingston: McGill-Queen's University Press, 2002.

Kostaniuk, Myron. "Recollections from the Life of a Ukrainian Pioneer." *Ukrainian Canadian*, October 1990, 35-38.

Krawchuk, Peter. *Interned without Cause: The Internment of Canadian Anti-Fascists during World War Two*. Toronto: Kobzar, 1985.

–, ed. *Our History: The Ukrainian Labour-Farmer Movement in Canada, 1907-1991*. Trans. Mary Skrypnyk. Toronto: Lugus, 1996.

–. *Reminiscences of Courage and Hope: Stories of Ukrainian Canadian Women Pioneers*. Trans. Michael Ukas. Toronto: Kobzar, 1991.

Kuhn, Annette. *Family Secrets: Acts of Memory and Imagination*. London: Verso, 1995.

Lambert, Barbara Ann. *Rusty Nails and Ration Books: Memories of the Great Depression and WWII, 1929-1945*. Victoria: Trafford, 2002.

Layman, Lenore. "Reticence in Oral History Interviews." *Oral History Review* 36, 2 (Summer-Fall 2009): 207-30.

Le Bourdais, D.M. *Sudbury Basin: The Story of Nickel*. Toronto: Ryerson Press, 1953.

Lindström, Varpu. *Defiant Sisters: A Social History of Finnish Immigrant Women in Canada*. Toronto: Multicultural History Society of Ontario, 1992.

Little, Margaret Jane Hillyard. "'A Fit and Proper Person': The Moral Regulation of Single Mothers in Ontario, 1920-1940." In McPherson, Morgan, and Forestell, *Gendered Past: Historical Essays in Femininity and Masculinity in Canada*, 123-38.

–. *'No Car, No Radio, No Liquor Permit': The Moral Regulation of Single Mothers in Ontario, 1920-1997*. Oxford: Oxford University Press, 1998.

Loewen, Royden. *Ethnic Farm Culture in Western Canada*. Ottawa: Canadian Historical Association, 2002.

–. *Family, Church and Market: A Mennonite Community in the Old and New Worlds, 1850-1930*. Toronto: University of Toronto Press, 1993.

Lucas, Rex. *Minetown, Milltown, Railtown: Life in Canadian Communities of Single Industry*. Toronto: University of Toronto Press, 1971.

Luciuk, Lubomyr. *In Fear of the Barbed Wire Fence: Canada's First National Internment Operations and the Ukrainian Canadians, 1914-1920*. Kingston: Kashten Press, 2001.

Luciuk, Lubomyr, and Stella Hryniuk, eds. *Canada's Ukrainians: Negotiating an Identity*. Toronto: University of Toronto Press, 1991.

Lupul, Manoly, ed. *A Heritage in Transition: Essays in the History of Ukrainians in Canada*. Toronto: McClelland and Stewart, 1982.

Luxton, Meg. *More Than a Labour of Love: Three Generations of Women's Work in the Home*. Toronto: Women's Press, 1980.

Lysenko, Vera. *Men in Sheepskin Coats*. Toronto: Ryerson Press, 1947.

Magocsi, Paul Robert. *A History of Ukraine*. Toronto: University of Toronto Press, 1996.

Manoff, Marlene. "Theories of the Archive from across the Disciplines." *Libraries and the Academy* 4, 1 (January 2004): 9-25.

Marks, Lynne. "Railing, Tattling, and General Rumour: Gossip, Gender, and Church Regulation in Upper Canada." *Canadian Historical Review* 81, 3 (September 2000): 380-402.

–. *Revivals and Roller Rinks: Religion, Leisure, and Identity in Late-Nineteenth-Century Small-Town Ontario*. Toronto: University of Toronto Press, 1996.

Martynowych, Orest. "The Hetmanite Movement and the Ukrainian Catholic Church in Canada, 1924-1940: Allies or Adversaries?" Paper presented at the annual conference of the Canadian Association of Slavists, Winnipeg, 1 June 2004.

–. *Ukrainians in Canada: The Formative Period, 1891-1924*. Edmonton: Canadian Institute of Ukrainian Studies Press, 1991.

Marunchak, Michael H. *The Ukrainian Canadians: A History*. Winnipeg: Ukrainian Academy of Arts and Sciences in Canada, 1982.

Massey, Doreen. "Places and Their Pasts." *History Workshop Journal* 39, 1 (1995): 182-92.

Matsumoto, Valerie. *Farming the Home Place: A Japanese American Community in California, 1919-1982*. Ithaca, NY: Cornell University Press, 1993.

Maynard, Steven. "Rough Work and Rugged Men: The Social Construction of Masculinity in Working-Class History." *Labour/Le travail* 23 (Spring 1989): 159-70.

McIntosh, Robert. *Boys in the Pits: Child Labour in Coal Mines*. Montreal and Kingston: McGill-Queen's University Press, 2000.

McKay, Ian. *Reasoning Otherwise: Leftists and the People's Enlightenment in Canada, 1890-1920*. Toronto: Between the Lines, 2008.

McPherson, Kathryn, Cecilia Morgan, and Nancy Forestell, eds. *Gendered Pasts: Historical Essays in Femininity and Masculinity in Canada*. Oxford: Oxford University Press, 1999.

Meyerowitz, Joanne. *Women Adrift: Independent Wage Earners in Chicago, 1880-1930*. Chicago: University of Chicago Press, 1988.

Mitchinson, Wendy. "The WCTU: 'For God, Home and Native Land': A Study of Nineteenth Century Feminism." In *A Not Unreasonable Claim: Women and Reform in Canada, 1880s-1920s*, ed. Linda Kealey, 151-67. Toronto: Women's Press, 1979.

Mochoruk, Jim, with Nancy Kardash. *The People's Co-Op: The Life and Times of a North End Institution*. Halifax: Fernwood, 2000.

Morawska, Ewa. *For Bread with Butter: The Life-Worlds of East Central Europeans in Johnstown Pennsylvania, 1890-1940*. Cambridge: Cambridge University Press, 1985.

Morton, Suzanne. *At Odds: Gambling and Canadians, 1919-1969*. Toronto: University of Toronto Press, 2003.

Myerhoff, Barbara. *Number Our Days*. New York: Simon and Schuster, 1978.

Nasaw, David. *Children of the City: At Work and at Play*. Garden City: Anchor Press, 1985.

Neatby, Blair. *The Politics of Chaos: Canada in the Thirties*. Toronto: Macmillan of Canada, 1972.

Nelles, H.V. *The Politics of Development: Forests, Mines and Hydro-Electric Power in Ontario, 1849-1941*. Toronto: Macmillan of Canada, 1974.

Newton, Janice. *The Feminist Challenge to the Canadian Left, 1900-1918*. Montreal and Kingston: McGill-Queen's University Press, 1995.

Nicaso, Antonio. *Rocco Perri: The Story of Canada's Most Notorious Bootlegger*. Toronto: John Wiley and Sons, 2004.

Noël, Françoise. *Family and Community Life in Northeastern Ontario: The Interwar Years*. Montreal and Kingston: McGill-Queen's University Press, 2009.

Nora, Pierre. "Between Memory and History: *Les Lieux de Mémoire.*" *Representations* 26 (Spring 1989): 7-24.

Norkunas, Martha. *Monuments and Memory: History and Representation in Lowell, Massachusetts.* Washington, DC: Smithsonian Institution Press, 2002.

Opp, James. "Re-imaging the Moral Order of Urban Space: Religion and Photography in Winnipeg, 1900-1914." *Journal of the Canadian Historical Association* 13 (2002): 73-93.

Opp, James, and John C. Walsh, eds. *Placing Memory and Remembering Place in Canada.* Vancouver: UBC Press, 2010.

Palmer, Howard. "Reluctant Hosts: Anglo-Canadian Views of Multiculturalism in the Twentieth Century." In *Immigration in Canada: Historical Perspectives,* ed. Gerald Tulchinsky, 297-333. Toronto: Copp Clark Longman, 1994.

Parr, Joy, ed. *Childhood and Family in Canadian History.* Toronto: University of Toronto Press, 1982.

–. *The Gender of Breadwinners: Women, Men and Change in Two Industrial Towns, 1880-1950.* Toronto: University of Toronto Press, 1990.

–. *Sensing Change: Technologies, Environments, and the Everyday, 1953-2003.* Vancouver: UBC Press, 2010.

Passerini, Luisa. *Fascism in Popular Memory: The Cultural Experience of the Turin Working Class.* Trans. Robert Lumley and Jude Bloomfield. Cambridge: Cambridge University Press, 1987.

–, ed. *Memory and Totalitarianism.* Oxford: Oxford University Press, 1992.

Patrias, Carmela. *Patriots and Proletarians: The Politicization of Hungarian Immigrants in Canada.* Montreal and Kingston: McGill-Queen's University Press, 1994.

Peake, F.A., and R.H. Horne. *The Religious Tradition in Sudbury, 1883-1983.* Sudbury: Downtown Churches Association, 1983.

Penner, D'Ann R., and Keith C. Ferdinand. *Overcoming Katrina: African American Voices from the Crescent City and Beyond.* New York: Palgrave Macmillan, 2009.

Perin, Roberto. *The Immigrants' Church: The Third Force in Canadian Catholicism, 1880-1920.* Ottawa: Canadian Historical Association, 1998.

Perks, Robert, and Alistair Thomson, eds. *The Oral History Reader.* 1st and 2nd eds. New York: Routledge, 1998, 2006.

Perry, Adele. *On the Edge of Empire: Gender, Race and the Making of British Columbia, 1849-1871.* Toronto: University of Toronto Press, 2001.

Petroff, Lillian. *Sojourners and Settlers: The Macedonian Community in Toronto to 1940.* Toronto: University of Toronto Press, 1995.

Petryshyn, Jaroslav. *Peasants in the Promised Land: Canada and the Ukrainians, 1891-1914.* Toronto: Lorimer, 1985.

Portelli, Alessandro. *Battle of Valle Giulia: Oral History and the Art of Dialogue.* Madison: University of Wisconsin Press, 1997.

–. *The Death of Luigi Trastulli and Other Stories: Form and Meaning in Oral History.* Albany: State University of New York Press, 1991.

–. *The Order Has Been Carried Out: History, Memory, and Meaning of a Nazi Massacre in Rome.* New York: Palgrave Macmillan, 2003.

–. "The Peculiarities of Oral History." *History Workshop* 12 (Autumn 1981): 96-107.

–. *They Say in Harlan County: An Oral History.* Oxford: Oxford University Press, 2011.

Pryjma, Theodore. "St. Mary's Ukrainian Catholic Parish: A History." Unpublished paper, n.d.

Prymak, Thomas. *Maple Leaf and Trident: The Ukrainian Canadians during the Second World War.* Toronto: Multicultural History Society of Ontario, 1988.

Radforth, Ian. *Bushworkers and Bosses: Logging in Northern Ontario, 1900-1980.* Toronto: University of Toronto Press, 1987.

Ramirez, Bruno. "Ethnic Studies and Working-Class History." *Labour/Le travail* 19 (Spring 1987): 45-48.

–. *On the Move: French Canadians and Italian Migrants in the North Atlantic Economy, 1880-1914.* Montreal and Kingston: McGill-Queen's University Press, 1991.

–. *Les premiers Italiens de Montréal.* Montreal: Boréal, 1987.

Rickard, Wendy. "Oral History – 'More Dangerous Than Therapy'?: Interviewees' Reflections on Recording Traumatic or Taboo Issues." *Oral History* 26, 2 (Autumn 1998): 34-48.

Riley, Mark, and David Harvey. "Talking Geography: On Oral History and the Practice of Geography." *Social and Cultural Geography* 8, 3 (June 2007): 1-4.

Riordon, Michael. *An Unauthorized Biography of the World.* Toronto: Between the Lines, 2004.

Ritchie, Donald. *Doing Oral History: A Practical Guide.* New York: Oxford University Press, 2003.

–, ed. *The Oxford Handbook of Oral History.* New York: Oxford University Press, 2010.

Robinson, Gregory. "Rougher Than Any Other Nationality? Ukrainian Canadians and Crime in Alberta, 1915-1929." In *Age of Contention: Readings in Canadian Social History, 1900-1945,* ed. Jeffrey Keshen, 214-30. Toronto: Harcourt Brace, 1997.

Roediger, David. *The Wages of Whiteness: Race and the Making of the American Working Class.* New York: Verso, 1991.

Rouverol, Alicia. "Collaborative Oral History in a Correctional Setting: Promise and Pitfalls." *Oral History Review* 30, 1 (January 2003): 61-85.

Rutherdale, Myra. *Women and the White Man's God: Gender and Race in the Canadian Mission Field.* Vancouver: UBC Press, 2002.

Ryan, Mary. *Civic Wars: Democracy and Public Life in the American City during the Nineteenth-Century.* Berkeley: University of California Press, 1997.

Saarinen, Oiva W. *Between a Rock and a Hard Place: A Historical Geography of the Finns in the Sudbury Area.* Waterloo: Wilfrid Laurier University Press, 1999.

–. "Sudbury: A Historical Case Study of Multiple Urban-Economic Transformation." *Ontario History* 82, 1 (March 1990): 53-81.

Sager, Eric W., and Peter Baskerville, eds. *Household Counts: Canadian Households and Families in 1901.* Toronto: University of Toronto Press, 2007.

Samuel, Raphael, and Paul Thompson, eds. *The Myths We Live By.* New York: Routledge, 1990.

Sangster, Joan. *Dreams of Equality: Women on the Canadian Left, 1920-1950.* Toronto: McClelland and Stewart, 1989.

–. "*Robitnytsia,* Ukrainian Communists, and the 'Porcupinism' Debate: Reassessing Ethnicity, Gender, and Class in Early Canadian Communism, 1922-1930." *Labour/ Le travail* 56 (Fall 2005): 51-89.

–. "Telling Our Stories: Feminist Debates and the Use of Oral History." *Women's History Review* 3, 1 (March 1994): 5-28.

Saxberg, Kelly, dir. *Letters from Karelia.* Montreal: National Film Board of Canada, 2004.

Seager, Allan, and John Thompson. *Canada, 1922-1939: Decades of Discord.* Toronto: McClelland and Stewart, 1985.

See, Scott W. "The Orange Order and Social Violence in Mid-Nineteenth Century Saint John." In Iacovetta, Draper, and Ventresca, *A Nation of Immigrants: Women, Workers, and Communities in Canadian History, 1840s-1960s,* 5-34.

Sheftel, Anna, and Stacey Zembrzycki. "Only Human: A Reflection on the Ethical and Methodological Challenges of Working with 'Difficult' Stories." *Oral History Review* 37, 2 (Summer-Fall 2010): 191-241.

–, eds. *Oral History off the Record: Toward an Ethnography of Practice.* New York: Palgrave Macmillan, 2013.

Sheller, Mimi, and John Urry. "The New Mobilities Paradigm." *Environment and Planning* A 38 (2006): 207-26.

Shopes, Linda. "Sharing Authority." *Oral History Review* 30, 1 (January 2003): 103-10.

Sitzia, Lorraine. "A Shared Authority: An Impossible Goal?" *Oral History Review* 30, 1 (January 2003): 87-101.

Solski, Mike. *The Coniston Story.* Sudbury: Journal Printing, 1983.

Srigley, Katrina. *Breadwinning Daughters: Young Working Women in a Depression-Era City, 1929-1939.* Toronto: University of Toronto Press, 2010.

–. "Stories of Strife? Remembering the Great Depression." In "Special Issue: Remembering Family, Analyzing Home: Oral History and the Family," ed. Katrina Srigley and Stacey Zembrzycki. *Oral History Forum d'histoire orale* 29 (2009): http:// www.oralhistoryforum.ca/.

Srigley, Katrina, and Stacey Zembrzycki. "Introduction." In "Special Issue: Remembering Family, Analyzing Home: Oral History and the Family," ed. Katrina Srigley and Stacey Zembrzycki. *Oral History Forum d'histoire orale* 29 (2009): http://www.oralhistoryforum.ca/.

St. Mary's Ukrainian Catholic Church Centenary Committee. *Centenary of the Ukrainian Catholic Church in Greater Sudbury.* Sudbury: St. Mary's Ukrainian Catholic Church, 2009.

Stanger-Ross, Jordan. *Staying Italian: Urban Change and Ethnic Life in Postwar Toronto and Philadelphia.* Chicago: University of Chicago Press, 2009.

Steedman, Carolyn. *Dust: The Archive and Cultural History.* New Brunswick, NJ: Rutgers University Press, 2002.

–. *Landscape for a Good Woman: A Story of Two Lives.* New Brunswick, NJ: Rutgers University Press, 1986.

Steedman, Mercedes. "Godless Communists and Faithful Wives, Gender Relations and the Cold War: Mine Mill and the 1958 Strike against the International Nickel Company." In *Mining Women: Gender in the Development of a Global Industry, 1670-2005,* ed. Jaclyn G. Gier and Laurie Mercier, 233-53. New York: Palgrave Macmillan, 2006.

Stefura, Mary. "Aspects of Culture in the Ukrainian Community of the Sudbury Area." *Polyphony* 5, 2 (Fall-Winter 1983): 29-32.

–. "The Process of Identity: A Historical Look at Ukrainians in the Sudbury Area Community." *Laurentian University Review* 15, 1 (November 1982): 55-64.

–. "Sudbury Ukrainian Time Line." *Polyphony* 10 (1988): 66-74.

–, ed. "Sudbury's People." *Polyphony* 5, 1 (Spring-Summer 1983): 71-81.

Stelter, Gilbert. "Community Development in Toronto's Commercial Empire: The Industrial Towns of the Nickel Belt, 1883-1931." *Laurentian University Review* 16, 3 (June 1974): 3-53.

–. "The Origins of a Company Town: Sudbury in the Nineteenth Century." *Laurentian University Review* 3, 3 (February 1971): 3-37.

Stoler, Ann. *Carnal Knowledge and Imperial Power: Race and the Intimate in Colonial Rule.* Berkeley: University of California Press, 2002.

Strange, Carolyn. *Toronto's Girl Problem: The Perils and Pleasures of the City, 1880-1930.* Toronto: University of Toronto Press, 1995.

Sugiman, Pamela. "'Life Is Sweet': Vulnerability and Composure in the Wartime Narratives of Japanese Canadians." *Journal of Canadian Studies* 43, 1 (Winter 2009): 186-218.

–. "Passing Time, Moving Memories: Interpreting Wartime Narratives of Japanese Canadian Women." *Histoire sociale/Social History* 37, 73 (May 2004): 51-79.

–. "'These Feelings That Fill My Heart': Japanese Canadian Women's Memories of Internment." *Oral History* 34, 2 (Autumn 2006): 69-84.

Summerfield, Penny. *Reconstructing Women's Wartime Lives: Discourse and Subjectivity in Oral Histories of the Second World War.* Manchester: Manchester University Press, 1998.

Sutherland, Neil. *Children in English-Canadian Society: Framing the Twentieth Century Consensus.* Toronto: University of Toronto Press, 1978.

–. *Growing Up: Childhood in English Canada from the Great War to the Age of Television.* Toronto: University of Toronto Press, 1997.

–. "When You Listen to the Winds of Childhood, How Much Can You Believe?" In *Histories of Canadian Children and Youth,* ed. Nancy Janovicek and Joy Parr, 19-34. Oxford: Oxford University Press, 2003.

Swyripa, Frances. "Negotiating Sex and Gender in the Ukrainian Bloc Settlement: East Central Alberta between the Wars." *Prairie Forum* 20, 2 (Fall 1995): 149-74.

–. "The Politics of Redress: The Contemporary Ukrainian-Canadian Campaign." In Iacovetta, Perin, and Principe, *Enemies Within: Italian and Other Internees in Canada and Abroad,* 355-78.

–. *Wedded to the Cause: Ukrainian-Canadian Women and Ethnic Identity, 1891-1991.* Toronto: University of Toronto Press, 1993.

Swyripa, Frances, and John Herd Thompson, eds. *Loyalties in Conflict: Ukrainians in Canada during the Great War.* Edmonton: Canadian Institute of Ukrainian Studies Press, 1983.

Tadmor, Naomi. "The Concept of the Household-Family in Eighteenth-Century England." *Past and Present* 151 (1996): 111-40.

"There Were No Strangers": A History of the Village of Creighton Mine. Lively: Anderson Farm Museum, 1989.

Thompson, John Herd. *Ethnic Minorities during Two World Wars.* Ottawa: Canadian Historical Association, 1991.

Thompson, Paul. *The Voice of the Past: Oral History.* Oxford: Oxford University Press, 1988.

Thomson, Alistair. "Four Paradigm Transformations in Oral History." *Oral History Review* 34, 1 (2007): 49-70.

Thomson, Ashley. "The 1890s." In Wallace and Thomson, *Sudbury: Rail Town to Regional Capital,* 33-57.

Tirabassi, Maddalena. "Bourgeois Men, Peasant Women: Rethinking Domestic Work and Morality in Italy." In Gabaccia and Iacovetta, *Women, Gender, and Transnational Lives: Italian Workers of the World,* 106-29.

Ukrainian National Federation of Canada, Sudbury Branch, Anniversary Book, Twenty-Five Years of the Branch. Trans. Larissa Stavroff. Sudbury: Ukrainian National Federation, 1957.

Ukrainian Rifleman's Community in Canada, 1928-1938. Trans. Myron Momryk. Saskatoon: *Novyi shliakh,* 1938.

"The ULFTA Branch, Sudbury, Ontario." In *Almanac, 1918-1929,* trans. Larissa Stavroff, 130-32. Winnipeg: Ukrainian Labour Farmer Temple Association, 1930.

Valverde, Mariana. *The Age of Light, Soap, and Water: Moral Reform in English Canada, 1885-1925.* Toronto: McClelland and Stewart, 1991.

Vecchio, Diane. *Merchants, Midwives and Labouring Women: Italian Migrants in Urban America.* Chicago: University of Illinois Press, 2006.

Wallace, C.M. "The 1930s." In Wallace and Thomson, *Sudbury: Rail Town to Regional Capital,* 138-67.

Wallace, C.M., and Ashley Thomson, eds. *Sudbury: Rail Town to Regional Capital.* Toronto: Dundurn Press, 1993.

Walsh, John C., and Steven High. "Rethinking the Concept of Community." *Histoire sociale/Social History* 32, 64 (November 1999): 255-73.

Weaver, John. *Crimes, Constables, and Courts: Order and Transgression in a Canadian City, 1816-1970.* Montreal and Kingston: McGill-Queen's University Press, 1995.

White, Luise. *Speaking with Vampires: Rumor and History in Colonial Africa.* Berkeley: University of California Press, 2000.

Woodsworth, James S. *Strangers within Our Gates or Coming Canadians.* Toronto: University of Toronto Press, 1909.

Yans-McLaughlin, Virginia. *Family and Community: Italian Immigrants in Buffalo, 1880-1930.* Ithaca, NY: Cornell University Press, 1982.

–. "Metaphors of Self in History: Subjectivity, Oral Narrative, and Immigration Studies." In *Immigration Reconsidered: History, Sociology, and Politics,* ed. Virginia Yans-McLaughlin, 254-90. Oxford: Oxford University Press, 1990.

Yasnowskyj, Phillip. "Internment." In *Land of Pain, Land of Promise,* ed. Harry Piniuta, 179-95. Saskatoon: Western Producer Prairie Books, 1978.

Zaslow, Morris. "Does Northern Ontario Have a Regional Identity?" *Laurentian University Review* 5, 4 (September 1973): 9-20.

Zembrzycki, Stacey. "Bringing Stories to Life: Using New Media to Disseminate and Critically Engage with Oral History Interviews." *Oral History* 41, 1 (Spring 2013): 98-107.

–. "'I'll Fix You!': Domestic Violence and Murder in a Ukrainian Working-Class Immigrant Community in Northern Ontario." In Hinther and Mochoruk, *Re-Imagining Ukrainian-Canadians: History, Politics, and Identity,* 436-64.

–. "Memory, Identity, and the Challenge of Community among Ukrainians in the Sudbury Region, 1901-1939." PhD diss., Carleton University, 2007.

–. "Sharing Authority with Baba." *Journal of Canadian Studies* 43, 1 (Winter 2009): 219-38.

–. "'There Were Always Men in Our House': Gender and the Childhood Memories of Working-Class Ukrainians in Depression-Era Canada." *Labour/Le travail* 60 (Fall 2007): 77-105.

Zucchi, John. *Italians in Toronto: Development of a National Identity, 1875-1935.* Montreal and Kingston: McGill-Queen's University Press, 1988.

Index

Printed and bound in Canada by Friesens

Set in Galliard and Minion by Artegraphica Design Co. Ltd.

Copy editor: Deborah Kerr

Proofreader: Helen Godolphin